Wolf's Rest

AND OTHER TALES OF SOUTHWEST NEBRASKA

Jean Smith

BY D. JEAN SMITH

1st ed.

Library of Congress Control Number: 2009941940

Published by Medicine Creek Press
74460 Road 395
Curtis, NE 69025

Printed in the United States of America

Design by Expertise Inc
www.IWillAdvance.com

Cover design by Gail Geis & Martin Mora

Summary: Historical accounts of surveyors, Native Americans, frontiersmen and settlers in early southwest Nebraska. Journals, letters, and reminiscences reveal the personal side of their struggles, failures, and triumphs.

ISBN: 9781449538569

To
The current owner and keeper of
Wolf's Rest Ranch,
And to the memory of his wife.

Table of Contents

TABLE OF CONTENTS IV

ILLUSTRATIONS VI

FOREWORD VII

ACKNOWLEDGEMENTS AND PREFACE VIII

INTRODUCTION X

1   THE SURVEYORS 1

2   JOHN Y. NELSON 17

3   IN CAHOOTS WITH THE CLIFFORDS 28

4   EENA TEGLAKA "SHE'S GONE HOME" 41

5   MONTE & JULIA CLIFFORD 49

6   KINAZI WEA "STANDING WOMAN" 60

7   PADDY MILES COMES WEST 68

8   PADDY MILES OF WOLF'S REST 83

9   AMBROSE SHELLEY 108

10   ENA OF WOLF'S REST 121

11   CARVER IN THE CROSSHAIRS 140

12   DOC CARVER THE CRACK SHOT 155

13   CHEYENNE OUTBREAK 178

14   JOHN "STORM" KING 190

15   COWBOY SHOOTOUT 195

16   THE HANGING TREE 199

17   THE DEATH OF ANNIE E. MCCLARY 211

18   THE REDEMPTION OF MCCLARY 224

19   THE BODY IN THE WELL 248

20   COULTER BALLANTINE JR. 268

21   THE WOMAN IN THE TREE 288

22   OF MEN AND SNAKE SKINS 302

BIBLIOGRAPHY...I

AUTHOR'S BIO..VII

Illustrations

Abbreviations used:
AMHMM = Anna Marie Hansen Memorial Museum
DPL = Denver Public Library, Western History Collection
FCHS = Frontier County Historical Society
NSHS = Nebraska State Historical Society
RVP = Robert Van Pelt Estate

Cover:
Photo of original Frontier County Jail (Gail Geis)

Other:
Page 3: Little Wound (RVP)
Page 10: John Y. Nelson (RVP)
Page 21: John Y. & Family (DPL, Nate Salsbury Collection: NS -118)
Page 27: Drawing of "Longman, Killing Pawnee" (NSHS, RG1730)
Page 36: Drawing of Richard Seymour by *Pay Ute* (NSHS, RG1730)
Page 40: Drawings of Buffalo & Flying Crane (NSHS, RG1730)
Page 47: Moccasins made by *Eena Teglaka* (FCHS)
Page 48: *Eena Teglaka's* headstone (Gail Geis)
Page 54: Orlando Clifford (FCHS)
Page 62: Barrett & Wheatley marriage license (RVP)
Page 70: Wm. H. Palmer (Miles) (NSHS, RG1730: PH 9-8)
Page 74: Dempsey & Anne Palmer (Norman Miles)
Page 76: Paddy Miles' Starr revolver (Gail Geis); Paddy Miles' Colt revolver (Norman Miles)
Page 78: Paddy Miles' heart-shaped branding iron & Wolf's Rest sign (George Cheek)
Page 80: Wm. H. Miles (RVP)
Page 86: Wm. H. Miles (RVP)
Page 87: Laura Murphy & Nellie Murphy (RVP)
Page 88: Laura Miles, William P. Miles & Nellie V. Miles (RVP)
Page 94: Center Avenue in Curtis, Nebraska (AMHMM)
Page 96: Paddy Miles displaying fish catch (Norman Miles)
Page 102: Miles Sale Bill (Norman Miles)

Page 104: Miles house circa 1880s (FCHS); Miles house, 2005 (Gail Geis)

Page 106: Map excerpt from 1905 *Standard Atlas of Frontier County, Nebraska*

Page 107: Tent camping pictures (Norman Miles)

Page 110: Ambrose Shelley (Cheryl Muilenburg)

Page 116: Shelley log cabin (FCHS)

Page 118: Shelley homestead (RVP)

Page 119: Ambrose Shelley (Cheryl Muilenburg)

Page 120: 1898 Frontier County Fair advertisement

Page 124: Ena Raymonde (NSHS, RG1730: PH 2-1)

Page 130: Texas Jack Omohundro (Buffalo Bill Historical Center, Cody, Wyoming; Original Buffalo Bill Museum Collection, P.69.715)

Page 141: Wm. F. "Doc" Carver (DPL, F-43044); Neiswanger monument in memory of Doc Carver (FCHS)

Page 145: Excerpt & drawing from Ena Raymonde's journal (NSHS, RG1730)

Page 157: Wm. F. "Buffalo Bill" Cody (RVP)

Page 161: Wm. F. "Doc" Carver & medals (NSHS, RG1730: PH 5-1)

Page 165: Doc Carver in *Harper's Weekly* etching (DPL, Harper's no neg. #)

Page 169: Carver's diving horse (NSHS, RG1730: PH 5-4)

Page 173: Carver in showman's attire (NSHS, RG1730: 4797 QC-193)

Page 175: Neiswanger monument in Cottonwood Canyon (FCHS); Old Texas-Ogallala Trail marker (www.waymarking.com)

Page 205: Coroner's Inquest

Page 207: Map excerpt from 1905 *Standard Atlas of Frontier County, Nebraska*

Page 210: Rudolph Wendelin's drawing of Stockville (RVP)

Page 212: D. C. Ballantine Sr. (NSHS, RG1730: PH 1-4); D. C. Ballantine's headstone (D. Jean Smith)

Page 214: Ena Raymonde (NSHS, RG1730: PH 2-1); Annie E. McClary's headstone (Gail Geis)

Page 226: W. L. McClary (FCHS); McClary monument (D. Jean Smith)

Page 232: The Enterprise Store (RVP)

Page 240: Stockville Main Street about 1905 (RVP)

Page 250: Thomas Jensen (RVP)

Page 252: Andrew Hawkins' sod house (RVP)

Page 254: County officers in front of courthouse (RVP)

Page 256: E. S. Case & R. D. Logan (RVP)

Page 258: 1898 Stockville street scenes (RVP)

Page 262: First Frontier County Jail (FCHS)

Page 266: Courtroom & banister in Frontier County Courthouse, 2009 (Gail Geis)

Page 270: Coulter Ballantine Jr. (NSHS, RG1730: PH 1-3)

Page 274: Mima (Leach) Ballantine (NSHS, RG1730: PH 17-12)

Page 276: Ballantine sod house (NSHS, RG1730: 0-18)

Page 278: Hunting camp (NSHS, RG1730: 11-16)

Page 282: Coulter Ballantine Jr. with horse & cart (NSHS, RG1730: PH 1-8)

Page 290: Mima (Leach) Ballantine (NSHS, RG1730: PH 3-1)

Page 294: Mima & Coulter Ballantine & Nellie Miles (NSHS, RG1730: PH 18-4)

Page 296: Ballantine house, 2005 (Gail Geis)

Page 300: Coulter & Mima Ballantine (NSHS, RG1730: PH 11-14)

Page 301: Ballantine monument at Sunset Point Cemetery (Gail Geis)

Page 304: Robert McKnight (AMHMM)

Foreword

Jean Smith is a storyteller. In *Wolf's Rest* she tells the early stories of Medicine Creek and Frontier County in southwest Nebraska – in all, twenty-two stories of Native Americans, trappers, bull-whackers, surveyors, cowboys, and homesteaders – the real men and women who invested their lives and energy to tame the Wild West.

It is said that everyone and every place has a story. Small communities in rural America have certainly produced many outstanding citizens – more, proportionately, than larger cities. However, Frontier County and its county seat, Stockville, have more than their share. The small character stories in *Wolf's Rest* capture each individual, their experience and their times. The context of those experiences tells the overall story of the development of the West: the beginning of the Indian Wars at the Grattan Massacre near Fort Laramie in 1854; the founding of Frontier County by John Bratt and Hank and Monte Clifford; Julia Clifford and her mother, the old Medicine Woman, *Eena Teglaka*. For some Medicine Creek was a fresh start after the Civil War, for others it was a new beginning as they built their farms, communities, churches, law enforcement, courts and the rule of law.

The life we enjoy on America's prairie did not just happen. We benefit from the hard work and investment of generations of men and women who came before us. Smith gives the reader twenty-two poignant tales of early pioneer life and love. You will find buffalo, wild horses, outlaws and scoundrels. You will also find the behind-the-scenes story on Buffalo Bill Cody and the Wild West show's sharpshooter, Dr. W. F. Carver, the legendary scout John Y. Nelson, Paddy Miles, and Ena Raymonde. If the book was not so well researched, many of the characters would be beyond belief; however, they are real, very real. You will enjoy *Wolf's Rest*.

~ Cloyd Clark

Acknowledgements and Preface

Historical accounts, of necessity, build on the works of previous storytellers. The writing of *Wolf's Rest* would not have been possible were it not for the forethought and diligent effort of any number of people and entities throughout the years in collecting and preserving the stories of an earlier time.

The journals of Ena Raymonde and W. L. McClary touch on everything from the mundane events of the day to the writer's innermost feelings. The writings and letters of Mima Ballantine offer insight into the thought patterns of a woman on the brink of full-blown insanity. Along with related correspondence and photographs, these journals, essays, and letters are preserved in the collections of the Nebraska State Historical Society in Lincoln, Nebraska.

It was the combined efforts of a number of the Cliffords' descendents that led to the publication of a booklet containing the stories of Monte and Julia Clifford, *Eena Teglaka*, and Nancy Barrett or "Standing Woman." Though largely a trumped-up story, Doc Carver's 1878 *Life of Dr. Wm. F. Carver of California: Champion Rifle Shot of the World* would surely be lost to only but a few readers were it not for a digitized version made available to the general public via the Internet.

The Frontier County Historical Society has done a fine job of gathering stories of area interest. A number of individuals, as well, have played an important part: W. H. "Paddy" Miles' great-grandson Norman Miles, who has "the Miles' box"; Henry Koch, who salvaged the court records pertaining to the murder of Eugene Sherwood and subsequent hanging of Jonas Nelson; the late Reiney Martins, who had the foresight to tape-record the recollections of William S. McKnight; Marion Johnson, who recalled various stories pertaining to Wolf's Rest and was on the scene during the final years of the lives of Coulter Ballantine Jr. and his wife, Mima. Many others have contributed stories and anecdotes.

The author is indebted to Samuel Van Pelt, who has graciously shared the papers and photographs from the estate of his father,

Robert Van Pelt. One of those with Nebraska small town roots who "made good," Robert Van Pelt was a lifelong collector of regional history. The once-missing link in the *Wolf's Rest* story, the collection also includes correspondence of historical interest between Robert Van Pelt and others who were intrigued by the fascinating people whose stories are told in this book. In addition, Robert Van Pelt was instrumental in the Nebraska State Historical Society's obtaining McClary's journals.

Finally, thanks to anyone who has ever rescued a vital piece of history – the handwritten note tucked away in the family Bible; a musty, water-stained, mouse-chewed journal; or the article in an old newspaper found lining the bottom of a drawer or trunk.

~ D. Jean Smith

Introduction

Located close to a branch of the heavily traveled McPherson Trail along the picturesque Medicine Creek in southwest Nebraska, Wolf's Rest Ranch was the stage for a fascinating panorama of events and people in the late 1800s. The colorful W. H. "Paddy" Miles could assume the guise of either an upstanding citizen or a scalawag with equal ease. W. F. "Doc" Carver, who later achieved worldwide fame as a marksman, often hung his cartridge belt at Wolf's Rest, whereas Ena Raymonde, a southern belle and expert shot in her own right, added a romantic flourish to the mix. Despite the fact that her story has been told in *Medicine Creek Journals*, it was necessary to touch on the essential elements of Ena Raymonde's life in *Wolf's Rest* in order to further develop her relationship with Doc Carver and W. L. McClary as well as the incidents surrounding her untimely death. While this may seem redundant to those familiar with the previous book, it is hoped the retelling will serve merely to refresh the memory.

John Y. Nelson, "Buffalo Bill" Cody, and "Texas Jack" Omohundro were among the notable frontiersman who crossed paths with the Wolf's Rest residents. At the same time Whistler and his band of Cut-off Sioux – encamped a stone's throw away – served as a reminder to the whites that they were, indeed, on the raw edge of the frontier.

Even though there are new characters in the cast, *Wolf's Rest* is, in some respects, an epilogue to *Medicine Creek Journals*. The author has further developed the narrative of some of those who received little more than a passing reference in the earlier work. With the discovery of additional information, a new light has been shed on old stories and previous assumptions have been challenged. Moving into the twentieth century, the life of the eccentric Coulter Ballantine Jr. is explored as well as that of his wife, who ultimately became a victim to the ravages of mental illness.

Other tales of early southwest Nebraska have been included for two reasons: they are intertwined with the lives of those who frequented Wolf's Rest and they are good stories. Like Indian beads in an anthill, certain stories that make up the history of any area have a way of continually working their way to the top.

1

The Surveyors

The Indians understood the importance of the men walking the divides and canyons with their chains and flags even if they did not understand the intricacies of surveying. And although there was still tension between the surveyors and the Indians in southwest Nebraska by the summer of 1872, a news item in the August 14, 1872 *Lincoln County (Nebr.) Advertiser* reflected the changes that had occurred since Indians under Pawnee Killer and Whistler massacred the Nelson Buck surveying party in 1869: "We received a visit on Monday from Pawnee Killer, one of the Sioux Chiefs. His band is located on the Republican Valley. He has seen several surveying parties, and in answer to our question would not allow his men to molest them in any manner."

In spite of Pawnee Killer's reassurances, the Indians caused plenty of "worry" for the surveyors that summer of 1872, beginning with their departure from the agencies or reservations where many of them had spent the winter. In late February F. D. Yates, an Indian agent at Sidney, Nebraska, telegraphed General Smith at the Whetstone Agency on the Missouri River in Dakota Territory:

> Had council with Indians before I left camp, about [their] returning [to the agency]. They are opposed to it. Little Wound wants to roam and catch wild horses all summer. Pawnee Killer with twenty-five lodges [wants] to go on the Arkansas [River]. They are bent on scattering when grass comes. Black Bear only, with forty lodges talks

of returning. I think if you could talk with them it would stop it…[1]

As spring gave way to summer, the uneasiness increased. The surveying parties working on the Blackwood, Stinking Water and Frenchman – all tributaries of the Republican River in southwest Nebraska – were especially concerned about the presence of Pawnee Killer and Whistler. A party under the leadership of Fairfield and Wells wrote to E. E. Cunningham, Surveyor General for Nebraska, on August 14, 1872, from "in camp on the Republican" in present day Dundy County. Fairfield and Wells stressed that they would not be able to continue their work without an escort as the Sioux were camped about four miles away "and say that they are going to stay here and hunt until they hear from Washington and get some pay for this land."[2] In addition, there was a rumor that a large band of Cheyenne was expected in the area in a few weeks. Charles Emmett, or "Dashing Charley," an interpreter with the Indians, bolstered the cause for concern by saying he expected there would be trouble if the Cheyenne came.

A few days later Lieutenant Smallwood of the Second Cavalry reported on a scout he had made through the upper Republican country. He had encountered the surveying party of Keyes and Jameson camped on the Blackwood. Mr. Keyes indicated that several Indians from Whistler's band that had been camped on the Stinking Water came into the surveyors' camp and demanded they leave by sundown – a demand the surveyors ignored. When Lieutenant Smallwood came across the Fairfield and Wells surveying party, he was told it was Whistler's understanding from what the interpreter told him that the surveyors did not have authority to be there, and when Whistler told them to leave they would have to go. Smallwood's report continued:

> [Whistler] says that he will give them plenty of warning, after he finds out whether they are here by authority

---

1 Paul D. Riley, "Frontiersmen of Fort McPherson, 1870-1875, and the Writings of Ena Raymonde Ballantine," circa 1970s, unpublished, Ballantine Collection, MS1730, Nebraska State Historical Society (hereafter cited as Ballantine MSS).
2 Ibid.

As Spring of 1872 approached, Little Wound, a sub-chief of Red Cloud, wanted to leave the reservation to "roam and catch wild horses." Though it is not known how or where she acquired it, Ena Raymonde tinted the original portrait with water colors. *Courtesy Robert Van Pelt Estate.*

or not…The surveyors here seem to be alarmed; as they say Pawnee Killer's Band of Brule Sioux is here, besides Whistler, and that the Indians tell them that 100 lodges of Ogallala's Sioux will be at this place within three or four days; and that there are 160 Lodges of Cheyennes coming from the South; these Surveyors have Thirteen (13) men with them…

I…found Whistler's Camp…I left my men on the side of the hill (so that I should give the Indians no cause for alarm or offense) and went myself into the Indian camp. I had a talk with Whistler. He says he has been told that surveyors have no business here; that they are without authority; I assured him to the contrary; but so far as I could judge by his manner and that of the Indians around him, they did not believe me. He says General Reynolds told him when the surveyors came, not to stay away from them, but to go to their camps, and show them that they are peaceable. I told him that the General must have meant for the chiefs to go, and not that the young men should go there at any and all times, and trouble the [surveying] parties. He promised to keep his young men away. I think Whistler and his [principal men are] disposed to be friendly and behave themselves; the young men appear dissatisfied… I also saw Pawnee-Killer…who is here with his band. He would not say much; only showed me his papers…[3]

Smallwood's report was sent on to Colonel Reynolds, Headquarters, District of the Republican, at Fort McPherson. Reynolds, in turn, forwarded the report to the Department of the Platte, Omaha, with his own cover letter:

The warning to the surveyors to leave the country has since been explained by "Pawnee Killer" as being a mistake. It was probably unauthorized by "Whistler" and meant to extort provisions.

Whistler seems disposed to follow my instructions given last March in anticipation of his meeting surveying parties, viz.: to keep his people away from the surveyors;

3 Ibid.

simply communicating in a friendly way thro' one or two
of his principal men...[4]

The Whistler, or Whistler, as he was commonly known, was a
chief of the Cut-off band of Oglala Sioux that had split with the
main group of Oglala in the 1850s. It seems that Whistler's band of
Cut-off Oglala had received temporary permission to remain south
of the Platte. Whistler had been in the area all winter, and while a
part of his band were encamped on the Medicine Creek in present
day Frontier County, Whistler and his braves roamed farther west
much of the time. Though he had been involved in a number of
earlier attacks on whites, Whistler was considered a peaceful Indian
by 1872, and his band probably never presented a significant threat
to the surveyors. On the other hand, it remained Whistler's opinion
that the surveyors were putting their stakes in his territory. Stephen
McElroy, who was with a party of surveyors on the Frenchman in
1872, recalled that Whistler's band would slip in at night and move
the stakes and stones that the surveyors had left to mark the section
corners.[5]

The disastrous conflict between the Nelson Buck surveying party
and the Indians had occurred three years earlier in 1869. Robert
Harvey, who was with the party that surveyed thirty-six miles of
what would later become the northern boundary of Frontier County
and the eastern twelve miles of Hayes County the same summer,
also encountered Indians but lived to tell his story.

Robert Harvey was a young Civil War veteran when he came
to Nebraska from his native Ohio in 1869 in hopes of being hired
on with a surveying party. He convinced the surveyor general of his
good intentions and was hired by Mr. Allison, a deputy surveyor
who had the contract for the designated area in western Nebraska.
It was the middle of May when Harvey and several other members
traveled by rail from Omaha, with Willow Island as the destination
for several parties to rendezvous. From there they went on to Brady
Station where they left their war sacks, containing their extra cloth-

---

4 Ibid.
5 Edna Christensen, telephone conversation with author, Sept. 18, 2008.

ing, to be forwarded on to North Platte. It was about a month later when they found their war sacks had been lost, but the "entire force resolved to make their present suits last the entire trip – a resolution every man kept…"[6]

The first major challenge the surveying party faced was fording the south channel of the Platte River, which was particularly high due to snow melt in the mountains. Each surveying party had a wagon, and there were three parties in the group that crossed the ford on the Platte that day. The teams from all three wagons were hitched to the first wagon to cross the river. Mr. Harvey wrote of the teamsters and their proficiency at spewing out profanity: "In those days it was current that a teamster who could not make the air blue with profanity when his mules got stuck, could not hold his job, and my recollection is that the man who handled the strings on that trip across the Platte fully upheld the credit of his calling…"

The newcomers were told that when they plunged into the river they were to "holler like hell" to give the mules courage. The river was wide – about 1900 feet – and the water was waist deep, swift, and cold. The deep channel on the south side of the river swept the men off their feet, and they could only reach the shore by swimming. In addition to hollering, it took a lot of strength, persistence, and strategic maneuvering to get three wagons and the teams of mules across the river. When it was finished, Robert Harvey said very few of the men had much "holler" left in them. As the wet and bedraggled surveyors stood in their underclothing on the bank trying to catch their breath, one of the deputy surveyors tapped into a two-gallon whiskey keg and offered the men a bracer. It was Mr. Harvey's recollection that all but three men accepted the offer.

Leaving the Platte Valley, the party ascended to the table land. Shovels and manpower were employed to build a temporary trail by which to pull the wagons up the steep hill. Once this was accomplished, and the entire outfit was "atop," the work of surveying began. Robert Harvey recalled the June morning the work began

---

6 Robert Harvey, "The Unwritten Story of the Establishment of the Second Standard Parallel," 1910, reprinted in Frontier County Historical Society (hereafter cited as FCHS) newsletters, Vol. 17, issues 1, 2 & 3 (2002).

as being clear with a gentle breeze causing "the luxuriant growth of blue joint grass to roll and ripple in gentle waves." The detail of surveyor's work can only be described in the words of the surveyor:

> At the corner, the latitude and the sun's declination was calculated, the instrument was set up and adjusted according to indications. The parallel according to the indications of the department, was to be run west on a true line and corners established at intervals of forty chains, or every half mile.

> The work began at eight o'clock, by running west, the leading chain beginning with a full chain [66 feet], followed by the rear chain of fifty links, or half a chain length, and adding the fifty links to the fortieth chain [½ mile] to even up the leading chain; if there was then any difference, it was divided by allowing one-third to the first on account of previous experience and two-thirds to the rear chain.

> At the first mile or quarter corner, the corner-men were instructed how to build the corner by digging a hole at the corner point, post set therein and charcoal placed in the hole on the north side. Witness pits were then to be dug twenty-four inches square and one foot deep, one east and one west of the post, about six feet distant and the earth piled around the same in the form of a cone, the post to be hewed and flattened on the north side and marked with the wood scribe "¼ S.S.C." [Quarter standard section corner].[7]

> Because they did not have the prescribed charcoal, charred or burned stakes, or sharpened posts, a fire was quickly built, and the sharpened ends of a number of posts were charred and one set for the corner.[8]

The country along which the line ran was very rough – the high table land or divides broken by a number of deep canyons. When the power of the mule teams was not enough to pull the wagons out of

---

7 Ibid.
8 Mr. Harvey felt this was a grave error and led to a number of "lost corners" in later years. He wrote: "An experienced practical surveyor would never have given such authority to

the canyons, a prolong or length of heavy rope, was run out ahead of the team and the men pulled on the rope. In addition, a road often had to be made by cutting down the rugged banks and "cat steps." On June 12, the second night on the survey, camp was made on the left bank of a beautiful little creek, about five or six feet wide, of cool, clear water. The creek, which was later named Fox Creek, was referred to at the time as "Cluxton Creek" after the Cluxton boys. Being the junior member of the party, Mr. Harvey felt it was out of place to ask who the Cluxton boys were, which is unfortunate, as the Cluxton boys surely spawned some interesting stories.

It was not until the surveyors had worked their way west and crossed what is now known as Well Canyon, which leads down into the town of Curtis, Nebraska, and were beyond the "Mud" or Medicine Creek Valley that they had their first encounter with Indians. Harvey and a fellow by the name of Johnson had gone back across a deep canyon to re-measure, when the men on the other side yelled "Indians" and began running along the ridge. Not having seen any Indians, Johnson yelled something to the effect that he thought they were fooling. Frank Burgess, who was taking some mighty long steps to the south, in turn yelled, "We're not kidding a God damned bit." The rest of the story as Harvey told it:

> Frank, being a school teacher was very precise in his language, especially in the case of adjectives. We wheeled about to the north and saw a band of twenty or thirty [Indians] burst from behind a clump of cedar trees, and seeing us to the south, headed in our direction and came down on the edge of the canyon on a gallop. To the best of my recollection, I made just one jump and landed in the bottom of the canyon, and Johnson was there ahead of me, running across the canyon. We threw the chain and our pins into the cat-steps and pulled our revolvers. In this brief time, I rehearsed the thrilling stories of Daniel Boone…and others of the old time Indian fighters and re-counted the tragedies of burning and scalping. I remem-

---

witness a corner by such precarious methods." He further felt that the root of such errors in judgment was the practice of appointing politicians, who lacked knowledge of the principles of surveying, to offices having the supervision of public surveys.

ber running my fingers through my hair to see if there was a chance of scalps. It had been clipped short and stood straight up.

We flew up the bluff, ran along the edge in the direction the men had taken; thinking they had seen the wagon where our guns were. The course of the canyon was south…for a quarter or half a mile then turned sharply to the west for thirty or forty rods, then swung around in a horseshoe curve to the south and east, then southeast. At the point where it turned west, a canyon or "pocket" with cut banks entered from the east. We descended into the south bluff and met the wagon directly on top of the ridge in the horse shoe curve. We were the third and fourth men there, Mr. Allison and one other being ahead of us.

The teamster quickly unhitched his mules, baggage was thrown out and a barricade formed, guns and ammunition stacked within the enclosure. One or two other men had come in by this time. In the meantime the Indians had galloped along the brink of the canyon and ran into the angle between it and the pocket from the southeast and not daring to cross at this point, galloped back around the pocket. Johnson, seeing the movement, grabbed a gun and spade and said, "Come with me." I, too, picked up a gun, box of cartridges and a spade and ran to the highest ground about fifty feet away where we began digging rifle pits.

On looking up, I saw the enemy coming down the ridge. I said to Johnson, "That Indian with the big head dress is mine."

"Dig, damn you, dig, or he'll get your top-knot," screamed Johnson. I dug. The Indians were now a hundred or hundred and fifty yards away and, on hearing a commotion, I ventured to look up and saw that they had wheeled and were rushing back along the ridge to the east. Fearing a trick was being pulled, we reconnoitered our position and found it a splendid one for defense. We again gave our attention to the fleeing Indians, when another party was seen in the northwest, which united with the first and all fled southeast as far as we could see…

> In about half an hour, we returned to the line, each man taking his gun, some of them their revolvers, also, and had we cannon, we would have taken them also…[9]

When they returned to Fort McPherson a few days later, the surveyors learned that a detachment of soldiers had been in pursuit of the fleeing Indians. Still shaken, the men carried guns and a good supply of ammunition with them the following day. By mid-afternoon their work had taken them to a point on a ridge where they crossed a military road running from North Platte to the Republican. All of a sudden, an Indian's head appeared above a hill to the south followed by a dozen or more. As the Indians scampered down the hill, Mr. Allison, the deputy in command of the surveying crew, whistled to rally his troops. The men working near enough to heed the command all laid down in the grass and took their positions. Seeing the Indians break to the right and left as though to surround them, Allison gave the order: "Boys, pick your buck, and don't miss a shot. Wait until I give the command, one, two, fire, them pump it into them hard, stop the rush, and then fall back to the wagon." Harvey continued:

> I called out that the fellow on the right with the red bandana was mine, Johnson took the next one, and we waited for the command. When about a hundred yards away came the count, one, two, I had the red bandana in my gun sight and was pulling on the trigger, at every breath expecting the command to fire – the Indians were not a hundred yards away when up flew a white handkerchief and "Don't shoot."

> "For Lord's sake," said Allison, "they are soldiers." We were stupefied but yet on our mettle for we still lay there with our fingers on the triggers until an explanation was demanded. An officer came up and explained they were escorting the paymaster from the cantonments on the

---

9 Harvey.

> Republican to the railroad, that he thought we were In-
> dians until they broke to right and left, which was for the
> purpose of surrounding us, when he discovered the instru-
> ments and then knew we were surveyors but thought he
> would give us a little scare for the fun of it.

As with the real threat of Indian attack a day earlier, this practical joke could have had serious consequences. By the end of the
eight days it took to finish the forty-eight mile survey, a new concern faced the surveying party as rations ran low. Harvey noted in
his journal that on the morning of June 18, 1869, each man had for
breakfast: one biscuit, a slice of fat bacon and a cup of coffee – and
a handful of parched (dried) corn. That was the last "morsel of food"
he tasted for three days.

It was later in the summer of 1869, while surveying the Holiday
Stage Line that Robert Harvey met H. B. McGregor, a cattle herder, who had recently quit the Nelson Buck surveying party because
they were so poorly armed. It would be some months before either
Harvey or McGregor learned the fate of the Nelson Buck party –
a story that has become legend in Nebraska history. Nelson Buck
from Illinois had been in the surveying business for thirty-four years
when he applied for a surveying job in western Nebraska. Though
not oblivious to the potential dangers, he wrote in a letter to P. W.
Hitchcock, the Surveyor General, that he was prepared to "employ
such force as will be likely to protect our party (of 12) surveyors. It
is not profit alone that would induce me to make this attempt, but
the desire to be employed where I can see the West – so then as far
as the fear of Indians is concerned, that has little or no weight in
the matter."[10] Before setting out in late July 1869, Buck put in a request to the military for the necessary arms and ammunition. When
the armaments were not forthcoming, Buck again wrote to the Surveyor General: "I regret now that I did not procure arms, etc. at
Plattsmouth. I made application through Capt. Pollock for leave to
draw such as were needed, but did not get them. Some, and indeed
several of my company, feel discouraged at hearing of Indians…and

---

10 Wayne Price, "The Mystery behind the Nelson Buck Massacre," *Rural Electric Nebraskan*,
Vol. 60, No. 7 (July 2006), pp. 6-8.

want arms so that if we must fight Indians, all can take part in the matter."[11]

H. B. McGregor remembered that Nelson Buck had a fine rifle, but that it was muzzle loading, while one fellow had a rusty shotgun and another an old army revolver. As for himself, McGregor had an army Springfield carbine but only ten cartridges. McGregor further recollected, "Our party were [*sic*] at Fort Kearney several days awaiting the arms ordered at an earlier date. The officers repeatedly warned us we would be killed if we ventured far poorly armed and without escort. Mr. Buck made [every] effort to arm an escort but without avail."[12]

Because of the remoteness of their work, it was quite some time before anyone realized something was amiss with the Buck surveying party. In the middle of September several companies of U. S. Cavalry under the command of Lt. Colonel Duncan along with Major Frank North and his Pawnee Scouts left Fort McPherson on a patrol in pursuit of a stubborn remnant of Cheyenne and Sioux along the Republican. This was just two months following the Battle of Summit Springs in which the command of General Eugene A. Carr had killed Tall Bull and decisively defeated his Cheyenne Dog Soldiers – a fierce conflict in which both Whistler and Pawnee Killer had participated. Wm. F. "Buffalo Bill" Cody had been a scout for the military in that engagement, and though his claim to having brought down Tall Bull has never been conclusively proven, he did come away with Tall Bull's horse. Cody was once again employed as scout on this expedition to the Republican along with the old frontiersman John Y. Nelson, who was married to an Indian woman. Cody recalled that late in September while in pursuit of a fleeing band of Sioux:

> We came upon an old squaw, whom they had left on the prairie to die. Her people had built for her a little shade or lodge, and had given her some provisions, sufficient to last her on her trip to the Happy Hunting grounds.

---

11 Ibid.

12 E. S. Sutton, *Sutton's Southwest Nebraska and Republican River Valley Tributaries*, (Benkelman, Nebraska: E. S. Sutton, 1983), p. 49.

This the Indians often do when pursued by an enemy, and one of their number becomes too old and feeble to travel any longer. This squaw was recognized by John Nelson who said that she was a relative of his wife. From her we learned that the flying Indians were Pawnee Killer's band, and that they had lately killed Buck's surveying party, consisting of eight or nine men; the massacre having occurred a few days before on Beaver Creek.[13]

Cody continued, "We knew that they had had a fight with surveyors, as we found quite a number of surveying instruments, which had been left in the abandoned camp. We drove these Indians across the Platte river and then returned to Fort McPherson, bringing the old squaw with us, from there she was sent to the Spotted Tail Agency." It wasn't until sometime later that some of Nelson Buck's friends, with the encouragement of a generous supply of provisions and tobacco, obtained Pawnee Killer's story:

> He said that while they were hunting they discovered a party of surveyors near their camp. That the party was out working as the Indians supposed leaving a man in camp cooking the meal and some of the young men of Pawnee Killer's band approached him intending to ask for food as they were hungry and that some of the surveying party while concealed in a clump of brush fired on them wounding one Indian. This commenced the fight and Pawnee Killer's band killed eight of them and destroyed the camp and wagon and surveying instruments…[14]

Pawnee Killer and his band retreated for the winter to the Whetstone Agency, where he was questioned by Captain D. C. Poole and admitted that his band had killed six or eight white men on the Beaver. When asked about the fate of the other four members of the surveying party, Pawnee Killer replied, "Maybe killed by another party of Indians." Pawnee Killer absolved himself of blame by saying

---

13 Wm. F. Cody, *The Life of Hon. William F. Cody*, (1878, reprint, Lincoln, Nebr.: University of Nebraska Press, 1978), pp. 274-275.
14 Bayard H. Paine, *Pioneers, Indians and Buffaloes*, (Curtis, Nebraska: *The Curtis Enterprise*, 1935), p. 71.

that the white men began the fight and so enraged his braves that he could not restrain them.

While being held at McPherson, the Indian woman who had been found on the prairie and identified as being the mother of Pawnee Killer, was questioned through the interpreter, Leon Pallardy. She said that although she was a part of Pawnee Killer's band, she had been with Whistler's band when four white men were killed, after which they hurried across to Medicine Lake Creek where they hunted for awhile.[15] A January 6, 1870 report from the Whetstone Agency further confirmed that it was Pawnee Killer's band that killed the first six or eight surveyors, and Whistler's band that killed the remaining four:

> Pawnee Killer's band arrived at this Agency in September last after a summer campaign through the Republican Valley. His party all had more or less United States currency which they paid over very freely. Spotted Tail informs me that Pawnee Killer attacked on the Beaver a party of about twelve surveyors in August last and succeeded in killing six of the party, the balance retreating and entrenched themselves. The Indians attacked them and were repulsed with the loss of three Indians killed. Three braves were buried in trees. The Indians abandoned the attack and the [rest of the] whites escaped down the creek, encountering Whistler, and were killed.[16]

There were probably only six surveyors killed by Pawnee Killer's band and four by Whistler's band as two of the original twelve who went out had returned to the fort for arms and never rejoined Buck's party. At any rate, it was shortly after that a surveying party under the leadership of Wm. J. Daugherty encountered Whistler's band. The old Indian woman was in on this skirmish also, and she told the interpreter that after crossing over to the Medicine following the killing of the four surveyors, they went on over to the Stinking Water "where other bands joined us…We went on to the French-

---

15 Named for Medicine Lake, which was located near its headwaters, Medicine Creek was generally called Medicine Lake Creek in the early years.
16 Sutton, pp. 48-49.

man… A party of white men were seen. Whistler said we won't fight them, and some braves went forward with a white flag. The white men fired, then all our men, even women and children went after the whites. All we wanted was their horses and anything we could use."[17] Daugherty's report to the Surveyor General:

> On the 21st August about 6 a.m. a small party of Indians dashed into our camp, shot one horse and made off with five. We succeeded in retaking the stock, wounding two Indians. There was evident signs of a large body of Indians. We decided to go to the Platte for guns and ammunition, being short of both. We proceeded about two miles when suddenly surrounded by about 175 Indians, coming from the south. We unhitched the stock and turned them loose, knowing the Indians would make for them. In the meantime we were digging pits and throwing up entrenchments. As soon as they got the stock, they surrounded us and fought Indian style all day. None of us were seriously wounded, though one was slightly hurt in the forehead by a glancing shot. My brother was disabled from duty by the explosion of a Sharps rifle cartridge in his face, blinding him so could not see for nearly a whole day.
>
> We disabled several of their horses and know that we shot twelve Indians, three of whom were killed; two of them lay in our sight all day. After dark the firing ceased, and they seemed to be stationing sentinels. We commenced digging with vigor to make them believe we intended staying there, but half past nine o'clock, by crawling on our bellies almost a mile, the moon shone almost as bright as day, we left a ridge of sand between us and the Indians. We then skedaddled as best we could…[18]

A short time later Daugherty submitted a requisition for seven new Spencers with accoutrements and one thousand rounds of ammunition as well as an escort. The Indians, for their part, were well armed. Captain E. D. Emory of the Eighth Infantry questioned Daugherty and reported that the "Indians were magnificently

17 Ibid., p. 50.
18 Ibid., p. 51.

mounted and were well armed with late model guns, mostly Spencers, and with plenty of bows and arrows. Mr. Daugherty is positive that had the confident Indians made a concerted attack they would have overcome the surveyors. They would have preferred to capture the whites. The loss of three men and a dozen or more wounded discouraged Whistler."[19]

Captain Poole recorded his impression of various chiefs when they came into the Whetstone Agency before the winter of 1869: "So far as villainy can be depicted in the human countenance, it was to be found in Pawnee Killer's. His face had a lean and hungry look; he was long and lank and reminded one of a prowling wolf. He seldom smiled while talking to his companions but stalked about with his blanket closely wrapped about him, as if expecting at each turn to pounce upon an enemy or be himself attacked. He had a murderous looking set of followers…"[20]

This description aside – as long as the Indians saw the white men staking what they believed was their territory – surveying was going to be a dangerous occupation. No doubt an error in judgment, made in the blink of an eye, caused the massacre of the Nelson Buck surveying party. The frontier of southwestern Nebraska changed dramatically from 1869 to 1872. As the dominance of the white man became increasingly inevitable, what Whistler wanted – perhaps above anything else – was to be left alone so he could live in the old way as long as possible. That was not to be. It was another error in judgment and a hair-trigger decision that caused Whistler and two of his braves to lose their lives in a white trappers' camp in December of 1872. As for the surveyors –

> Mostly without military support, even poorly armed with their own, they suffered untold hardships, exposed to Indian raids at all times. Some lived to tell their story. Others vanished leaving no trace. ~ Anonymous[21]

---

19 Ibid., p. 52.
20 Paine, pp. 70-71.
21 Sutton, p. 49; Also: Louis A. Holmes, *Fort McPherson, Nebraska; Fort Cottonwood, N.T.,* (Lincoln, Nebraska: Johnsen Publishing Company, 1963); Don Russell, *The Lives and Legends of Buffalo Bill,* (Norman, Oklahoma: University of Oklahoma Press, 1960).

2

John Y. Nelson

ohn Y. Nelson claimed to have had nine wives; he could have easily and more truthfully claimed to have had nine lives. He was forty-four years old and had used nine lives several times over by the time he "ran up a hut" on the banks of Medicine Lake Creek in the winter of 1870. He was a master at spinning a yarn, and Buffalo Bill Cody once declared that Nelson was a good fellow "though as a liar he has but few equals and no superior."[1] That allegation aside, John Y. Nelson did live an eventful life in a time and place when making a split-second decision could mean the difference between life and death. After Ena Raymonde first met the old plainsman at Wolf's Rest in June of 1873, she recorded in her journal that John Y. Nelson was "an original of no mean order…"[2] If his tales didn't happen exactly as he told them – and it is doubtful many of them did – the fact remains; they were good stories.

He was born on August 25, 1826, at Charleston, Virginia, and named John Young Nelson. The name John Nelson is a common one, but on the frontier, there was only one John Y. Nelson. He ran away from home at an early age, headed west and was seventeen years old when he happened onto a caravan of prairie schooners headed toward the Nebraska and Kansas territories on a trading trip. He joined the wagon train, which eventually struck an encampment of both Oglala and Brule Sioux under the leadership of Spotted Tail

1 Cody, p. 272.
2 Annie "Ena" Raymonde's Journals, Ballantine MSS. All journal entries of Ena Raymonde Ballantine referred to in this book are from this source.

at Cottonwood Springs (later the site of Fort McPherson) on the Platte River. When the trading was finished, Nelson, ready for some real adventure, decided that he was going to join the Indians.

In the nonchalant manner that became his trademark, Nelson claimed that he "strolled amongst the tepees, when, making straight for a decent-looking one, I lifted up the flap, entered, and sat down."[3] The tepee was that of Spotted Tail, and Nelson, refusing to leave, finally made them understand his intentions to stay. He was christened *Cha-sha-cha-opoyeo* or "Red-Willow-Fill-the-Pipe" and in three months was adopted into the tribe.[4] In short order Nelson took a young Indian maiden as a wife, but she soon left him for a young Indian buck. This established a pattern in Nelson's life that would last for many years; the bonds of matrimony were easily severed.

In 1847 while Nelson and Spotted Tail's band were at Cottonwood Springs, Nelson encountered Brigham Young and his Latter Day Saints. Brigham Young was leading his people to find the Promised-land and asked Nelson if he would guide them on west. Nelson was a veteran frontiersman by this time and although he was reluctant to leave the Indians, he realized this party of whites was headed into certain trouble. With Spotted Tail's permission, Nelson sent his wives back to their family and joined the Mormon wagon train. With a lifetime's worth of adventure under his belt, his first Indian scalp, and a profound appreciation for his own scalp, Nelson returned from the Mormon expedition two years later. His wives – the whole kit and caboodle – had taken up with an Indian by the name of Long Man.

A period of relative peace between the westward bound wagon trains and the Indians – secured by treaties guaranteeing goods and provisions for the Indians – was broken with news of the Grattan Massacre over "the Mormon cow" incident in 1854. Nelson, who was with a band of Brule Indians, was sent to Fort Kearny to see

---

3 Harrington O'Reilly, *Fifty Years on the Trail*, (1889, reprint, Norman, Oklahoma: University of Oklahoma Press, 1963), p. 23. O'Reilly's telling of John Y. Nelson's story is the source for most of this chapter.
4 Cody, p. 272. Cody's translation is Red-Willow-Fill-the-Pipe, while O'Reilly used Redwood-Fill-the-pipe. Red Willow seems more accurate as they used the bark of the Red Willow.

Nelson—Scout, Guide and Interpreter.

Noted for spinning a tale, John Y. Nelson was, nonetheless, a frontiersman without equal. This "cabinet photo" was taken at Sheridan, Illinois, in the late 1800s while Nelson was touring with Buffalo Bill Cody's Wild West show. *Courtesy Robert Van Pelt Estate* if the reports were true. Finding that the reports of the massacre were true, Nelson remained at the fort as he could not fight against the whites. Like other white men who joined Indian tribes, John Y. Nelson seemed to be able to move back and forth from the Indian side to the white side as circumstances dictated. Nelson remained at Fort Kearny until the fall of 1855 as a government employee hauling wood for the building of a larger fort. He then did some trapping, during which time a small settlement named Dog Town sprang up near Fort Kearny. Saloons being profitable in Dog Town, Nelson and his trapping partner established a business named Robbers' Roost. Nelson claimed the down side to the saloon business was that quite a few fellows were being killed, so the two entrepreneurs decided to vamoose before they found themselves on the receiving end of a bullet.

After meandering in and out of a few more predicaments, Nelson went to work for Jeremiah "Jerry" and John K. Gilman at their road ranch (a trading establishment) east of Cottonwood Springs on the Platte River in about 1862. The Gilmans' road ranch was one of the largest ranches along the road, and they appreciated Nelson's knowledge of the Sioux language. After about three months, work began on the trans-continental telegraph line, and the Gilmans secured a contract to furnish poles. Nelson went out into the cedar-laden canyons along the river with a crew of men and wagons and "lumbered up" these poles. Likewise, when construction of Fort McPherson – originally named Fort Cottonwood – at Cottonwood Springs began in 1863, he was involved in the cutting and delivery of the red cedar logs used to build the fort.

In the early 1860s Nelson once again chanced matrimony, his last wife having long since made her departure. He had gone to visit the Oglalas when he met the attractive twenty-three-year-old *Op-an-gee-wee-ah*, or the Yellow Elk Woman. The terms of union came about only after much bargaining, as *Op-an-gee-wee-ah* was the daughter of Old Smoke, a big chief of the Bad Face band of Oglalas. Because he was also required to give gifts to her nine brothers, the prospective groom had to "shell out" liberally. Nelson named his new wife Jennie and gave due respect to her first husband for introducing

This photo of the legendary scout and plainsman, John Y. Nelson, and his family was taken while they toured with Buffalo Bill Cody's Wild West show. Nelson and his Oglala Sioux wife, Jennie, and their children were presented to Queen Victoria while the show was in England in 1887. The twin boys to the left and the youngest daughter were born after Nelson began touring. Doc Carver said that John Y. Nelson toured with his show for awhile after Carver and Cody split their "Wild West: Hon. W.F.Cody and Dr. W.F. Carver's Rocky Mountain and Prairie Exhibition" in 1884. *Courtesy Denver Public Library*

her to the ways of the whites and taking the rough edge off her. For her part, Jennie must be given credit for tenacity, as she was the wife John Y. Nelson would have until the end of his life.

While the United States was engaged in the Civil War, the forts along the main westbound route were inadequately manned. With the majority of Union soldiers being needed to fight the Confederacy, the soldiers remaining at the forts were at a disadvantage due to the overwhelming number of Indians. Because of his knowledge of the countryside and the Sioux language, Nelson was engaged as a scout, guide, and interpreter for the troops; therefore, he once again found himself in the position of fighting his Indian brothers. During the war and much of the volatile 1860s, John Y. and Jennie Nelson lived apart, for there was an implied understanding between them that when there was peace she lived with him, but when there was war, she lived with her people.

Along about this time Nelson had one of several adventures with his old friend and fellow frontiersman, George P. Belden, known to the Indians as the White Chief. Like Nelson, George Belden had run away from home as a boy and joined an Indian tribe. Belden described Nelson as a "roving, reckless, dare-devil sort of fellow, who always needed to be led, and who could never be intrusted [*sic*] to lead in any expedition, on account of his rashness and indiscretion."[5] On the other hand, Nelson described Belden as "a smart officer, as brave a man as ever stepped, and a magnificent shot… [who] was always getting into trouble…" Nelson further contended that Belden "had a lot of confidence in me."[6] Regardless of which one merited the most trust and confidence, both Belden and Nelson had the same nose for adventure.

Belden had been with one Indian tribe or another for twelve years when news of the strife between the Union and the Confederate States reached him at the Indian encampment far north on the Missouri River in Dakota Territory. The Indian who was the bearer of this news also said the government was enlisting the help of volunteer troops to replace the soldiers that were going East to fight the rebels. A sense of duty to his country overpowered his allegiance to the Indians, and Belden resolved to help with the effort. With his wives, lodge, and possessions he traveled south down the Missouri as far as Fort Randall. From there Belden sent his wives to live with their people and traveled by himself on down the Missouri River to Omaha where he was enrolled as a soldier in the United States Army, First Nebraska Cavalry.

This regiment rendezvoused with several other cavalry regiments at Fort McPherson with a Colonel Brown as the commanding officer. There were also a number of Indians in the command, including

5 George P. Belden, Ed. by General James S. Brisbin, Belden, *The White Chief: or Twelve Years among the Wild Indians of the Plains, 1870*, <http://mos.umdl.umich.edu.> p. 196.
6 O'Reilly, pp. 212 & 219.

a large body of Pawnee Scouts under Colonel Frank North. Reports had reached Fort McPherson that a large concentration of particularly troublesome Sioux Indians under Chief Spotted Tail was camped on the Republican. These Indians were traveling with their lodges, women and children, and with the snow lying deep on the plains, it was considered a good time to make an offensive attack. After crossing the Medicine and establishing a supply camp on the Republican, Colonel Brown – who Nelson claimed was anxious to bolster his own image – offered a reward to anyone who could locate and lead the command to a village of Indians. Both Nelson and Belden later told the story with Nelson giving the amount offered as being $1000 while Belden gave it as being $500. The discrepancy in the amounts may be said to fairly represent the difference in the storytelling style of the two men.

Belden – by then a lieutenant – wrote that Sergeants Hiles and Rolla took Colonel Brown up on his offer. The day after Hiles and Rolla left camp, Nelson proposed that he and Belden "go out and hunt an adventure." With permission from the colonel, the would-be adventurers packed a mule with supplies and headed out – traveling by night and hiding out in the brush along the creeks by day. After a few days with no Indian sightings, they were startled to come upon the horse that Sergeant Hiles had ridden from camp. Their conclusion was that Hiles and Rolla had been attacked by Indians, and because the horse had no saddle, they believed that at the very least, Hiles was dead. Soon after they came across "a heavy Indian trail" not more than five hours old and surmised that Sergeant Rolla had escaped, and the Indians must be pursuing him. For the next few days Belden and Nelson traveled night and day, stopping to sleep for only a few hours at night. By going far out of their way and using the finely honed instincts of the frontiersmen they were, they avoided encountering the hostile Indians. On the fifth day they met a company of cavalry out looking for them and returned safely to camp. Sergeant Rolla had been killed, and from Sergeant Hiles they learned how he had survived by tunneling deep into a snow bank for two days after his horse plunged into a snow-filled ravine while pursued by the Indians. Belden's perspective on the whole affair: "We had not found an Indian village, and none of us got the five hundred dollars, but we all had a glorious adventure, and that to a frontiersman is better than money."[7]

Nelson, for his part, recalled the response to the colonel's offer of a cash reward differently. He claimed that after several parties that took Colonel Brown up on the offer were attacked and killed by Indians, Colonel Brown persuaded Nelson to give it a try. Nelson's only request was the use of the Kentucky racehorse that the colonel had ridden at the Battle of Shiloh. The horse was tall and raw-boned with a reputation as a "flyer," which was why Nelson wanted him. Lieutenant George P. Belden was the only man to respond to Nelson's invitation to accompany him. With two half-breed Cherokee scouts, they struck out, hiding by day and traveling the banks of the Republican by night.

After several days with no signs of Indians, they grew brave and decided to reconnoiter up Short Nose Creek. Before setting out the next morning, however, they sent the Cherokees out to kill a buffalo for breakfast. When the hunters failed to return in the anticipated length of time, Nelson and Belden became anxious and decided to go look for them. Nelson had not yet ridden the Kentucky racer, but with the possibility of an Indian encounter eminent, he decided the time was right. They rode some distance and were surveying the area from an elevated piece of ground when they saw the two half-breeds galloping towards them and every now and then looking back over their shoulders at a party of Indians following them. Nelson and Belden "stuck spurs" to their horses and galloped towards the Cherokees, who signaled them to stop. Belden stopped; Nelson didn't. The Kentucky horse had his racing blood up and pounded over the prairie, oblivious to Nelson's efforts to stop him. The rest of the story as told by Nelson was printed in the July 4, 1883 *Omaha Weekly Bee*:

> My horse broke away from me, and before I knew it I was going pell mell straight for three braves who were astonished at my fool hardiness. I tried to stop the animal and whacked him over the head with my gun, but that

7 Belden, p. 317.

only made him go the faster. I made up my mind that before morning my scalp would be dangling at the end of some lance-poles. When I got within fifty yards of the red devils I commenced pumping my old rifle and raised the yell. By the time I sent out all the loads the reds were running the same way I was. One of them fired his pistol at me so close that the powder burned me as it whizzed by. On we went to the creek. With one mighty leap, the sole remaining brave cleared the stream and on. As I prepared to follow on the other side one other red deliberately drew a bead on me. I jerked out my revolver and fired, throwing myself on the other side of the horse as I did so arrows were sent quivering into my saddle. Continuing his wild dash up the hill, my frightened horse carried me into the midst of the reds, who scattered as if I were some evil spirit. The fact that the lieutenant [Belden] and his men were now following me made me feel safer of keeping my hair, but on looking at my rifle, I discovered that I had dropped the stock. As I did not care about facing the whole Sioux nation with a gun-barrel, I steered my now tractable animal down a long slope and back where my friends were playing whoop and hide with the Indians – the Indians doing the whooping and the soldiers the hiding. The old colonel got to see all the Indians he wanted, and I guess he's running yet.

It was presumably following this expedition and with a relative peace patched up with the Indians that Nelson put together a trading outfit and headed in the general direction of Medicine Creek. On the Medicine, he ran into a party of Indians that included Jennie and a daughter who was more than a year old. Nelson, of course, had not been aware of this addition to his family since he had not seen Jennie for nearly two years. The rest of the Indians went on, while Nelson's party traveled on to the mouth of the Stinking Water in present day Hitchcock County, Nebraska. In late winter a war party of Cheyenne Dog Soldiers surrounded Nelson's camp. They were unaware that a peace treaty had been made and were still on the warpath. Although Nelson had told them that if they killed him, the Sioux would avenge his death, he was forever thankful for the timely arrival of Jennie's brother Lone Wolf and a party of his warriors. John Y. Nelson was reminded that he was still a white man and as such was often an enemy of the Indian.

After another series of uprisings, the Fort Laramie or Sioux Treaty of 1868 once again brought a tenuous peace. While many of the Indians went to the reservations set aside for them, there were still a number of bands of raiding and pillaging Indians roaming about. Then again, in Nelson's estimation, many of the Indians did not understand the treaty obligations and simply wanted to do as they had always done and follow the buffalo.

As mentioned previously, Nelson, along with Buffalo Bill Cody, was a scout and interpreter for the expedition that set out from Fort McPherson in September 1869 with the intent of pushing the marauding bands of Indians onto the reservation at the Whetstone Agency in Dakota Territory. Nelson contended that this assignment was against his will, as he had made preparations to move with his family to the reservation. A few days in the guardhouse (the military brass at the fort surely had something they could hold over his head) caused him to take a different point of view. Nelson said they "ran the Indians round all the winter, eventually driving them into the Reservation." Nelson's version of finding the old Indian woman, who was with Whistler's band of Indians when the surveyors were killed, was stark in its simplicity: "Two days… [after a skirmish with the Indians] we found an old squaw on the prairie who was too decrepit to keep up with them, and they had left her to be devoured by the wolves."[8]

Following this expedition, Nelson joined Jennie and the children on the Great Sioux Reservation in northwest Nebraska and what was then Dakota Territory. Before long, as might be expected, the comparative peacefulness of reservation life began to take its toll; "peace troubled" John Y. Nelson. The Indians, of course, were having their own difficulty making adjustments to reservation life, but it was among the other white men with Indian wives that Nelson found willing partakers in plots to alleviate boredom.

---

8 O'Reilly, p. 244.

This drawing of "Long Man Killing Pawnee" was found in Ena Raymonde's journal. Long Man at one time reportedly made off with all three of John Y. Nelson's wives. Ena became a friend of Long Man's but apparently questioned his intentions when she wrote: "Suffice it to say that I was not sorry when 'Long Man' took down his lodge poles and started for 'heap Sioux.'" *Courtesy Nebraska State Historical Society.*

3

—

In Cahoots with the Cliffords

*L*ike a tumble weed borne by the wind, John Y. Nelson rolled through life on the plains with little thought for the outcome. Those who signed on for an adventure with the old plainsman were almost certainly in for a rough ride. It was around 1862 that Nelson drifted into the Gilmans' road ranch east of Cottonwood Springs on the Platte River. Most likely, this is where he first ran into Hank Clifford – and later Hank's brother Monte Clifford. Compared to Nelson, Hank and Monte Clifford were newcomers on the frontier, but given time – and a few experiences with John Y. Nelson – they, too, were "old frontiersmen" by the time they pitched their tepees on the Medicine Lake Creek in 1870.

Henry Clay "Hank" Clifford was born in Indiana in 1839, and his brother, Mortimer Harrison "Monte" Clifford, was born about three years later, probably in Missouri. They, along with a younger brother, John Marshall Clifford, came with their parents, Orlando Hines and Elizabeth (Knox) Clifford, to Otoe County, Nebraska Territory, in 1855. Family lore has it that Orlando H. Clifford had seven brothers, who all became Methodist ministers. He is also said to have been the first man in Nebraska City to make a business of putting up and selling ice. In conjunction with the ice business, he opened a hotel known as the Clifford House and later made oxen yokes.

The discovery of gold in the mountains of Colorado – then Kansas Territory – precipitated an increased need for commerce and transportation that impacted Hank and Monte Clifford in their westward migration. Along about 1858 Jerry and John Gilman, two livery stable operators in Nebraska City, became interested in the freighting business. With that in mind, John Gilman made a trip west by horseback and pack mule in the fall of 1858 to explore the feasibility of establishing a delivery service between Nebraska City and the mining territory. He was accompanied on this expedition by a couple of fellows, one of those being Jerome Dauchy, who was a recent migrant from the state of New York.

The following spring Gilman put two wagons on the trail with himself whacking the bulls on one and twenty-year-old Hank Clifford on the other. Clifford was strong, always on board for adventure, and handy at fixing things – attributes that would serve him well as he "gee-ed" and "haw-ed" a heavy, lumbering wagon pulled by six to eight yoke of oxen along the trail. John Gilman and Hank Clifford maneuvered their heavily laden wagons out of Nebraska City onto the westward trail in March of 1859. They encountered no more than the usual number of problems and arrived at the "diggings" without having lost either merchandise or their indispensable beasts of burden. Back in Nebraska City by June and with a new wave of gold fever spreading across the country, it was decided to make another trip yet that year.

The merchandise on the first trip had been contracted, but this time the Gilman brothers decided to invest in their own goods, and Jerry would join his brother in the freighting business. They sold their livery stables, collected old debts, and loaded the wagons with the standard trading stock of food, clothing, ammunition, and whiskey. In addition, they loaded one wagon with iron work, wheelbarrows, and tools, etc. Besides John and Jerry Gilman and Hank Clifford, Jerome Dauchy also made this trip. It was mid-summer when the whips cracked over the backs of the oxen, and the four men began the long westward trek. This second trip, though, did not go as smoothly as the earlier one had. With an ever-increasing number of wagons on the trail, it was difficult to find camping spots that provided adequate grazing for the oxen. These wagons had already been over the long trail before; consequently, there were more breakdowns, with the wheels being especially vulnerable to the hot, dry weather. When the wooden wheels shrunk away from the iron rims, the wagons had to be unloaded, jacked up, and the wheels removed and soaked in the river until the wood expanded to fit the rims. This was a time-consuming and back-breaking process, with the oxen being the only beneficiaries of the time off the trail.

Still dealing with wheel problems, they were a good distance west of the Plum Creek Station (now Lexington, Nebraska) and about fifteen miles east of Cottonwood Springs when an axle broke. They set up camp with the hope that some disheartened traveler would come along with a wagon for sale. Over the next few days, as the four men attempted to repair the wagon, they were besieged by Indians and travelers wanting to engage in trade. Fellow travelers eye-balled the merchandise that had been unloaded from the disabled wagon or wanted to trade two foot-sore oxen for one good ox. A load of firewood cut for their use was sold in a day. With no chance of getting to Denver before late summer and seeing the market for the necessities of the trail – water, firewood, supplies, and road-worthy stock – the Gilmans decided to build a road ranch. Their campsite on the broad, flat Platte Valley, with its high water table and proximity to the cedar-filled canyons was an ideal location for establishing a trading business along the great wagon trail.

With the assistance of Hank Clifford and Jerome Dauchy, the Gilmans built two sod houses from which to conduct their new business. They dug a well, lined it with cedar posts, and installed a fine, red iron pump that had been meant for the trading customers in the foothills of the mountains. A rarity in those days, when a windlass and bucket were the usual means for drawing water from a well, the pump became a drawing card for the Gilman road ranch. The Indians, who had never seen such a contraption, christened John Gilman, *We-Chox-Cha*, the "Old Man with a Pump."[1]

The remaining good wagon was sent back east to Nebraska City for more supplies to finish out the trading season. As the Gilmans

1 Musetta Gilman, *Pump on the Prairie*, (Detroit, Michigan: Harlo Press, 1981), p. 39. General information involving the Gilmans is from this source.

improved and expanded their road ranch, they continued to have an interest in freighting. Their own wagons were continually on the road securing supplies from Nebraska City, and they understood the ins-and-outs of the business. By 1861 they had acquired enough wagons and livestock to put their own bull-train of upwards of twenty wagons on the road hauling freight to the mines. Hank Clifford was the man they hired as the wagon master. Being pegged for this position was testimony that the trail-wizened Clifford had proven himself with the Gilmans. Shepherding a bull-train across the plains required steadfastness and the ability to make a quick decision, whether dealing with the hazards of the trail or with the varying temperaments of the teamsters or "bullwhackers." Hank Clifford continued to work for the Gilmans at least off and on until they discontinued the road ranch and returned to Nebraska City in 1868. Jerome Dauchy was the cook for a year or so before establishing his own road ranch and then freighting for the firm of Russell, Majors and Waddell. It is thought that both Hank Clifford and his brother, Monte, also freighted for a time with Jerome Dauchy.

A number of changes affected the freighting business during those years – the most important being the arrival of the railroad in the mid-1860s, which significantly reduced the traffic on the trail. Several major Indian uprisings also occurred in those years, making it too dangerous to freight. Although reports of where these fellows were at any particular time are sketchy and conflicting, John Y. Nelson, like Hank Clifford, seems to have been employed at various intervals by the Gilmans for a number of years. When winter slowed the activity on the trail and curtailed logging and other seasonal work that Nelson did for the Gilmans, he would load up a wagon with trade goods and set out across the prairie to trade with the Indians for hides and furs. Hank Clifford eventually engaged in similar endeavors and he, like Nelson, married an Indian woman – Maggie, a Cheyenne – and assimilated into the Indian way of life.

There is no record of just when Monte Clifford came West, but it was at least several years later than his brother. He was a bushwhacker during the Civil War, and because he had not taken sides with either the Union or Confederate cause, he delivered ammunition to both armies. It is said that Monte was initially shocked when he found his brother had married an Indian woman, but he soon grew accustomed to the idea, came up with the obligatory ponies and did the same. In any case, the Gilman road ranch became an integral link in the lives of John Y. Nelson, Hank and Monte Clifford, and Jerome Dauchy, all of whom would sooner or later migrate on south to the Medicine Lake Creek.

Life with the Indians at first seemed to offer a freedom that appealed to the adventurous white men. However, as the Indians' struggle with the whites continued to tip in the white man's favor, and the "squaw men" found themselves living on reservations, they chafed at the inactivity. It appears to have been early in 1870 that Nelson and the Cliffords moved with their Indian families to the Great Sioux Reservation in northwest Nebraska. Although the whiskey-selling scheme smells more like a John Y. Nelson proposal, he gave credit (or blame?) for the idea to the Cliffords. Nevertheless, five other white men at the reservation decided they wanted in on the action.

The Indians habitually stole horses from the whites and were quite willing to trade a horse worth $250 for a gallon of "tarantula juice," a cheap but potent doctored-up whiskey concoction. Nelson was fully aware of the devastation that alcohol brought the Indians, but he put aside any qualms of conscience on the basis that if he didn't do it, somebody else would. Trading whiskey to the Indians on the reservation was out of the question, but it was easy enough to find Indians off the reservation, for as Nelson said, "there were more out than in." In Nelson's words: "We got a few wagons together, laid in a good stock of firewater, and moved out into the open on the lookout for wandering parties. We ran across several of these, and did fairly well for some little time. The Indians would sell anything for whiskey, and parted readily with horses and mules, which had cost them nothing, for a few drinks."[2]

The whole thing began to unravel when they reached a large Indian village, and a Cheyenne came into Nelson's trading-lodge want-

2 O'Reilly, p. 245.

ing whiskey but without a horse to trade. Nelson recalled that he was lying down with his head against the cask while his brother-in-law Lone Wolf informed the Cheyenne there was no whiskey dispensed without trading stock. The Cheyenne's reaction was to put a couple of bullets through the cask of whiskey just above Nelson's head. (As with all of John Y. Nelson's stories, this one no doubt took on more twists and turns with each telling.) Anyway, Lone Wolf supposedly took a flying leap at the Cheyenne, grabbed the pistol, and knocked the fellow down. A couple of their cohorts came into the tepee and dragged the Cheyenne out while some of the others helped Nelson plug the holes in the cask with pieces of stick. Once the Cheyenne got his head about him, he high-tailed it back to his band and soon returned with reinforcements, demanding that Nelson be handed over to them. The Indians in Nelson's corner refused, and a few shots were fired through the top of Nelson's lodge, bringing his Indian brothers-in-law into the fracas, which soon turned into hand-to-hand combat. When one of the Indians was killed as the fighting became increasingly ugly, Nelson re-evaluated his position:

> I saw nothing funny in being killed over a row which was none of my seeking, and accordingly crawled into the tepee, where I remained until the poles, which were being persistently shot through fell upon me, and the whole place was becoming honeycombed with bullets. Then my friends brought me a horse, told me to put on a blanket, mount, and ride for life. I did so, but not without getting some holes shot through the blanket. After covering about three miles, I pulled up and waited until the firing had ceased. Then I made my way back quietly to camp.
>
> When I arrived I found about half the village gone, and my friends gathered round the spot where my tepee had stood. This had all been torn down in the scrimmage, but the Cheyennes had been beaten off.
>
> The first thing that attracted my attention was the head knocked out of my twenty-gallon keg, and the entire crowd drinking out of tin cups, buckets, dippers, in fact anything that would hold liquid. I knew it was no use say-

ing anything, so I looked cheerful under the depressing circumstances.[3]

The fellows that were imbibing at Nelson's expense told him that his brothers-in-law had taken the horses and headed towards the Platte, so Nelson took off in that direction. It was the next morning before he caught up with his brothers-in-law and found that thirty-two of Lone Wolf's band had "passed in their chips." Nelson got back to the reservation with thirty-seven head of horses – about one horse per dead Indian. The Cliffords and the other white men also had run-ins with the Cheyenne and lost all of their whiskey and horses, barely escaping with their lives.

Revived by a few weeks rest, Nelson said he again began to yearn for more "active occupation." Hank Clifford and Art Ruff went in on an enterprise to kill buffalo and sell the meat on consignment to Chicago markets. Between the three of them they acquired six wagons, hiring teamsters to drive the additional wagons. They hunted on the south side of the Platte where they found the buffalo to be plentiful. As the wagons were loaded, the teamsters would deliver the meat to a railroad station where it was delivered to its destination by rail. Nelson estimated they made over $2000 in the first six weeks. When the weather got too warm to ship meat, they sent Hank Clifford to Omaha to lay in a supply of groceries and whiskey.

Upon Clifford's return with the trading stock, each family loaded their wagon and set off to trade with the roving bands of Indians that were eluding the government troops. The plan was that they would meet at a given point near Fort McPherson in two-month's time. John Y. and Jennie found a secluded Indian village and traded successfully for a length of time. When it was discovered that some government troops were in the vicinity, the chief, *Che-wax-sah*, was convinced Nelson had put the soldiers on his track. Nelson's protests fell on deaf ears, but he and Jennie were permitted to strike camp, load the wagon, and leave the village. As the old frontiersman told it, before *Che-wax-sah* and his band fled the area, they set the prairie on fire behind Nelson. With no shelter but the wagon, and the

3 Ibid., p. 247.

prairie being rapidly consumed by fire, the outlook for John Y. and Jennie looked grim. Nelson credited his wife with the quick response that saved their lives, as she immediately set backfires in the long grass around them. They threw water on the wagon covers and on themselves, escaping death as the fire roared over them. Jennie was unharmed, but Nelson said he didn't fare as well. His hair was burnt off, and he was burned severely enough that it was some time before he was well enough to resume travel.

Shortly after the trading parties arrived at the rendezvous site near McPherson, Buffalo Bill Cody rode in with instructions to "arrest John Nelson and outfit going with a party of Indians down South to hunt." The implication was that Nelson was aiding the Indians in their endeavor to avoid the troops. Nelson protested, and although Cody considered Nelson his friend, orders were orders. While Nelson was held under guard, Hank Clifford was the one who made the long trip horseback to Omaha where the general who had command of the district was headquartered. Nelson claimed Clifford returned with an order commanding his release, provided he did nothing to prevent the Indians from being driven into the reservations.[4]

After that they went to the Red Cloud Agency near Fort Robinson for awhile, following which, Nelson recalled his next move as being with the Cliffords and Arthur Ruff down to Fort McPherson. "A few miles south of the Fort was Medicine Creek… This was a favorite spot of mine, and I had long wished to pitch my tent and live there. We moved out, and I ran up the first log hut that ever adorned its shores. Hank Clifford followed, and then Arthur Ruff started one. The place soon became known as 'Pleasant Valley,' and the rendezvous of all the hunters in the vicinity…"[5] This was the first known settlement by white men on the Medicine, although George P. Belden, the "White Chief," had trapped and hunted on the Medicine earlier in 1870. Because efforts to successfully adapt the Indians to reservation life were not helped by some of the shenanigans of

---

4   Paul D. Riley at the NSHS found no documentation to support Nelson's claim.
5   O'Reilly, p. 260.

This picture was drawn by *Pay Ute*, a member of the Cut-off band of Oglala Sioux, and titled, "The man who killed many wolves, when he was starving to death." The drawing is of Richard Seymour, an educated easterner who mingled with the inhabitants of Wolf's Rest in 1872 and 1873. The items in the drawing as labeled by Seymour are: 1. Bottle of Strychnine; 2. White man; 3. Wolf, dead; 4. Trap. Seymour was interested in learning the Sioux language and accompanied Hank Clifford on several trading missions with the Indians in what is present day Hitchcock County, Nebraska. He recorded the details of these missions on the unused pages of Ena Raymonde's journals. *Courtesy Nebraska State Historical Society.*

these squaw men, their departure from the reservation was no doubt welcomed.

It was at about the same time that Whistler and his band of Cut-off Sioux also established a village on the Medicine Creek. One historian wrote that Whistler's was one of several bands of raiding Indians that the military placed on the small streams feeding into the Medicine while the Bureau of Indian Affairs prepared a permanent reservation for them elsewhere. It has also been indicated that Hank and Monte Clifford were put in charge of this village.[6] If that is the case, it was a later development, for it does not appear that the Cliffords' initial move to the Medicine was in connection with the Cut-off Sioux.

The primary endeavors during the first years on the Medicine Creek were hunting and trapping. Although the days of the buffalo were numbered, there was still good hunting into the winter of 1871. Paddy Miles was on the Medicine by the middle of the year and noted in his journal on November 18, 1871, that he had gone into partnership with the Cliffords to kill buffalo. Unfortunately the buffalo meat never made it to the railroad sidings, and Paddy Miles learned a basic fact of Indian life: "We killed the buffalo and the squaws tanned the robes until we had ten thousand pounds of meat and a thousand tongues dried that we expected to ship east. But alas! A shadow came over the spirit of our dreams of wealth, in the shape of sixty Indians that came to spend the winter with us, which they did. The meat went to entertain our guests."[7]

If the Cliffords and John Y. Nelson played a part in hunting the buffalo to extinction, it was not without just cause. Because they were obligated to provide for their wives' relatives, who were likely to show up for a stay of indefinite length, the squaw men were in a predicament. Although they were poor, they were usually better off than the Indians who were increasingly being denied access to the buffalo, their traditional means of survival. At the same time, the rations provided by the government were often of poor quality, in

---

6 Sutton, pp. 60-65
7 W. H. Miles and John Bratt, *Early History and Reminiscence of Frontier County, Nebraska*, (Maywood, Nebraska: *The Eagle*, 1894), p. 10.

short supply, or stolen by dishonest Indian agents. The whites had the additional advantage of being able to get credit at the trading posts while the Indians could not.[8] Nelson lamented that a party of his wife's relatives came out to visit "and brought their families, their horses, dogs – everything. This was rather a big order for me, but I was bound to show them every hospitality. They had no sugar, coffee, flour, or bacon and I had to furnish them with these."[9]

During these early years on the Medicine, Hank Clifford often served as a scout and guide and was directly involved in the activity of the Cut-offs. Paddy Miles, who was on the Medicine at the same time, credited Clifford with having the influence over the band that prevented the escalation of trouble when Whistler, chief of the Cut-offs, was murdered by whites in December of 1872. Dick Seymour, who accompanied Hank Clifford on two trading missions with the Indians, described him as being a man of medium height and muscular build. From that description and Seymour's journal entry for January 16, 1873, one can visualize Hank Clifford in his everyday mode: "Hank mounts a mule, two [buffalo] robes and one blanket this time, same old rope for stirrups, and goes trotting off." Hank Clifford's mother-in-law, Silver Woman, was among the band of Indians Clifford and Seymour traded with in the winter of 1873. Seymour's journal entry for January 23, 1873, illustrates the rough-edged familial bond that had developed between the white man and his Indian mother-in-law: "She loves her son-in-law, Hank Clifford, and knowing three words in broken English, she gives vent to her feelings with them. Her own language is insufficient to give an idea of the love she bears him. Speaking of this son-in-law of hers, she breathes gently the whole of her English vocabulary, and the white listener hears, 'Gaud dam um…'"[10]

Of the two Clifford brothers, Hank Clifford's personality emerges as being more out-going. John Nelson once compared another acquaintance to Hank, saying that, "He knew everything, and

8 Nellie Snyder Yost, *Buffalo Bill: His Family, Friends, Fame, Failures and Fortunes,* (Denver: Sage Books, 1979), pp. 37-38.

9 O'Reilly, p. 261.

10 Richard Seymour's journals, January and February 1873, Ballantine MSS. Seymour's description of the trading missions with the Indians can be found in *Medicine Creek Journals.*

everybody's business except his own." Reserved by nature, Monte Clifford engaged in frontier farming and stock-raising as trapping and hunting became less lucrative. Frontier County was organized in Hank Clifford's tepee in January of 1872, and both Hank and Monte Clifford were active in the early affairs of the new county. Hank Clifford was the first sheriff; moreover, always on the lookout for the possibility of profit, he was granted the first liquor license for a fee of twenty-five dollars. It is also on record that he was the first county attorney. He had no legal background, but there were so few white men in the area at the time that being alive and present were the requisite qualifications. Monte Clifford was a commissioner and also served as justice of the peace. Whether they were involved in hi-jinks with Nelson, acting as traders and mediators between the Indians and the whites, or participating in the government of the new county, the names of Hank and Monte Clifford are synonymous with the earliest activity of white men on the Medicine Creek frontier.

Neither Hank Clifford nor John Y. Nelson, however, stayed in the little trapping settlement on the Medicine for more than a few years. Nelson said that they "were there altogether three winters." Nelson and Hank Clifford then moved with their Indian families to the reservation. Monte Clifford stayed in Frontier County until 1888 or 1889 when, because his family was Indian he, too, was forced to move to the Indian lands in Dakota Territory – soon to be South Dakota. On the marginal land of the Badlands of Dakota, the Cliffords, as well as the Indians, continued to endure privation and hardship. Life on the frontier was hard for everyone, certainly, with a variety of responses and outcomes to the opportunities – or importunities – that existed. John Y. Nelson made no secret of the fact that he would lose a pocketful of money playing poker in an evening's time. Monte Clifford, on the other hand, was by all accounts industrious and frugal. Regardless of the direction they leaned, the white men who took Native American wives cast their lines into a different pond.

Ena Raymonde was a neighbor to a band of the Cut-off Sioux when she came to southwest Nebraska in 1872. Some of the pictograph style drawings found in her journals appear to have been drawn by her Native American friends. *Courtesy Nebraska State Historical Society.*

This drawing is labeled "Flying Crane" in Ena Raymonde's handwriting. *Courtesy Nebraska State Historical Society*

4

Eena Teglaka "She's Gone Home"

R iding across the prairie, Marguerite *Yauqueae* Lucian saw in
the distance the body of a man and his horse shot so full of
arrows they looked like giant pincushions. As she drew closer, her
worst fears were confirmed; Augustine Lucian, her husband and
the father of her children, died where he had fallen. She pulled an
armful of arrows from the body of her husband and his horse and
returned to her home, screaming the Indian's death chant. It is said
the grieving woman vowed never to speak to another Indian other
than those in her immediate family for as long as she lived. A full-
blood Oglala Lakota, Marguerite *Yauqueae* was born in the Black
Hills in December of 1808 and is commonly referred to as *Eena
Teglaka – Eena* meaning "Mother," and *Teglaka* being a derivative
of her Indian name, *Titokonlati*, which is interpreted to mean "She's
Gone Home." She was given this name when she fled to the Black
Hills following the death of her husband [1]

Augustine Lucian – known to the Indians as "Yuse" – was a
French-Indian who came to Nebraska Territory as a trapper and
fur trader. It is not known when or where Augustine Lucian and
Marguerite were married, but in the mid-1840s they lived near the
current location of Sidney, Nebraska, where they had some type of

---

1 Emma V. Ruff Jacobs, *Dimming Trails, Fading Memories*, (Kyle, South Dakota: Little
Wound Day School, 1983), p. 4. The Clifford/Ruff family Bible gives Marguerite's English
surname as being Swaggerman. Augustine Lucian's surname is also spelled variously.

a ranch and supplied beef and buffalo meat for the army. They were living in the Fort Laramie area when their daughter Julia was born in 1851 and yet at the time of Lucian's death in 1854. Given the times, he probably continued to hunt and trap to provide for his family, however, he was also serving as a scout and interpreter for the army at Fort Laramie.

Although tension existed between the Indians and the travelers on the Oregon Trail, there had for some time been relative peace in the Fort Laramie region of Nebraska Territory. This peace had been procured by the provisions of the Fort Laramie Treaty of 1851, which promised an annual payment of food and goods to compensate the Indians for the hardship caused by the passage of the white man's wagon trains through their hunting grounds. In exchange, the Indians were not to molest the traffic on the Oregon Trail. This changed with the August 17, 1854 tragedy credited with giving the Indians a taste of the white man's blood and precipitating the Great Sioux War that would rage across the Great Plains for forty years.

Thousands of Indians – Brule, Oglala and Minneconjou Sioux – had come together and were camped on the North Platte River just east of Fort Laramie as they waited for the supplies promised them. The man who touched the match and ignited the explosive situation was Second Lieutenant John L. Grattan. A short-tempered young West Point graduate who was contemptuous of the fighting ability of the Sioux warriors, the inexperienced Lieutenant Grattan was spoiling for a fight. There are more detailed and perhaps more accurate versions of the story, but this is the account of Grattan's Massacre or the Mormon Cow Incident as passed down by the descendents of Augustine Lucian:

> One day a caravan of Mormons was passing through in route to the Salt Lake area. A man of the company had with him an old crippled cow. He traded it to Conquering Bear for a buckskin suit. That spring the cow was butchered for beef. It was reported to Grattan by a jealous Indian that Conquering Bear had stolen the cow. The soldiers were sent out by Lt. Grattan to bring in Conquer-

ing Bear. He refused to surrender because he hadn't done anything wrong.

Meantime Lucian was trying to make Grattan understand what had happened, but to no avail. In the meantime the soldiers were getting drunker and more aggressive. Conquering Bear finally made his appearance, ready to lay down his gun and surrender. Without heeding Lucian's pleading and warning, the drunken soldiers shot and killed Conquering Bear.

When the Indians saw the injustice of what had been done, they decided to go after Grattan and his men. Just then Lucian came over the hill from the Fort and met the angry Indians. He was returning with a message from Lt. Grattan. The Indians were so angry over Conquering Bear's fate that they charged Augustine Lucian, blaming him for the fatal incident. Living with the Indians and being married to one of them, they were sure he should have been able to prevent the death of Conquering Bear. So far he had been unsuccessful but hadn't given up. When the Indians met Lucian coming back from the Fort, they killed him with their bows and arrows.

Lucian had known his mission would not be completed, that he'd never return alive. As he mounted his horse to make the final and fatal trip to the fort to plead the case of Conquering Bear once again, he called to his cousin, Leon Pallardy, to take care of his wife and family and to send the children to school.[2]

After killing Augustine Lucian, the Indians – including a young brave by the name of Red Cloud – rode against Lieutenant Grattan and killed him and all twenty-eight of his troops. When the fighting was over, and Marguerite *Yauqueae* Lucian went to look for her husband, she was mindful of his last words: "I am afraid you will be a widow before night."[3] There is conflicting information as to the number of children Augustine Lucian left, but Julia had just turned three. One story is that there was one older brother, and that Leon

2 Ibid., pp. 5-6.
3 Paine, p. 37.

Pallardy, as the guardian, did as Augustine had instructed and took the boy to St. Louis, Missouri, to school. Julia said she never saw this brother again, but she did receive a letter from him once. There are also references to other older children who were sent off to school, never to be seen by their mother again. The Indians living in the vicinity of Fort Laramie feared there would be reprisals against all Indians, regardless of their complicity in the massacre of Lieutenant Grattan and his men. Consequently, Marguerite's brother took her and little Julia and fled with them to their homeland in the Black Hills where they remained until Julia was nearly grown.

Because of Marguerite's refusal to associate with Indians outside of her family, she most likely lived in mixed-marriage trappers' camps when she returned to Nebraska Territory. Augustine Lucian's cousin, fellow interpreter and trapping partner Leon Pallardy was on the plains at least until the early 1870s. Numerous other white men who were married to Indian women moved about the plains, running trap lines and harvesting the rich bounty of fur-bearing animals. Following the dissolution of Julia's first marriage, she was married to Monte Clifford. This was about 1869, and the following year, in the early winter of 1870, Hank and Monte Clifford, John Y. Nelson, Arthur Ruff and possibly Dick Seymour moved to the Medicine Creek Valley in southwest Nebraska.[4] Julia Clifford's mother was most likely among this little group of white hunter-trappers who moved their Indian families, ponies, and lodges to the campsite on Coon Creek (later named Coyote Creek) at the point where it flowed into what was then known as Medicine Lake Creek.

From here on Marguerite *Yauqueae* Lucian will be referred to by the name engraved on the headstone at her burial site – *Eena Teglaka*. It seems that she spent her remaining years on the Medicine Creek in Nebraska. An Indian widow of over sixty years of age with no means of support, she had to depend on Monte and Julia Clifford for her livelihood. The old Medicine Woman became a fa-

---

4 Arthur Ruff married Mary Gary, half-blood daughter of Eldridge Gary who was a descendent of a signer of the Declaration of Independence. Mary Gary's stepfather was Lone Wolf. Arthur and Mary (Gary) Ruff's son, George, married Monte and Julia Clifford's daughter, Rosa Clifford.

miliar and much-loved figure during her years in Frontier County. She wandered along the creek banks, up the ravines, and onto the divides, collecting the herbs and digging the roots she needed for her medicine bag. Her potions and herbs brought relief when there was no doctor available – and sometimes when there was. She practiced midwifery, and her gnarled, brown hands were the first to touch many of the babies born to the early settlers.

Ena Raymonde first met the old Indian woman in early 1873. Though she sought to know and understand many of her Indian neighbors, Ena was especially fascinated with the *wee-nux-cha* (old woman or medicine woman). Ena wrote in her journal on March 12, 1873:

> The *wee-nux-cha* sat on a gunnysack, petting alternately the bright-eyed papoose and a little white dog that looked something like a prairie dog and something like a dwarfish coyote... I looked at that old, brown squaw with strange fancies making wild pictures in my busy brain. Suppose one could read her life. Must she not watch the changes that the whites have brought to pass with deep wonder? She remembers when these vast plains knew only the brown children of her race.

On another occasion in those early years on the Medicine, Ena wandered into the Indian camp while out hunting. She was struck by the appearance of the woman seated in front of her tepee looking as wrinkled and brown as a bag of leather and apparently "as indifferent and as ignorant of human sentiment or feeling as the Indian dog that crouched by her side." After spending more time with the old Indian woman and listening to the stories of her life, Ena realized the error of her first assessment. The old Medicine Woman told of Indian customs and spiritual beliefs and of the sorrow of losing the burial grounds of her people to the encroachment of the white man's homes. Although Ena understood a number of words in the Lakota language, much of what the old woman said was lost. The strength and pride that showed in her face, however, told the rest of the story.

In 1884 the William Hinton family settled near the Cliffords' place. At first they had to haul all of their water from a spring in the creek located a short distance from where the Cliffords lived. The Hintons necessarily got to know the Cliffords quite well and passed down an amusing anecdote about their old Indian neighbor. The Cliffords had for some time been bothered by some wild animal getting into the chicken coop at night and killing the chickens. The wizened old *Eena Teglaka* declared that she would get the trouble maker. She wrapped herself in a blanket, and taking a club as a weapon kept a vigil in the chicken house one night. Eventually the guilty creature – a skunk – stalked knowingly into the coop expecting to snatch its evening meal. If she hesitated at taking on the intruder, the Indian woman put her qualms aside, plunged into battle and killed the skunk with her club.[5] A skunk always leaves a calling card, and no doubt the Clifford family was thankful that the victorious woman slept in her own tepee.

Though she was both, *Eena Teglaka* was acting as neither a midwife nor Medicine Woman when she went to the Whitneys' home on the occasion of baby Olive's birth. The Whitneys had settled south of the Cliffords, and though they knew the family members, the old Indian woman was usually on the outskirts of any visits back and forth. Mrs. Whitney was startled when *Eena Teglaka* suddenly appeared in her house one day while she was still in the "sick bed" with the new baby. The old woman muttered an unintelligible greeting, walked over to the bed, and threw the covers back. Mrs. Whitney was by then quite frightened, wondering if perhaps *Eena Teglaka* was going to try to take her baby; Indians did sometimes have a peculiar fascination with white children. Without saying a word, the Indian woman simply held the baby's feet up, measured them with her thumb and a finger and left. A few days later *Eena Teglaka* returned with a pair of tiny moccasins made out of soft, tanned leather

---

5 *Curtis(Nebr.) Enterprise,* July 30, 1936

and beaded with turquoise and yellow beads, which she presented to baby Olive.[6]

In later years, Monte and Julia lived in dwellings of either sod or log, but *Eena Teglaka* continued to live in the traditional Indian lodge or tepee nearby. In the winter the children would take meals to her, but in the summer she prepared her own meals, usually over an open fire. Visitors to the Cliffords' recalled that when the old Indian ate in the house, she never sat at the table but would sit on the ground in the corner and eat from a tin plate. At the time of her death in April of 1888, *Eena Teglaka* was the only full-blood Indian left in the community. Nevertheless, she had touched the lives of many, and it is said that the neighbors for miles around attended the funeral. There is a story told in the Robert Cole family of little Clara Cole, too young to walk the entire distance from the family home on Spring Creek, being carried part of the way to Arbor Cemetery on her father's shoulders.[7] Located along the old McPherson Trail, *Eena Teglaka's* grave was one of the first in what became Arbor Cemetery, the town cemetery for Stockville, Nebraska. *Eena Teglaka* – "She's Gone Home" – was buried with her bow and arrow, tomahawk, and Indian blankets.

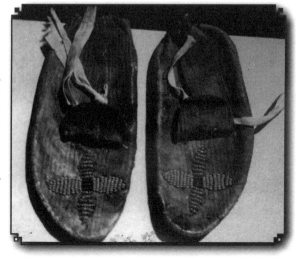

Mocassins made by *Eena Teglaka* for baby Olive Whitney. *Courtesy Frontier County Historical Society*

6 Kenneth Phillips, conversation with author, Cambridge, Nebr., Dec. 7, 2004.
7 Email from Gene Cole, June 19, 2009.

Area citizens raised the funds for this native stone monument marking the grave of *Eena Teglaka* at Arbor Cemetary near Stockville, Nebraska. D. F. Neiswanger of Cambridge crafted and erected the monument in the late 1920s. Although the date of death on the headstone is 1884, it is generally believed *Eena Teglaka* died in 1888. *Photo by Gail Geis*

5
—

Monte & Julia Clifford

Two very different cultures pressed their demands upon those who descended from white fathers and Indian mothers. Strong, hard-willed, they lived and worked to contribute their part to our pioneering past.[1]   ~ Emily H. Lewis

*A*s an Indian married to a white man, Julia (Lucian) Clifford was often required to make adjustments, giving up many – but not all – of the Indian ways. But then, Julia's life had always been lived at odds with her Native American heritage; her father's death at the hands of Indians guaranteed that. Born on July 4, 1851, at Fort Laramie, Julia had just turned three when her father, Augustine "Yuse" Lucian, was killed in the notorious Grattan Massacre. Nothing is known of her life in the wilderness of the Black Hills during the years following her father's death. It is known, however, that she did not receive the education her father had wanted his children to have. When Julia and her mother, Marguerite *Yauqueae* Lucian, finally returned to Nebraska Territory, Julia could not read, write or speak English. In 1866 when she was only fifteen years old, Julia Lucian was married to a man – either white or half-breed – by the name of Peter Peno. They had one child, a boy by the name of Wil-

---

1 Emily H. Lewis, "Shadows of the Brave," circa 1962, reprint, FCHS newsletter, Vol. 7, Issue 4 (1992).

liam Peno, who was born in 1867. This marriage was unsuccessful and short-lived.

It was about 1869 when Julia married the white newcomer to the frontier, Mortimer Clifford – known variously as Monte, Monty or Morte. In the company of a small group of other white men who were married to Indian women, they pitched their lodge on Medicine Creek in southwest Nebraska in the winter of 1870. The settlement on the Medicine remained primarily a hunters and trappers' camp for several years. After the band of Cut-off Sioux set up camp adjacent to the trappers' camp, the nearby whites referred to the Indian village as "Sioux City." A first-hand observation of the daily activity in the little settlement is provided by Ena Raymonde. She wrote of her visit to the Indian village in a journal entry on March 12, 1873:

> I have just returned from a visit to "Sioux City." The squaws were out fishing; or at least Monte's squaw was fishing; and the "California Woman," and the *wee-nux-cha* or Medicine Woman were out digging Indian turnips. Monte met me with his usual kindness and without dismounting, I went with him to the creek for water and to hunt up his wife, Julia, also. We found her fishing, her two papooses playing in the road nearby. Monte got the water and she chattered in Sioux, telling me of her luck, etc., Monte interpreting when I could not understand. She returned to the house with me, and here we met Mrs. Wheatley and the *wee-nux-cha*! How an Indian can blush. They tried to show me that their intentions were hospitable, but with what blushing embarrassment…

> I saw but one white man besides Monte. He was a "bull-whacker" and I could hear him long before he came into view. "Gee-haw! Who-haw, God damn you!" – were the gentle sounds wafted on the soft spring air! The squaws laughed, repeating with gusto the language of this white civilian!

It was Julia's mother who Ena referred to as the *wee-nux-cha* or Medicine Woman and the "California Woman" was Julia's Aunt Nancy Wheatley. Julia's children, six-year-old William "Johnny"

Peno and Delilah Jane Clifford – not yet two years old – were the papooses playing in the road. (Julia Clifford gave birth to nine children – eight of whom lived – in the eighteen years they were on the Medicine Creek. The first two Clifford children were born in tepees – Delilah Jane in June of 1871 and Orlando Hines in 1873. Born in Ambrose Shelley's log cabin in 1877, Rosa Clifford was the first of Julia's children to be born in the way of the white man. Hannah, on the other hand, was born without ceremony in the corral while Julia was helping with the evening chores.)

When domestic harmony went awry in the early years on the Medicine, Julia and Hank Clifford's wife, Maggie, left their husbands to fend for themselves for a spell. The John C. Gammill family, living ten or twelve miles to the south, recalled that when the men stayed away too long on a hunting trip, the wives would "take all the ponies and drive them up to the reservation and stay there 'till the men got tired of cooking for themselves, and they'd go up and get them and bring them all back home again – children, ponies and all."[2]

Although Julia was mixed-breed and had been raised Indian, she adapted to the ways of the whites, and used both the methods of the Indians and those of her white sisters to provide food for her family. She dried, salted, and smoked meat. She raised a garden and preserved or dried the wild fruit and learned to bake bread, pies, and cookies. In her spare time, Julia Clifford tanned leather and made moccasins for which she found a ready market among the Mormons, who traveled the McPherson Trail, which passed near the Cliffords' place. Julia paid a white woman in eggs, butter, and milk to come twice a week to teach her English. It was quite awhile, though, before Julia was confident enough to try out her English in public. One neighbor remembered that when the Indians came to visit her mother, it was apparent they could understand English, but Julia would enlist the aid of her son William "Johnny" Peno as an interpreter, saying, "Johnny, you talk."[3]

It was a priority of Monte and Julia Clifford that their children have the education the parents had missed. School sessions only last-

2 Kristine H. Smith, Compiler, "Burt Grant Moulton and Ann Isabella Gammill Moulton," circa 1960, reprint, FCHS newsletter, Vol. 15, Issue 3 (2000).
3 Smith.

ed two or three months in those early years and were held in various locations – often in a room of a settler's house. Some years the Clifford children had to get up at four o'clock in the morning in order to get their chores done in time to travel the seven or eight miles to school before nine o'clock. Sometimes they walked, sometimes they rode horse-back, and sometimes they drove a horse-drawn sled or wagon, depending on the weather.

The oldest of Monte and Julia's children, Delilah, and her half-brother "Johnny" Peno attended several sessions of school in one room of Sam Gammill's sod house located some distance from their home. Frank Griffith's daughter Mae recalled being fond of pretty little Delilah Clifford or "Lili," but it was Johnny Peno who left the most vivid impression. Even though he was a favorite with almost everybody in the school, Johnny Peno had only two favorites – Mae Griffith and Will White. Johnny called Mae "his sister" and Will "his brother." There was a definite advantage in being Johnny Peno's favorites. The half-breed Indian boy was wiry and tough, and he would fight like the dickens for Mae and Will.[4]

Johnny Peno – or William as he as properly called – made an impression in another school he attended. A one-armed man by the name of Westgate taught in Stockville's first school along the wagon trail that was the main street. Apparently the winds of freedom had been blowing through the black hair of the Indian boy for too long before he started school. Among the students that Mr. Westgate taught were the Dauchys, Sanders, and Fentons, but it was William Peno, who presented a memorable challenge to Mr. Westgate. As told by his brother Berl Westgate: "When my Bro would ring the bells, or rather, tap the bell for recess, noon or night; he [Will] would jump up and run over the top of the seats to get outside till

---

4 Mae (Griffith) Wilmeth, "History of Orafino Post Office," 1936, reprint, FCHS newsletter, Vol. 10, Issue 2 (1995).

my brother had to change his ways, and that was pretty hard to do sometimes."[5]

Although their needs were not extravagant, Monte Clifford found it increasingly difficult to provide for his family and Indian relatives. He had taken out a homestead, but when he found himself deeply in debt at McDonald's store at Fort McPherson, Monte had no other option but to deed his land to Charles McDonald. Ambrose Shelley was temporarily away, so Monte moved his family to Shelley's log cabin. In due time, Monte relocated and established a frontier farming operation. Although these very early Medicine Creek settlers with a bent toward agriculture soon broke out some land and planted crops, it was on a very small scale. Even as the buffalo disappeared, the cattle were allowed to free range so any successful crop grower had to fence his fields. With the good pasturage and running streams for water, livestock seemed to hold the most promise. Cattle, hogs and sheep were all introduced early on, with varying degrees of success.

Both Paddy Miles and Ena Raymonde wrote of the excitement of the first chickens brought to the settlements. As Paddy Miles told it, he and the Cliffords went in together and had a dozen chickens shipped from the east at a cost of seventy-five cents each. He said they were a "wonder to the natives who came from far and wide to see them." Ena Raymonde recalled the arrival of the chickens and the general feeling of community on the creek in a March 1873 journal entry:

> We had fried eggs for dinner! Less than a year ago a hen on the Medicine would have been a curiosity! When we got our chickens and really saw them scratching among the leaves, how domesticated we felt! And then, when we bought three pigs why it was the climax to civilization. Although we slept in tents – cooked by a campfire, and sat about on the grass to eat! When the Cliffords put up a <u>hen-house</u>, what an excitement! I went to see them and

---

5 Berl Westgate to *Curtis Enterprise*, 1932, reprint, *Hi-line (Curtis, Nebr.) Enterprise*, Jan.1973.

scarcely had I entered their "Lodge" when we all started for the hen-house.

As time went on, Monte Clifford built up a small herd of Durham cattle and a line of Hamiltonian horses. In addition to practicing as a veterinary, he had a fine stallion for which he was able to command a twenty-five-dollar stud fee. During the breeding season and other times when Monte was away, Julia, along with the older children and a hired man, did the farming and tended the stock, which had to be

The oldest son of Monte and Julia Clifford, Orlando H. Clifford (right) was nearly eighty years old when this photo was taken at the time of a visit to Stockville in 1952. *Courtesy Frontier County Historical Society*

herded during the day. The children had to be especially resourceful when their father was away from home. The horses were always corralled in the evening, but several times one spring the Cliffords got up in the morning to find the horses had supposedly been in the neighbor's cornfield. Having corralled them, the neighbor held the horses and demanded a choice colt for damages. Orlando, who by then was about twelve or thirteen years old, told his mother he was going to find out what was going on. He took his gun and concealed himself in sight of the corral. It was nearly daybreak when the neighbor came over, turned the horses loose, and drove them to his place. When Orlando, with his gun in hand, confronted the neighbor, there was no defense; he had been caught in the act. Orlando returned home with the herd of horses plus the colts the neighbor had been skimming off for damages.

Orlando "Lando" Clifford took another matter into his hands. Having discovered a meadowlark nest on their way to school, the

Clifford children were beside themselves with excitement the morning they found the eggs had hatched. The scrawny baby birds were duly named, and each day the children caught insects and poked them into the five wide-open mouths. They were horrified one morning at the discovery that someone had skinned the baby meadowlarks alive. Lando was furious and promised to find the culprits and "wale the stuffing out of them." The bullies who had committed the crime revealed themselves by taunting the Clifford children when they arrived at school. Orlando waited until noon when the teacher went to lunch, and then he posted the little kids at the corners of the schoolhouse to keep watch. It didn't take very long to give one of the offending boys all he could stand, but it took a little longer with the bigger one. One of the culprits got away and ran up town screeching that Lando was killing "Neezer." Rosa Clifford later recalled, "The teacher came running back to the schoolhouse, panting like a lizard and pulled Lando off and got us all into the schoolhouse. Then one of us little kids got to bawling and told her what the fight was about. Teacher thought it was pretty fine of Lando to take up for the birds…"[6] It was frontier justice on the school ground.

The Clifford children were inadvertently involved in pursuing justice in another situation. They had often taken extra lunch along to school or when herding cattle and shared with a neighbor boy, who never seemed to have enough to eat or adequate clothing. One winter day the boy got caught in a blizzard when he went after the milk cows and never returned home. When his skimpily clad body was found at the head of a canyon the following spring, charges were brought against the stepfather. Monte Clifford was justice of the peace at the time so he held the man's hearing at his home. The children were all sent outdoors, but little Rosa pressed her ear against the keyhole and caught most of what was said. Orlando was allowed to testify: "He told how he and his brothers and sisters used to share their lunch with the boy. The townspeople were called upon for their testimony. They told how they had seen the boy eating from

---

6 Rosa (Clifford) Ruff, "The Indians' Story," *Curtis, Nebraska: The First 100 Years*, (Dallas, Texas: Curtis Media Corporation, 1986), pp. 2-4.

the garbage cans at the back of the hotel and stores. The stepfather was found guilty of abuse and neglect and fined."[7]

The Cliffords' fortunes in Frontier County changed in 1885, when Monte Clifford took on a contract to build a certain portion of the grade for the railroad. He bought the necessary equipment, the mules, and horses and hired the help he needed. Unfortunately he was unable to meet the specified deadline; therefore, he was not paid for the work he had done. By the time he paid his help and what he could of the bills he owed, he was broke – saving only their household goods, a few head of cattle, some horses, the wagons and teams. Land was being allotted to the Indians in Dakota Territory, and since Julia Clifford was Indian, the family decided to relocate.

While Monte stayed behind to settle his affairs, Julia, the children, and a couple of fellows who had worked for Monte made the trip with the household goods and livestock. Julia Clifford was thirty-seven years old when she set off with her nine children – one only a year old – and two wagons on the trek across the Nebraska prairie that would take them more than two months. It was October 20, 1888, when Julia and her caravan left their home on the Medicine Creek – the season when the golden leaves of the cottonwood shimmer and tease – when the warmth of the late afternoon sun beguiles one into forgetting the harsh reality of winter on the Great Plains. It was not unusual in those days for migrants to spend several months traveling by foot, horseback or wagon to reach the desired destination. It was unusual to set out on such a trip when winter loomed ahead.[8]

Julia Clifford was no fool, however, and she would not be caught by surprise if a blizzard should roll across the plains. The deadly "Blizzard of 1888" had occurred only ten months earlier, following a succession of storms that had locked in much of the Great Plains during the entire winter of 1887 and 1888. Though such a winter

---

7 Jacobs, p. 12.
8 Rosa (Clifford) Ruff gave differing accounts. In one she said they left in 1887 and in another she said it was 1888. The 1888 date is most likely the correct one as it is believed Julia's mother died in the spring of 1888, and Julia would not have left her aged mother behind. Rose also indicated that they arrived in South Dakota after the great blizzard of 1888.

was not likely to be repeated, Julia loaded the wagons with buffalo robes and adequate fuel and food to insure her family's survival should a surprise storm force them to make an emergency camp. Traveling in the fall had its advantages as the first frost eliminated most of the insects, and they were spared the threat of lightning and hail storms. Providence was apparently kind to the travelers for they spent all of November and December on the road and there were no untoward incidents reported. They arrived at Wolf Creek just east of Pine Ridge on the first day of January 1889, where they set up camp in a deserted dugout. Julia then took eleven-year-old Rosa and set out to find her Aunt Nancy, who she had not seen for many years. After the visit to Nancy's, Julia and her family went on into the Badlands where they stayed in an extra cabin of Hank Clifford's on the Big White River. Here she remained until spring when Monte joined the family.

Considering the deep black soil and the timbered banks of the Medicine Creek Valley in Nebraska or the fine hay land and grass-covered plains they passed in the Sand Hills on the way to Dakota Territory, the Badlands was a barren and desolate place. The new home had one similarity to the Nebraska home site; it had a nearby creek that bore the name Medicine – Medicine Root Creek, a tributary of the Big White River. In addition to the log house, barns and corrals, Monte built roads and bridged the Medicine Root Creek. Recognizing that the land could be more productive, he constructed an extensive irrigation system and grew corn, oats, and alfalfa. Through perseverance and hard work, the Cliffords turned their Badlands' home into a welcoming haven for family and friends.

Mortimer Harrison Clifford never had the opportunity to enjoy the fruits of his labor in old age. He passed away in August of 1904 at the age of sixty-two and was laid to rest at Grace Church, Lacreek, South Dakota. Five months later his daughter Hannah and her infant daughter were buried in the same cemetery. Monte Clifford was not a veteran, so his widowed wife and minor children were not eligible to receive a pension. Therefore, the heirs decided the estate should be given to their mother for her lifetime use, and the sons who lived nearby would help care for her and the livestock.

Julia Clifford was fifty-four years old when her husband died, and of necessity, she created a life of her own. She continued to live in the family home – a two-story log cabin – until her children were grown. The youngest, Mortimer Shelley Clifford, was only ten years old when his father died. Julia's oldest child, William "Johnny" Peno, having burned out his candle early, had died a year earlier at age thirty-six, and Julia finished raising his children. (It is said William Peno was a rough rider in Buffalo Bill Cody's Wild West show at one time.)

In later years Julia had a little two-room frame house built on the south side of Medicine Root Creek several miles from the MHC Ranch, the original home site, which was named for their M-C brand. She always kept her own buggy and team and would go by herself to visit relatives or to shop at the area towns. In the fall of the year when she shipped her cattle to Sioux City or Omaha, Julia would buy a wagon-load of groceries. On her way home from town, she would leave groceries for any of her children who might be in need. When she butchered a beef, she shared the fresh meat with the children living nearby and dried and cured the meat for those at a distance. And of course, there was always good food for her visitors – a pot of soup on the stove or homemade bread with plum, choke cherry or buffalo berry preserves, which she made and stored in five-gallon crocks.

Julia had a long-stemmed Redstone clay pipe that she would smoke a couple of times daily. She usually smoked *cha-sha-sha*, a sweet smelling tobacco made from the bark of the red willow, but she also used a tobacco that was made up of plug tobacco, red willow and herbs. This she claimed was for medicinal purposes only ("Her Asthma"). Although Julia Clifford was a Medicine Woman, she did not pass the authority on to the next generation as her mother had done. While she adhered to certain Indian rituals and superstitions, she became a Christian of the Catholic faith. One year she furnished some beef for the Christmas dinner at the Saint Stephen's Catholic Church. Someone in the church told those serving the meal to be careful to give Julia beef, as she did not like the traditional "dog soup" that was usually served. Her native tongue remained the one

Julia spoke the most easily; however, she and Monte apparently used English in their home. Because of the government assimilation policies in the years after the Cliffords moved to South Dakota, the Indian children were sent to boarding schools and not allowed to use their native tongue. Consequently, Julia never taught her children or grandchildren to speak Lakota. She also would forbid anyone in the family to "speak Indian" in the presence of her English speaking in-laws and grandchildren.

Julia (Lucian) Clifford died in April of 1934 at the age of eighty-two. Counting her oldest son, William Peno, she had given birth to thirteen children over a period of twenty-eight years (three more children were born after the move to South Dakota). Two she lost as infants, including Emily Julia, her lastborn. Julia buried three of her adult children and grieved at the loss of several grandchildren. Over the years if there was a death in the family and no money for a coffin, her son James would build the coffin, and Julia would furnish the material for the lining. Wishing to be prepared for her burial, Julia would buy a new purple "burial" dress each year and wear the old one as her "good" dress. But when Julia died, times were particularly hard, and there was no purple dress.

Julia Clifford was laid to rest at the St. Barbara's Catholic Church where she had been designated the "Grandmother of the Church." Although Julia was not a tall lady, she became quite heavy as she grew older, and people affectionately gave her the name "Julie Tonka"; the word tonka meaning big or great in the Lakota language. In the eyes of her children, grandchildren, and great-grandchildren, she had fulfilled the name "Julie Tonka" in every sense of the word. One of her grandchildren succinctly phrased the qualities that were the key to Julia's success in integrating her Indian life with her "white" life: "She had no formal education, but she had the intelligence, ability, and resourcefulness to learn from others and the ambition to do it. Her character was exemplified by her everyday living."[9]

---

9 Jacobs.

6
—

Kinazi Wea "Standing Woman"

Antoine "Andy" Barrett, known as the California Horse Tamer, and Nancy Wheatley, known as the California Woman, each had a story that connected them to that far-off land of California. The half-breed, Andy Barrett, was supposedly captured while still a child and taken west by the Mormons, where he gained fame as a roper and horse trainer. After twenty years or so, he came back to the Nebraska plains in search of his Sioux mother, but she had gone to the Happy Hunting Grounds. On June 4, 1873, Frontier County Probate Judge Samuel P. Watts issued the first marriage license in the young county to thirty-four-year-old Antoine Barrett and thirty-two-year-old Nancy Wheatley. The place of birth listed for the prospective groom was Prairie, Dakota, which, given that Andy Barrett was born about 1839 means simply that he was born on the prairie in Dakota Territory. The place of birth for the bride-to-be was given as North Platte River. The marriage took place on June 8, 1873, at Wolf's Rest with Samuel Watts and E. G. Nesbitt as witnesses. As Paddy Miles told it:

> The first wedding in the county was at the ranch of W. H. Miles on June 4, 1873. The happy parties were Andy Barrett and Mrs. Nancy Wheatley, both half Indian. It was a grand social affair, attended by ranchers, cowboys and Indians… After congratulations, Judge Watts wished that their lives would be on a sea of happiness, that the white wings of love and peace would fan away every trou-

bled thought, that their path thru life be ever strewn with fairest flowers. Everyone wished the new couple a happy married life. The wish never came to pass. An Indian had a dream that he must kill the first person he met or he would never get to the happy hunting grounds in the hereafter. By chance, he met Andy Barrett and shot him dead. His bride, Mrs. Barrett, was lost on the plains and died. This ended the earthly pilgrimage of the contracting parties to the first marriage in the county of Frontier.[1]

This story of the wedding has become a local legend. It is, indeed, the way the marriage was launched, but it is not the way it ended – at least not for the bride. Nancy Wheatley Barrett was not lost to death on the plains but lived a long life. For that matter, she had lived what surely must have seemed like a long life before her marriage to Andy Barrett. Although Nancy had given her age as thirty-two when she married Andy Barrett, family records show her as being at least forty. Like most women, Nancy was discreet about her age – especially when marrying a younger man.

It was twenty-four years earlier in 1849, that the young Indian girl was married to a white man by the name of Thomas Wheatley, probably in the vicinity of Sidney, Nebraska. Thomas had previously been married to a Mexican woman and had a daughter by that marriage. After Thomas and Nancy were married, he informed his bride that he was going to California; the gold rush was in full swing, and he wanted to be a part of it. Furthermore, they were going by way of Mexico so he could get his daughter, who was now living there with her mother. Not presuming to ask questions, Nancy climbed into the wagon beside her husband for a trip that would take them halfway across the continent. Upon arriving in Marysville, California, Thomas set his family up in a small cabin and then left Nancy to manage on her own while he went off to become a prospector. It didn't take the young Indian girl long to figure out whose initiative it was going to take if she and the little step-daughter were going to survive. Nancy Wheatley was young, strong, and industrious, and she set to work immediately. She built a corral and chicken coop and

---

1 Miles and Bratt, pp. 16-17.

STATE OF NEBRASKA, }
Frontier COUNTY. } ss.

The People of the State of Nebraska.

To any Person Legally Authorized to Solemnize Marriages, Greeting:

You are Hereby Authorized, *To join in the Holy Bands of Matrimony and to celebrate within this County the rites and ceremonies of Marriage between Mr.* *Antwine* *Barrott* *of Stockville Neb* aged *34* *years, born at* *Pierce Dakota*, *son of* *John Barratt* *his mother's maiden name was* *Jane Black* *and Miss* *Nancy Wheatly* *of San Francisco Cal* *aged 32 years, born at* *North Platte Riv daughter of* *J. B. Strike* *her mother's maiden name was* *Nancy Walton and this shall be your good and sufficient warrant, and you are required to return this License to me within three months from the celebration of such marriage, with the certificate of the same appended thereto, and signed by you, under the penalty of five hundred dollars.*

In Witness Whereof, *I have hereunto set my hand and official seal* this *4th* day of *June* *A. D.* 18*73*

Samuel F. Watts

Probate Judge.

The first marriage license issued in Frontier County, Nebraska, was to Antoine "Andy" Barrett and Nancy Wheatley, both at least half Native American. The marriage took place on June 8, 1873, in the log cabin at Wolf's Rest. Wm. H. "Paddy" Miles' father, Justice of the Peace Dempsey B Palmer, signed the marriage certificate to which Miles added a note that the couple wanted to be married like white people and it was "You bet". Although it is commonly believed that both Andy Barrett and his bride met with sudden death soon after their marriage, Nancy Barrett (several years older than her stated age and an aunt of Julia Clifford's) returned to her native Dakota territory and lived to be quite an old woman.

by some means was able to purchase four head of milk cows, some laying hens, and turkeys. She milked the cows and found the miners' families living in the tent cities to be a ready market for the milk, cream, and butter. She also sold eggs and raised and sold turkeys.

It appears all Thomas Wheatley contributed on his infrequent home-comings were the crude and vulgar habits he had learned in the mining camps. His departures left Nancy with more work, less money, and sometimes a pregnancy. She gave birth to two sons,

Charlie and Thomas Jr., and to at least one baby that never lived. (In a March 1873 journal entry Ena Raymonde wrote that the "California woman" had shown her the tiny pattern she had made of a baby's foot, explaining "I cut it, where me can look far, far Caller [California] way! And me cry!" Ena was touched at the insight into the inner life of this Indian woman who had kept the measure of the tiny foot of a baby who had died so long ago.)

Almost twenty years passed, and Nancy became very ill – so ill that she was confined to her bed. In the words of her great-grand niece, "When an Indian remains in bed because of illness, one knows he or she is very ill." On his return home and finding his wife gravely ill, Thomas hired a Digger Indian – as that particular tribe of California Indians is known – to come in and do the work. After a time, Nancy's health improved, and she woke up one morning feeling well enough to help prepare breakfast. She went into the kitchen, and much to her surprise found her husband in bed with the Digger Injun. Thomas was no prize, but his wife's pride was hurt at finding him in the bed of another woman – and one she considered lower class at that. Nancy's disgust is best described in her words: "Dirty Digger Indians. No good – eat grasshoppers."

Nancy's reaction was quick and decisive. The stepdaughter was grown and had married a Sacramento doctor and Nancy's own sons, Charlie and Thomas Jr., were apparently old enough to fend for themselves. Nancy Wheatley packed her few belongings, said goodbye to her sons, and left by horseback for Sacramento, where she sold her horse and riding gear to her stepdaughter's husband. She then bought a train ticket to Salt Lake City, Utah, which was the end of the railroad from California to the east. Nancy found a job at a tavern in Salt Lake City and settled in to wait for a freight or bull-train to come in from the east. This was within a year of the driving of the Golden Spike at Promontory, Utah – the official recognition of a transcontinental rail system – and the bull-train was about to fade into history. The story is that it was almost a year before Nancy left Salt Lake City headed east on a bull-train – probably one of Jerome Dauchy's – under the hand of Hank Clifford as wagon master. When the weary wagon master and his crew came into Salt Lake, they washed the trail dust from their tonsils at the tavern at which Nancy was washing dishes. Perhaps a conversation was struck, and Hank Clifford mentioned Julia Clifford's mother – Nancy's half-sister – Marguerite. Nancy, of course, had no way of knowing that her sister had lost her husband, Augustine Lucian, in 1854 in the Grattan Massacre. It was following her return from California that Nancy went to live with her half-sister, Marguerite or *Eena Teglaka*. There is no indication that Nancy ever saw either her sons or step-daughter again.

This is where we again pick up the story of the marriage of Nancy Wheatley to Andy Barrett. Ena Raymonde first mentioned meeting Mrs. Wheatley in March of 1873. In the same journal entry in which she mentioned the paper tracing of the dead baby's foot, Ena wrote, "The California Indian tried to amuse me in every way she could! Got me a letter to read from Salt Lake. It was from a woman of education and quite entertaining…" The journals of Ena Raymonde also add detail to Paddy Miles' brief description of the wedding. On July 1, 1873, Ena noted in her journal that on the eighth of June a remarkable event had occurred on the Medicine – the solemnization of the first marriage in Frontier County:

> Quite a number of the "creek people" were gathered here at "Wolf's Rest" to see Mr. Andy Barrett and Mrs. Nancy Wheatley joined in the "Holy Bonds of Matrimony!" Both of them are half-breed Indians; and the bridegroom is better known as "Andy, The Half Breed," or the wonderful "California Horse-Tamer," than Mr. Barrett. I have known the bride for some time and think her quite a nice woman…

> One year ago, I saw the Horse-Tamer for the first time. He was with that "Saratoga Man's Outfit." The party that passed here on the 7th of June for the purpose of lassoing buffalo. I did not expect to see him the principle actor at a wedding out here, in a year's time! There was not a woman in 30 miles of us then – and only one cabin on the creek!

> There were five or six ladies present, 20 or 30 gentlemen, and 10 or 12 Indians. We got up a right good dinner,

for the <u>prairie</u>, and everything passed off charmingly (I hope!!!). I was kept very busy, being the <u>prime minister</u> for the whole "out-fit."… I think I did my duty to people and things that day – even to prompting the bride at the all-important moment! Standing a little behind the bride, I had a fine opportunity to hear the congratulations! The <u>styles</u> were quite varied! Our humorous Judge W[atts] really surprised me with his rhetorical eloquence! Wish I could remember just how his congratulation was worded.

Paddy Miles' handwritten note appears on the marriage certificate: "The above named parties was Indians, the first wedding in Frontier County. They was married in our house at Wolf's Rest. They wanted to be married like white people and [it] was 'You bet.'" There is little to affirm or disaffirm the narrative surrounding the death of Andy Barrett, The California Horse-Tamer, although A. T. Andreas' *History of the State of Nebraska* states that the newlyweds parted after a couple of months. On July 4, 1873, Ena Raymonde noted that she'd had a visit from the "bridal pair." Beyond that, no further mention is made of Andy Barrett. The Clifford family history offers only W. H. "Paddy" Miles' version. Nancy Barrett later told some of the story of her grueling California years to family members, but for reasons of her own, she apparently never mentioned the fate of Andy Barrett.

Whether she was widowed or suffered the humiliation of another ill-fated marriage, it seems Nancy soon left Nebraska for Dakota Territory. When Julia Clifford made her three-month trek from Frontier County to the reservation the winter of 1888 and 1889, the first thing she did on arrival was locate her Aunt Nancy, who she found living in a tepee. Although she was actually an aunt to the Clifford nieces and nephews, grandnieces and grandnephews, etc., Nancy refused to be called "Aunt" so everyone, family and friends alike, called her Grandma Nancy. In South Dakota, Grandma Nancy made her home either near or with various relatives. Like her sister, she preferred to live in a tent. She prepared her food on a small cook-stove, ate at a table set with a checkered tablecloth, and slept on a bed. During the coldest part of the winter, she lived in the house with a relative – usually Monte and Julia Clifford.

When Grandma Nancy did eat in the house, everyone at the table was on their best behavior. If table manners were not observed, she would walk up to the culprit, tap him or her on the shoulder, and speaking in a false indignant tone of voice, say, "What, you can't say please?" "You don't know the words thank you?" "Got no fork, have to use fingers?" "Look at me, full-blood Injun, and I know better than that." Grandma Nancy took pride in her ability as a housekeeper, in her good manners, and in being able to converse in the English language; however, as she grew older she reverted more and more to the Indian traditions or superstitions. Every spring while she was able, Grandma Nancy would climb to the top of Sugar Loaf Butte – so named because it was almost square in shape like a lump of sugar and covered with tiny white flowers in the spring of the year. She would tie a little tobacco in a new piece of pink calico, point it to the four winds, and repeat this prayer: "Oh, God, I thank thee for letting me live to a ripe old age. Let me live to put my feet on green grass in another year." After that she would push the end of the stick into the ground and leave. [2]

Grandma Nancy – the Indians gave her the name *Kinazi Wea* or Standing Woman – passed away in January of 1909 at the home of her grandnephew on Big White River in South Dakota. She was, as nearly as can be determined, about seventy-seven years of age. Though she was never considered a good-looking woman, Julia Clifford would point out, "Looks are only skin-deep. It's what's inside that counts." A woman of strong character, Nancy was deeply loved and respected by her relatives and friends. She was also conservative and thrifty, and it was those characteristics that allowed her, at the time of her death, to leave a mystery as intriguing as that of her marriage to the California Horse-Tamer. As a result of necessity and a general inclination to never indulge herself – beyond a cup of good tea – Nancy spent very little money on herself over the years. After the bare necessities were taken care of, she put the rest of her

---

2 Jacobs.

money in a baking powder can and hid it. The story passed down through the years is that she hid the can of money under a certain large stone. Efforts to find the hidden stash have been in vain. But, of course, her family knew that Grandma Nancy's greatest legacy was her tenacity.

7

Paddy Miles Comes West

The image of Paddy Miles riding into town on a Saturday night – reins in his mouth and a pearl-handled gun in each hand, firing them all the way down the street – captures the very essence of the frontiersman's legend. Certainly no one lent more color to the stage of early southwestern Nebraska history. William Herbert "Paddy" Miles, however, did not begin life with the surname of Miles. Born near the Georgia and Florida border, he began life on January 6, 1846, as William Herbert Palmer, the only son of Dempster B. and Anne Marie (Timmons) Palmer.[1] By the time the young veteran of the Confederate Army reached the windswept plains of Nebraska in the early winter of 1869, his surname was Miles. Perhaps the name "Miles" came to mind as he trekked – mile after mile halfway across the continent – a man evidently on the run. Although it has never been proven or disproven, it is generally believed that Miles left his native Georgia after shooting and killing his sister's former fiancé, one Dr. Hilliard H. Harley, on the night of August 24, 1869.

Whether William Herbert Palmer fired the shot that left Dr. Harley's brains splattered on the wall that fateful night, or whether someone else was astride the horse that sped away in the dark is irrelevant. Young Palmer was implicated, and in short order he disappeared. As the story is told, he left his clothes on a Georgia riverbank hoping to create the impression he had drowned. It was, in any

---

1 Birth date was incorrectly stated in *Medicine Creek Journals*.

case, the end of William Herbert Palmer. The man who emerged on the other side of the river, dressed in dry clothes, picked up his gun and war sack, slid a bowie knife into his boot-top and headed west would from thereon be known as William Herbert Miles. Although his original destination had been California, the young fugitive was writing from Brady Island, Lincoln Co., Nebraska, when he made the following entry in his journal on November 6, 1869: "I find myself in Nebraska, working on the U.P. Railroad, with chills and fever, nearly dead from exposure. This is a miserable sandy and windy country."[2] A month later he met Buffalo Bill Cody who was on the government payroll – as a scout in the spring, summer and fall and as a herder in the winter:

> December 5, 1869 –
>
> At Fort McPherson going on a hunt on the Lo[u]pe with Buffalo Bill…to catch wild horses and cattle. Spent the Winter on the Lo[u]pe hunting [and] fighting Indians. And freezing nearly to death. One of our party frozed off both legs and arms. I find this country rather cool compared with the South.
>
> Thousands of game on the Lo[u]pe, buffalo, elk, deer, antelope. [Also] cattle and horses. Last but not least the Indians.

Certainly the reality of winter on the Nebraska plains was a new experience for the young adventurer. The contrast between Miles' upbringing in an atmosphere of culture and privilege and the harsh life on the frontier is reflected in his lone journal entry for the year of 1870:

> Fort McPherson, Lincoln County, Nebraska, May 1, 1870 –
>
> I am herding horses, scouting, etc. for Uncle Sam. Do anything I can, for I must get money enough to get a home for Mother and Sister.

---

2 W. H. Miles' journal is on file at FCHS. All references to Miles' journal are from this source. Original spelling is retained with some changes in punctuation for clarity.

Wm. H. Palmer in a photo probably taken before he left Georgia. After his arrival in Nebraska in 1869, he was known as Paddy Miles. *Courtesy Nebraska State Historical Society*

I get homesick and so tired at times. "No one to love and caress, roaming over this wild wilderness."

Every day, long lines of white covered wagons pass up the Platte, going west to hunt homes. I think of going on myself, soon. I don't like this country. I see no one but rough men, soldiers, etc. w[h]ich is no company for me. But I must not give up, bear all and be brave...

Miles eventually became one of the rough men to which he referred, but on Christmas Day 1869 he was just a homesick young man writing home. Miles and three other cowboys, on the trail of a herd of cattle pushed toward the Platte by a late December blizzard, found themselves at the railroad siding of the Union Pacific Rail Road at Plum Creek (now Lexington, Nebraska) where they had a fine dinner at the eating and rooming house. Paddy took advantage of a few hours respite from the weather and wrote a letter to his sister:

I left my camp on the Lo[u]pe river two days ago on the trail of twelve hundred head of cattle that left in a snow storme. There is fore of us – had a cold time...I have my ears and hands frozen, we had to get water by melting snow.

We came to this station to water our horses, and get a fresh sup[p]ly of food and will leave in the morning after the cattle – don't know when we will find them and when we do will return to the Lo[u]pe.

I have just partaken of a splendid Christmas dinner rather unexpected...I wrote you I thought of having a ro[a]sted <u>deer</u> only.

I am getting along very well only sick parte of the time to see and hear from you...Darling Ones, My thoughts have been with you all the time today thinking over the changes, since a few shorte Christmases ago we spent in such glee – and this I mostly spent riding over snow covered mountains in a wilde c[o]untry so far away...[3]

---

3 Wm. H. Miles, Ballantine MSS.

The letter was signed simply – just an "H" for Herbert – and no doubt sent by a circumspect route. By the following Christmas, Paddy Miles would be an experienced frontiersman living on the Medicine Creek. He first set foot on the Medicine in July of 1871:

> My first trip on the Medicine Lake Creek. Bill Read [i.e., Reid or Reed] [and] James Lodderdale [i.e., Lauderdale] and me came out to take claims. I am delighted with the Medicine. We take claims by starting a house on each. The land is not surveyade yet. Our rights, there is none to dispute, from the [ ] all round to the creek. We are the First.

> There's a band of Sioux Indians here. Whistler is the Chief. There's some white men with them who have squaws for wives – John Nelson, Hank and Monty Clifford. They have taken claims also. We go back to the Fort to fix up to come out for good and grow rich.

Paddy Miles soon joined the small enclave on Medicine Lake Creek – known at the time as "Pleasant Valley." There were many hunts, of course, but Miles' story of one he took part in that first summer is worth retelling. The object of this particular hunt was to catch some live buffalo calves. The hunting party, which included the old plainsman John Y. Nelson, was on the Mitchell several miles to the east of their camp when the action began. They had caught three buffalo calves and were off their horses tying the calves when:

> An immense herd of buffalos came running along "pell-mell"…almost running over me and sending a thrill of fright coursing through our anatomy, which almost paralyzed us and scared our horses so that Dick Seymore [*sic*], Hank Clifford and [Wilk] Snell's horses broke away and went with the rushing, surging herd toward the Sunny South, bridled and saddled but riderless.

> John Nelson and myself followed to try and overtake the fugitives, but they were soon lost to our view in the herd of thousands of buffalo, though we followed in hopes of coming up with the horses.

> Near the mouth of the Mitchell we found where the

buffalo had run over a bluff, at one place nearly a hundred feet down to the bottom where there stood a large elm tree in which the gentle zephyrs had moaned the evening requiems of solitude, among its leafy branches for many long years in the flight of ages, undisturbed. But in the wild rush of the bison of the plains, a huge buffalo was crowded off the perpendicular cliff and lodged in the old elm. This was the only time I ever saw a buffalo up a tree.[4]

From here they continued down the Medicine to the Republican in hopes of finding the runaway horses. They were unsuccessful in this regard, but at nightfall they came upon a log house occupied by Bill Colvin and George Love and his family. Paddy Miles continued:

> As our horses were tired out, we told them we would camp for the night with them. We unsaddled, picketed out our ponies and began looking around for some meat for supper. As luck was to our hand in that line, a herd of buffalo came along nearby. I took up my needle-gun and started after them, when one of the men called to me saying, "We wish you would not kill any of those animals inside the town site, as it might be hard for us to remove the carcass."
>
> I apologized, saying, "I did not know that I was in town but grant your request and would not intentionally violate any city ordinance."[5]

The stakes the weary hunters mistook for picket pins were actually the stakes marking the lots and streets of the new town of Arapahoe in present day Furnas County. George Love went on to explain that Captain E. B. Murphy had staked out the town and named it Arapahoe. Another telling of the story indicates that there was actually a little set-to between Miles and the captain over buffalo hunting in the area. If so, Paddy Miles got off on the wrong foot

4 Miles and Bratt, p. 23.
5 Ibid., pp. 23-24.

with Captain Murphy, a highly es-
teemed veteran of the Indian wars,
who later became his father-in-law.[6]

By winter, hunting and trapping were the major endeavors for
the newcomer on the Medicine and
on November 18, 1871, Miles wrote
that he had gone into partnership
with the Cliffords to kill buffalo. Indicating that Reid and Lauderdale
had "weakened and gave up their
claims," Miles was resolute: "But
I never weaken and will stay alone.
There is no way for me to live but
to trap and hunt, and I have gone in

Dempsey B. and Anne Palmer
and their daughter Ena (Palmer)
Raymonde joined their son Wm.
Herbert "Paddy" Miles on the
Medicine Creek in March 1872.
Courtesy Norman Miles

with the Squaw men and Indians." And then Christmas was upon
them. Paddy Miles' tale of the first Christmas on the Medicine has
been related numerous times; however, no telling of his story is com-
plete without it:

> The Indians that camped on the Medicine…were Whis-
> tler's band, that had been cut off from the tribe of Spotted
> Tail, the big Sioux chief. Hank and Montie Clifford and
> John Nelson were with them and had Indian families; [I]
> found them and built a smoke-house, dried buffalo meat
> and trapped during the winter…
>
> We prepared for a "big time" on Christmas; so Clifford
> went into town [Fort McPherson] and brought out some
> "fixin's" such as currants, sugar, etc.; and last but not least,
> a keg of whiskey, of which Indians and all indulged freely.
> The Indians had a war dance, which came very near to be-
> ing a "killing off," but we had a good time all the same.
>
> The Indians said they would celebrate Christmas too, by
> killing and eating all the dogs in the village. I had a fine
> dog and told them to spare him; but the first thing I saw
> Christmas morning was poor Dodge roasting on the fire.

6 Edward B. Miles to Robert Van Pelt, Dec. 27, 1986, Robert Van Pelt Estate.

There were ten dogs eaten at the first Christmas celebration in Frontier County.[7]

The year to come – 1872 – was an eventful one on the frontier, and Paddy Miles, by now a permanent player in the area, answered roll call at a number of important occasions. One of the events of significance was the buffalo hunt held for the benefit of the Grand Duke Alexis, the son of Alexander II, the czar of Russia. At the time, buffalo hunting was the sport of choice and would remain so until the huge herds that had once roamed the plains were decimated. Although there were a number of buffalo hunts involving well-heeled easterners and prominent dignitaries, this particular hunt, because of the international importance of the duke, was the one that would capture the attention of the press. As the guest of General Phil Sheridan, a Civil War commander for the Union cause, Duke Alexis would have the opportunity to see a panorama of the West played out before his eyes.

When the company of cavalry and dignitaries that met the duke's special train at North Platte on January 13, 1872, started south with their guest and his entourage, they picked up the McPherson military trail and followed it to the Medicine where a little excitement was added by the staging of a sham battle between the soldiers and some of Whistler's band of Indians. When the Indians made their "attack," Buffalo Bill Cody, Duke Alexis, and others of the party "escaped" and laid in hiding on an island on the creek bottom until the all-clear signal was given. Once assured that the "hostile" Indians had been driven away, the party continued on to the campsite on the Red Willow Creek in present day Hayes County.[8] It was on the Willow that the war dance that Buffalo Bill Cody had arranged with Spotted Tail's band of Indians as well as other exhibitions and the buffalo hunt took place.

Several of the residents of the Pleasant Valley camp on the Medicine took part in the festivities on the Willow, and Paddy Miles

7 Miles and Bratt, p. 11. In Miles' reminiscence, written in 1894, he gives 1870 as being the year of the first Christmas, however, he was not on the Medicine until the summer of 1871.
8 C. D. Hayden, "Frontier County Trails," *Curtis (Nebr.) Enterprise*, July 30, 1936.

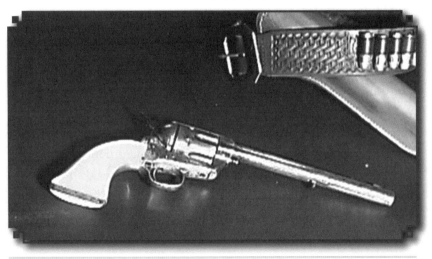

The .44 caliber revolver pictured in the upper two photos was manufactured by the Starr Arms Company of New York City. The patent date is January 15, 1856. Starr revolvers of this type were used by both Union and Confederate soldiers during the Civil War. It is believed the gun and the concealed carry holster once belonged to Paddy Miles. This gun was in poor condition when it came into the possession of the current owner by a long and curcuitous route. The lower photo is of Paddy Miles' .45 caliber long Colt revolver with ivory grips, which is still in the Miles family. The serial number dates this gun to 1884. *Top photos by Gail Geis. Lower photo courtesy Norman Miles*

came away from the hunt with a couple of good stories. The son of the Russian Czar, the duke was royalty and expected to be treated as such even on the wild frontier; only those of rank or a certain importance were to address him. Paddy, on the other hand, figuring the frontier was a level playing field, strolled up to Duke Alexis and said, "How do you do, Duke?" The Russian visitor took affront at the nerve of the bold frontiersman, to whom he had not been officially introduced, but Miles persisted in his greeting, saying, "It don't make any difference to me, how do you do, Duke?" The flustered duke appealed to General Sheridan, indicating that perhaps the general was too familiar with his inferiors. General Sheridan did some quick thinking and decided that royalty or not, Duke Alexis was in America, a land without class barriers, and he answered: "By God Sir, we are Americans."[9] Duke Alexis may not have been amused by the demeanor of the brash frontiersman, but that did not prevent Miles from appreciating his souvenir of the hunt. A short time later Paddy Miles was seen packing a bone-handled six-shooter, which he claimed had belonged to Duke Alexis. The duke came up missing it following the hunt but didn't know where he had lost it. Paddy said he did.[10]

It was also in January that another important event took place – memorable at least to the founders of Frontier County, Nebraska. John Bratt, a big cattleman on the Platte, had cattle ranging as far south as present day Red Willow County. Bratt was anxious to have the area organized into a county so that a vote could be held to repeal the herd law, which had been enacted in Nebraska in 1871. (The "herd law" required the cattlemen to fence their grazing areas, unless the people of the county voted to have a "fence law," which would put the burden of fencing on those who wanted to keep livestock out of their fields.) In spite of adverse winter weather, which very nearly prevented John Bratt from making the long, treacherous trip from Fort McPherson with the "county books" on the night preceding the date set for the organization – and despite the fact that the newly

---

9 Miles and Bratt, p. 23.
10 J. N. Gammill, "Jim Gammill Writes Interesting Early History of Frontier County," circa 1941, <http://rootsweb.com.>

Paddy Miles' heart-shaped branding iron was found some years ago in a field near his old Wolf's Rest home.
Photo by George Creek

"The Wolf's Rest Ranch" no trespassing sign punctuated with a skull and cross-bones was painted on the side of Paddy Miles' barn in the late 1800s. Now on the inside of a roof and protected from weathering, the crude sign bears silent testimony to the early history of Wolf's Rest. *Photo by George Creek*

appointed county clerk, John Kirby, had to be left behind at Bratt's Fox Creek Ranch because of injuries received in a wild wagon ride down an icy hill – Frontier County was duly organized in Hank Clifford's lodge on Coon Creek. Paddy Miles recorded his take on the event in this diary entry:

> We organized a county seven of us and named it Fron-tier County and the county seat "Stockville." The county officers all we had men enough to fill was John Bratt, W.H. Miles, M.H. Clifford, Commissioners; Sam Watts,

Judge Probate; John Nelson, Surveyor; John Kirby, Clerk; E.G. Nesbitt, Supt. Public Instruction.

> We did not have enough to fill all of the offices, but we got on fine. There was no oppersition to anything. We was appointed by Gov. W. H. James. We went on each other's bonds when we did not own anything. [11]

Other industry occupied the white settlers in those early months of 1872. Paddy Miles said he built the first bridge across the Medicine, and he and Ambrose Shelley both built log cabins. Paddy mentioned in his journal on February 7, 1872, that his 18 ft. by 25 ft. log house, though not yet lived in, was the first in the county. He also noted in February the construction of the first courthouse "to put the county books in," which called for a celebration. Paddy wrote that they had a big feast for which he killed two deer and the Indians killed and ate five dogs. He made a journal entry in early March noting that Hank Clifford was starting to Fort McPherson with two loads of meat to sell, while he and Monte Clifford were hard at work drying more meat. Beyond that, Indian activity seemed to be foremost on his mind:

> Mar. 7 – The Pawneys stole 7 Sioux ponyes from our camp.
>
> Mar. 8 – I start in to the Fort to get horses to follow the Pawneys – a fearful snowstorm; owing to the storm I did not get any help from the Fort.
>
> Mar. 12 – Went hunting – had a fine chase at a large band of elk – killed a good many.
>
> Mar. 13 – Monte and I started on trail of the stolen horses – came up with them – had a fight. Got all the horses back but one.

---

11 Andreas' *History of the State of Nebraska* gives January 5, 1872, as the date of the organization in H. C. Clifford's lodge and January 18, 1872, as the date County Clerk John W. Kirby received his commission. John Bratt's account gives the impression the organization was approved by Acting Governor Wm. H. James on January 17, 1872, and that the organization in Clifford's lodge was the following day. Andreas also lists the names of fourteen white men as being present.

Mar. 16 – In an Indian lodge smoked half to death. Tiard of their sosiety. March is half gone. I long to see Spring. I am tiard of storm after storm and suspence, ever changing and wating me down. Will my loved ones ever come out here?

Mar. 18 – All the boys is in camp. Hank Clifford, Dick Seymour, and John Kirby, our Co. Clerk – his first visit to Frontier County.

John King is here, the only man on the Republican Valley. I have traided him 2 cows for a mule and start this morning to drive the cows to his camp.

Mar. 19 – On the Republican Valley – it is a fine country. We plowed the first furrow in that splendid valley. The buffalo will soon go and perhaps in a few years, these hills and valleys will know the Indian, buffalo and us, the hunter and trapper, no more. The plowman will turn the grass under, and cities will spring up. Railroads will follow in our track.

Mar. 20 – I found a man lost and starving on the prairie, and saved him.

Paddy Miles in a photo taken about 1890. *Courtesy Robert Van Pelt Estate*

Paddy Miles later told the story of the starving man. It seems Miles and one of the Cliffords were trapping and poisoning wolves when they found the fellow near death after having eaten some of the poisoned meat. They took him into their camp and proceeded to apply every remedy they could think of: "We forced grease, whiskey and everything we could get down him. After a great deal of work with him, he was relieved from the effect of the poison; and when conscious, he looked around with astonishment on the Indians and longhaired men with buckskin suits on. He thought he was a subject for a war-dance or a scalping-bee. We told him he was with friends and that he would not be hurt. He said that he had come out with a hunting party from away down East, [and] got lost..."[12]

The news he had been waiting for finally came when Paddy Miles got word in late March that his family was in at McPherson, waiting for him to go after them. Two days later he added, "I meet my loved ones once more." On March 28, 1872, he wrote of this momentous occasion: "We start for the Medicine. Ma is quite sick but says she will go with me if she dies on the way. Near night we are in camp under some elms on the Medicine. The first white women ever in Frontier Co. Lots of Indians came to see us. A new life has commenced for us." A few weeks later, as the relentless spring winds battered their meager shelter, the decision was made to move. Again, in the words of Paddy Miles:

> The first house I built was upon a high hill, being far from water and the winds blew so hard that we concluded to camp near the timber. Our choice place for a home was under the protecting branches of a large spreading elm tree.
>
> When we made this selection, from nature's grove for our abode, near by was a large white wolf, dead with a big steel trap on his foot, which he had dragged over many miles of prairie grass until he became hungry and worn out with life's pilgrimage, [and] had quietly lain down like one that is weary and sweetly reposed forever. We named our home under the elm "Wolf's Rest." After some in-

---

12 Miles and Bratt, p. 29.

quiry, we found that our only neighbor in Red Willow County, Storm King, had set a trap at a dead buffalo, caught the wolf, which broke the chain and took the trap to Wolf's Rest.[13]

---

13 Ibid., p. 19.

8

Paddy Miles of Wolf's Rest

When Paddy Miles cashed in his chips in 1909, his death certificate listed him as a stock raiser. And so he was, though he began small as indicated by this January 1872 journal entry: "I have a cow, and she has a calf. I begin to feel like a stock man." Eventually Wm. H. Miles' heart-shaped brand was seen on a fine herd of cattle grazing the pastures of Wolf's Rest. Although trapping and hunting continued to be the primary means of livelihood for a few years, some farming and domestic livestock raising was attempted on a small scale almost immediately. Paddy recalled that the first flock of sheep provided a picnic for the wolves, and his first attempt at a garden was trampled by a herd of buffalo.

By the time his parents and sister joined him, Paddy Miles had been on the frontier for nearly two and a half years. Before that he had been toughened by service on the Confederate side in the Civil War – the late "unpleasantness," as he called it – in addition to a couple years of wandering before the murder incident that motivated him to leave Georgia in a hurry. He didn't take to the rough life in the West at first, but once acclimated he could ride as hard, draw as fast and spit as far as any frontiersman. And by all reports he never failed to swing the doors of the nearest saloon. Miles was a handsome man, though his appearance could assume the same chameleon-like changes as his personality. J. N. Gammill, an early Frontier County resident, recalled:

> The most unique and comical character of probably the whole west was W. H. (Paddy) Miles. Born in *Fla-a-da the land of flo-a-ers*, as he said it. He was in the Confederate Army and wanted to tackle ten Yanks at once. Until he got in a tangle, and then one was enough. He was a great storyteller and actor. Looked like a southern Colonel. And could look like a monkey. He enjoyed packing a bone handled six-shooter. Was liable to shoot up the town…[1]

The Southern Colonel persona – as well as a few other characterizations – would come in later years. In his early years on the plains, Paddy Miles was a hunter and trapper, and his scruffy appearance befitted that profession. Dick Seymour was trading with the Indians in present day Hayes County when he encountered Paddy – sometimes referred to as the Lone Trapper. Seymour was on *Eau de Cologne Creek* or the Stinking Water on March 1, 1873, when he wrote, "I…saw the back of a man who wore long unkempt hair, a buckskin shirt with ragged looking fringe appending there from, and a pair of pantaloons that showed signs of diligent work with the needle and rivaled Joseph's coat in the grotesque blending of heterogeneous colors. Judge of my surprise when he turned, to find that he was a white man…the 'Lone Trapper.'"[2] Miles had departed on this particular expedition on New Year's Day – three months running a trap line and no doubt wearing the same outfit of clothes!

Ena Raymonde's journal entries enhance the robust image of her brother on the frontier. On March 18, 1873, she wrote of his arriving home following the above sighting, "The 'Lone Trapper' came driving up yesterday afternoon! Looking in fine health and wild as an Indian! Buckskin and dusky!" In another instance Ena stated that "Bert looked like a hearty good-natured savage!"

Paddy Miles was particularly pleased to have his sister with him on the frontier. An accomplished horse woman and a crack shot, Ena

---

1 Gammill. It has never been determined for certain whether Miles was born in Florida or Georgia.
2 Seymour.

was always game for sport and adventure. There were a number of unattached young men on the Medicine – all of them keenly aware of the presence of the spirited Ena Raymonde – and quite willing to include her in their various activities. A few of the young people from the Medicine went into the fort on July 3, 1872, where Ena remained for most of the summer. A week or so later she received a letter from Paddy, or "Bert," as she often called him, accompanied by the corpse of her wild-cat. Bemoaning the death of her "pet," she wrote: "Poor Brute! It died a most ignoble death – chained in a barrel, and then choked and smothered out of the world. I suppose the men that had my pet in charge got a little afraid of it and concluded to put themselves out of harm's way! Well, 'twas a handsome, fierce looking creature and I'm sorry they did not keep it at Wolf's Rest until my return, [even] if it did catch a chicken now and then!" In time Paddy changed his attitude towards wild cats and later kept his own cage of bobcats. When he wanted a little extra excitement, Miles would take a whip, get into a cage with the bobcats and in the words of one neighbor, "have a big time."

The heady excitement of living on the advancing edge of civilization wore off, and as hunting and trapping became less lucrative, the general concerns of life weighed on those in the little settlement on the Medicine. Invariably, some of them looked for new horizons. Although Ena disappeared from the Medicine for at least part of 1874, she was back at Wolf's Rest by February of 1875 and made several references to her brother's comings and goings. On the first of May 1875 she noted, "Herbert has gone to the Black Hills with Col. Mills' 'out-fit'. Left here today, three weeks ago. Have heard from him once. Sixty miles north of North Platte – camping at Sand Beach Lake..." Miles was most likely headed for the Black Hills as a prospector. The Black Hills Gold Rush, which began in 1874, drew prospective miners by the thousands in spite of the fact that the Fort Laramie Treaty of 1868 recognized the Black Hills as belonging to the Sioux. If Paddy Miles and Mills' outfit were, in fact, in search

William H. "Paddy" Miles in a photograph taken in his later years. About 1903, Miles left Wolf's Rest and moved alone to Long Beach, California, where he died in 1909. Although a monument bearing his name and date of birth was erected in Sunset Point Cemetery overlooking the Medicine Creek in Frontier County, Nebraska, Miles was buried in Sunnyside Cemetery at Long Beach, California.
Courtesy Robert Van Pelt Estate

Laura Murphy, daughter of Captain E. B. Murphy, Civil War captain and Indian fighter who founded the town of Arapahoe, Nebraska, was married to Wm. H. Miles circa 1878. She was about twenty-two years of age when she died two years later. *Courtesy Robert Van Pelt Estate*

Nellie E. Murphy, younger sister of Laura, was married to her sister's widower, Wm. H. Miles, on January 21, 1882. *Courtesy Robert Van Pelt Estate*

Laura Miles, daughter of Wm. H. & Laura Miles, was born about 1880. *Courtesy Robert Van Pelt Estate*

William Palmer Miles, son of Wm. H. & Nellie E. Miles, was born in 1885 and went by the nickname Prairie Dog Bill. *Courtesy Robert Van Pelt Estate*

Nellie V. Miles, daughter of Wm. H. & Nellie E. Miles, was born in 1887. *Courtesy Robert Van Pelt Estate*

of gold they must have struck out for the Black Hills excursion was never referred to again.

Ena Raymonde was united in marriage to D. C. Ballantine on October 5, 1875, and gave birth to a son the following August, which soon brought an end to her journaling. Ann Palmer – the mother of Wm. H. "Paddy" Miles and Ena Ballantine – died on April 21, 1877, and was the first to be buried at Sunset Point overlooking the Medicine Creek. In September of the same year, Ena made the last journal reference to her brother: "Herbert went away last week, on a little trip, or perhaps a big one. His plans were uncertain." This may be the same trip Ena referred to in a letter written to her brother a year or so later:

> I write to you, because I pledged my word at our last settlement that I would never talk over [money] matters again, and my experience here of late has only strengthened my resolution…

> I persisted in taking your cattle, in buying your place – against his [Mr. Ballantine's] wishes – as you know, and it is my place…to shoulder the responsibility of a settlement…

> Mr. Ballantine said when you first came home, "You had better have a settlement or understanding at once." I told him to let me alone – that I had had no peace all the winter from Pa – that I had tried to act honorably in every particular, and that if I had failed, I'd find out soon enough. I will not enter into any recrimination with you, Herbert. Poor Ma's last request to me was to have no money matters with Willie. I have been warned of this, but what is the use to talk to you. Do not think I am angry, or want to make you so, but you must certainly know that I know, you can talk one way today and another way tomorrow; you contradicted your own word without any compunction a thousand times over…

> You said it was not that little cow-case that was driving you away – that you felt it was better to go and stay –

that you wanted nothing but the Smith claim, even if you
came back…

Although the draft of this letter found in Ena's journal is undated, it was clearly written after the death of their mother in 1877
but before the death of their father, Dempsey Palmer, in February
1880 and likely before Paddy Miles' marriage in 1878. This letter
also indicates a rift in the once close relationship between brother
and sister. Dempsey Palmer, who died at Wolf's Rest on February
25, 1880, is a nearly invisible figure in Paddy Miles' story – Paddy
never mentioned his father in his journals or later when he wrote his
reminiscence. That be as it may, the sins of the father were visited
upon the son, for heavy drinking was given as the cause of the Palm-
ers' "problems" back in Georgia, and excessive drinking is seen as a
pattern throughout the life of Paddy Miles.

It is not known how long twenty-year-old Laura Murphy knew
the smooth-talking southerner – twelve years her senior – before she
accepted his proposal of marriage. Captain Edward B. Murphy had
homesteaded land close to Wolf's Rest during the 1870s, but Paddy
Miles may have met his daughters on the summer evening in 1871
when he inadvertently hunted buffalo too close to the newly platted
town of Arapahoe. Laura also taught the first session of school to be
held in the area in the log home of Andrew and Johanna Webb, who
lived on the Medicine about two miles east of the present town of
Curtis. Regardless of how they became acquainted, and in spite of
her father's strong objections, Laura Murphy was married to Wm.
H. Miles in 1878. About two years later, Laura Miles gave birth to
a daughter, also named Laura. Shortly thereafter, the young mother
died; just how isn't certain, but those closest to the horse's mouth
recall hearing of a wagon accident. Nellie Murphy was living in the
Miles' home at the time of her sister's death and with little Laura
needing a mother, perhaps it was inevitable that she would follow in
her sister's footsteps. Nellie E. Murphy was twenty-one or twenty-
two years of age when she married the charming widower – her
brother-in-law – on January 21, 1882. Young and impetuous, Nellie
made her bed – so to speak – and would have to sleep in it.

Over the next twenty or so years the life of the Miles' family can be sketchily tracked in two conflicting scenarios. On the one hand a scene of domestic harmony is presented, while on the other there are the alcohol-fueled exploits of Paddy Miles. Nellie Miles eventually divorced her husband and surely threatened to divorce him – or worse – many times before. Wm. H. and Nellie (Murphy) Miles had two children together: William Palmer Miles, nicknamed "Prairie Dog Bill," who was born in 1885 and Nellie V. Miles, born in 1887. Paddy Miles built two frame houses at Wolf's Rest, although the most that is known about the first one comes from an undated newspaper item describing its loss to fire:

> On Monday afternoon about 2 o'clock, the fine large residence of Mr. and Mrs. W. H. Miles was burned, together with all contents. Mr. Miles and family were at home at the time and cannot account for the origin of the fire, but think it possible that rats had carried matches between the walls. Mr. Miles had one of the finest houses in the country, the frame work being built of hard wood. It was the oldest frame house in Frontier county. They were unable to save anything from the fire as it had gained such headway before being discovered. Among the contents of great value to the owner were relics of old hunting days and the needle gun used by Mr. Miles to kill buffalo years ago. The loss on the house is about $1500 and $500 on furniture. It is a severe loss to Mr. and Mrs. Miles and their many friends sympathize with them. They will rebuild at once.

It is generally believed that the loss of this home and the building of the second – a large, two-story house – was during the early 1880s. Another newspaper item probably refers to the second home, and the mention of three children would place the date after 1887:

> On last Sunday the fat scribe of this great moral weekly paid a visit to the home of W. H. Miles, over there by the classic waters of the Little Medicine. Here is where the romantic "Paddy" and his estimable wife dwell in peace and happiness with their three lovely and obedient children, surrounded by all the comforts of life. It is a spot one

may well look upon with admiration; situated in the midst of a most lovely natural forest…Mr. Miles owns about a thousand acres of as fine land as the sun ever shone upon, and [his] is one place that is not for sale. His residence is built after the plan of the southern planters' home – large and commodious…

And then there are the stories that have been passed down through the years. Paddy developed a reputation for riding his horse places normally reserved for foot traffic, and on at least one occasion did the same with his team and buggy. This incident occurred in April 1886 when the town of Curtis was in its infancy. Paddy Miles, or "Billie" as the storyteller referred to him, and his five-year-old daughter, Laura, drove into Curtis. Paddy's declaration that he was going to drive through the awning or as he called it, "that sheep's head" (something foolish), was a signal to those who heard him to be prepared for some excitement. After getting what he had come to town for, Paddy Miles started for home.

Now the most of us knew Billie, but never knew just what his next move would be. As he drove up in front of the shop in his platform spring wagon, he inquired what that was in front of Johnson's bank. On inquiring what he was talking about, we said that "bank fellow" Mr. Johnson had had his carpenters build an awning across the front of his bank, which was the first in town. What acquaintance he had with Johnson, the writer never knew. Billie said "I don't like that banker; I know he don't like me. I sure will drive through that sheep's head when I go home."

As he drew up his lines, he took an extra grip with his teeth on his cigar; he let out a yell that his horses seemed to understand and they started at full speed. Remembering what he had said, we looked to see if he would attempt such a thing. The floor of that awning was fully fifteen inches off the ground, and the space between the walls and the posts must have been less than eight feet and how he accomplished it without an accident was a mystery. His little girl was with him and seemed to enjoy it. The team ran for some distance before he got them stopped. Mr.

Johnson said he thought the whole front [of the building] was going to be torn out. [3]

One indispensible anecdote in the "Paddy Miles Legend" is of Paddy – dead drunk – riding up the stairway to the second floor of his house, tying his horse to the banister and falling into bed (an imprint on a stair step bearing the likeness of a horse's hoof has kept this story alive). And of course, he personalized a bedroom window by putting a bullet through it. It is has also been said that one of the second-story bedrooms was used as a temporary jail while Miles was sheriff. References to Miles being Frontier County sheriff sometimes give the impression that he was sheriff for a number of years. In fact, records show he was only sheriff for a term from 1884 to 1886 – and this after winning by just seven votes. Ena's October 31, 1883 letter to a cousin indicated it took more than one election race for Miles to secure the confidence of the voters: "Herbert called today on his way to Indianola. He is just about the same. Just through with an election fight – ran for Sheriff again, and against Jack Lynch <u>again</u>. Herbert beat!"

Another oft-told tale is of an incident said to have occurred while Paddy was sheriff, but it may have happened before or after his term, for Sam Watts was not the county judge at the same time Paddy Miles was sheriff:

On a warm afternoon in the spring, Sheriff Paddy Miles rode into Stockville and entered the Drug Store. He was searching for a reliable remedy for "Spring Fever." Having obtained a "surefire tonic," Paddy took a couple of good size doses, then sauntered to the front of the store, seated himself in a chair, tilted back against the wall, drew his hat down over his eyes and dozed off to enjoy the cure.

A little later the County Judge S. F. Watts came into the drug store and leaned over the showcase opposite Paddy. He was admiring some merchandise on display. Paddy came out of his doze enough to see what was going on, and urged by some mischievous impulse, drew his gun and

3 R. H. Booth, *Curtis (Nebr.) Enterprise*, Nov. 24, 1916. Minor corrections in punctuation.

It was an awning similar to one of these on the main street of early Curtis that Paddy Miles once drove a team and wagon through. *Courtesy Anna Marie Hansen Memorial Museum*

fired a bullet close above the head of the judge. The bullet went through the wall – the judge went through the ceiling – Paddy went through the door for home. Some say Paddy was riding out of town before the judge returned to the floor from the ceiling.[4]

Paddy's name has also surfaced in a story concerning a group of settlers who were going to meet in the log school house near the Webb place on the Medicine Creek for the purpose of organizing a church. The date had been set for a certain Sunday, but Paddy Miles sent word that if the settlers met, the cowboys would shoot up the school house. The would-be church organizers met, and as promised, Miles and a gang of ruffians came riding in and circled the school house shooting and yelling. As Judge W. H. Latham later told the story, Tyra Nelson, a settler located at the mouth of Curtis Creek, went outside and had a little talk with the cowboys. Level-

---

4 Dean Johnson, "A Paddy Miles 'Believe it or Not,'" *Curtis (Nebr.) Enterprise*, publication date unknown.

headedness prevailed and the cowboys left, having had their fun for the day.

Miles did seem to relish being characterized as lawless. One time the settlers were missing calves and suspected Paddy, saying jokingly that all of Paddy's cows had twins. Having no proof, they "got up a purse" and employed a detective who hired out as a cowhand to Paddy Miles. The suspicions were soon verified when Paddy dispatched the "cowhand" to take baby calves that were too young to be branded from their mothers. The charge brought against Miles was for stealing a calf belonging to Tyra Nelson. As the story is told, Paddy hired C. H. Tanner, a brilliant, silver-tongued attorney, for his defense. The feeling in the community was running against Paddy, so Tanner got a change of venue, and the trial was moved to Richardson County, which was heavily populated with homesteaders who disliked cattlemen. Nelson grew uneasy and began to think the jury was going to be convinced he had stolen his own calf, as Tanner painted Paddy Miles as being nearly a saint. Tyra Nelson was saved, however, when Miles, his reputation as a scoundrel at stake, finally jumped up and yelled at Tanner, "You are a God damned liar. I have been in every jail from Tallahassee, Florida, to Curtis, Nebraska."[5]

Many of the tales told about Paddy Miles involve guns – sometimes one – more often two. J. N. Gammill, who was a boy during the years of some of Paddy's wild capers, told one story:

> Once after trying some rifles at a shooting gallery, which he [Paddy] claimed were no good, he drew [a] six-shooter and shot the targets to smithereens. The scared owner who thought he was ruined financially, didn't know that Paddy carried a roll of bills that would choke a cow, to pay all and more of [the] damage done on these escapades. And by the way, this six-shooter had belonged to the Russian Grand Duke Alexis...[6]

---

5   Neva Lofton, unpublished manuscript, circa 1985. Another version of this story gives the attorney's name as Starr. Like Tanner, W. R. Starr was a heavy drinker, but he was considered a good criminal lawyer.
6   Gammill.

Growing up in Stockville, Robert Van Pelt often heard the story of Paddy Miles becoming so incensed over receiving an account due statement from R. D. Logan, proprietor of the Phoenix Drug Store, that he rode his horse into the store and shot up the ceiling. It was Van Pelt's understanding that, "Mr. Logan never again sent out a statement to any customer."[7] Another

Paddy Miles is to the right in this undated photograph displaying the day's catch. *Courtesy Norman Miles*

former Stockville area resident recalled: "When Paddy Miles came to town and rode horseback up and down our board sidewalks shooting off loud talk and his revolver, most any resident of the burg could have written a story that would have made Owen Wister's *Virginian* sound like a veritable primer of western society."[8] Others claimed that the stores in Stockville were boarded up as a preventative measure before Paddy Miles rode into town on Saturday nights.

One "Paddy Miles incident" reportedly took place while Andrew Hawkins was being tried for the 1897 murder of Thomas Jensen. As the story goes, Miles had been known to loan one of his pearl-handled guns to the eccentric old money-lender, who made his collecting trips around the countryside alone, on foot, and unarmed. District Court Judge George W. Norris put Paddy on the witness stand to find out if he knew anything about the murder. When the judge asked Paddy if he had one of his pearl-handled guns with him,

7 Robert Van Pelt to Edward B. Miles, March 25, 1987.
8 Paine, p. 59.

Paddy pulled out both guns, fired two shots over the judge's head and said, "You mean these?"[9]

If he played hard, Paddy Miles also worked hard. While all these shenanigans were going on, Miles was building up a successful farming and ranching enterprise. Nonetheless, regardless of the appearance of genteel living, the demon alcohol took its toll on the Miles' home life. Attorney W. S. Morlan filed a Petition for Divorce on Nellie Miles' behalf before Judge W. H. Latham on August 5, 1890:

> The defendant regardless of his marital duties and obligations, on or about the 30th day of July, 1890, was guilty of extreme cruelty towards this plaintiff without any cause or provocation on her part, violently throwing the plaintiff from a wagon in which the plaintiff was riding with the defendant and others, threw her to the ground and attempted to run the team and wagon hitched thereto over her; drew a knife on her and threatened to kill her…, and at diverse other times prior to said 30th day of July, 1890 and within the last year the defendant has assaulted the plaintiff and threatened to kill her and attempted to beat and wound the plaintiff, and has been guilty of such acts of extreme cruelty that the plaintiff is afraid if the defendant is allowed to be with her or in her company that he will kill and murder her.
>
> Second: The defendant wholly regard[less] of his obligations as a husband, soon after said marriage commenced the excessive use of intoxicating liquors, and has for two years last past been an habitual drunkard. The following children are the issue of said marriage, to-wit: William Miles, aged five years; Nellie Miles, aged three years. The defendant is a man of vicious habits and violent and cruel disposition and is wholly unfit to be entrusted with the care, custody and education of said children. The plaintiff as the wife of the defendant has had living with her a child by a former marriage of said William H. Miles, to-wit Laura Miles, aged ten years. The defendant is of such cruel, vicious and vulgar habits and so given to the use of intoxicating drinks, that the plaintiff believes that it would

9 Lofton.

be unsafe for said Laura Miles to be left in the custody of said William H. Miles.

The plaintiff is the owner of about ninety head of neat cattle in her own right, and ninety-five head of hogs, and about twenty-eight head of horses, and a lot of farming implements and the land on which they are kept. The defendant has threatened to kill said cattle and horses and swine – burn up the buildings on the land owned by the plaintiff where the plaintiff and the defendant have resided together, and to prevent the plaintiff from in any manner caring for or having the custody of said property and to kill any person who would take care of or manage said property, and has sold and disposed of a portion of the neat cattle, horses and swine so owned by the plaintiff.

The plaintiff therefore prays that she may be divorced from the defendant, and that she may be given the custody of said children, and that the defendant be enjoined from in any manner intermeddling with the personal property herein before mentioned, and that he be restrained from coming upon the premises where the plaintiff resides…[10]

Although there was a protracted court suit, the Miles reached a tenuous reconciliation that held for at least a decade. It may have been during this time period that Paddy suddenly became inhospitable and painted "The Wolf's Rest Ranch" no trespassing sign on the side of his barn, punctuated with skull and crossbones.

During the 1890s and early 1900s, the newspapers reported various social calls made by the Miles as well as "socials" held at their home. The Miles' large plantation style home was the setting for entertainments such as this one, which most likely took place in the 1890s: "The home of Mr. and Mrs. W. H. Miles was the scene of a very pleasant party and social ball last Friday evening. About seventy-five invited guests were present and everyone enjoyed themselves to the fullest capacity. There were games for the old people and dancing for the young…At midnight ice cream and cake were

---

10 Divorce petition is an exhibit in a land abstract. Some obvious typographical errors have been corrected.

served…" On another occasion it was reported: "Several buggy loads of young people from Stockville and Curtis spent a very pleasant evening at the Miles' Ranch, Tuesday. Social lawn and parlor games, vocal and instrumental music, and last but not least water melons and musk melons galore served to pass the hours all too swiftly for the merry crowd." The Miles also played an important part in community theater, where Paddy easily assumed the role of villain:

> Star Home Talent Comedy Co., Stockville, played two nights, Friday and Saturday, last week, to good audiences. The Company, under the management of Paddy Miles and Wm. Anderton [*sic*], is an exceptionally strong one, and won popular favor from our citizens…

> The acting of Paddy Miles was true to life, and won for him favorable comment from the audience. Paddy possesses the make-up for the part of heavy villain in a deep plot, as he can assume the sober and sarcastic expression so admirably adapted for that character…

> Prairie Dog Bill was a mirth-provoking imp, always on the alert for mischief. He will make a dandy all-round actor…

> Mrs. Nellie Miles as "The Maniac," displayed marked ability in *The Coming Man*. Study and practice will make an actress of her…

The Miles' son, Wm. P. "Prairie Dog Bill," amused the crowd at an event held at a rural school in 1891: "The scholars…were assisted by Paddy Miles, Prairie Dog Bill, Lulu Serles and Robert Serles. The comedy play, entitled *Clams* was rendered in a most pleasing manner. The six year old specialty artist, Prairie Dog Bill, was a favorite from start to finish. His 'take-offs' were received with great enthusiasm…"[11]

By 1898 a revolution in Cuba over oppressive Spanish rule was making headlines in the United States. On February 15, 1898, an explosion blew up the battleship *Maine*, which had arrived in Ha-

---

11 Undated news items are either from the Stockville or Curtis, Nebr., newspapers.

vana Harbor to indicate national interest. Believing that the Spanish
had blown up the *Maine* and with pressure from those who wanted
the United States' flag to fly over Cuba and the Philippines, war
fever was building. The February 18, 1898 *Curtis Enterprise* reported
that W. H. Miles, Frontier County's "enterprising pioneer ranchman, was in town Tuesday, and telegraphed Governor Holcomb that
Frontier was ready to furnish 100 men at a moment's notice to help
whip the Spaniards." On June 17, 1898, the *Curtis Courier* reported
that Wenzel Patzelt, along with sixteen other young men had volunteered to fight for their country's honor. Though the Spanish-Amer-
ican War lasted little more than three months, the recent conflict
was on Miles' mind as the clock ticked away the final minutes of the
year. Otherwise, Wolf's Rest was a scene of domestic tranquility on
December 31, 1898, as Paddy Miles reflected:

> We are all here watching the old year out. All except
> Wenzel Patzelt who was with us one year ago – But is
> now on his way to Cuba with the 3rd Nebraska Regiment.
> Yes, we are all here, our little family – Papa, Mama, Laura,
> Bill and Nie [Nellie] sitting around a warm stove all well
> and happy. Reading over the records of each day of 1898.
> We find that we have done well financially. Had some loss,
> and some gain. Our stock is fine. The Ranch and house
> is in good shape. So if we have no bad luck the coming
> year, we will be able to make lots of improvements on our
> little house. It is very cold tonight. [1898] has been harde
> – stormes everywhere. We whipped Spain this year. Will
> take charge of Cuba, tomorrow. The old year is fast dieing
> [*sic*] – only a few moments to live and I must say Good
> Night…[12]

By the turn of the century, Wm. H. Miles was spending his winters in a warmer climate. The December 8, 1899 *Curtis Enterprise* indicated the Miles were going to winter in Florida. The February 26,
1903 *Enterprise* printed a long letter that Paddy Miles had written

---

12   Single page of 1898 journal found in Miles' papers, copy on file with FCHS. Spelling
variations are Paddy's.

from Florida. The letter was signed "Col. W. H. Miles" and lavished praise on the virtues of the south as a winter retreat:

> You see I am down here yet, in the land of flowers, and am having a good time as usual. I just came off a hunt, we killed three fine deer. It is spring time here, everything is in bloom. Ripe strawberries, tons of fish and oysters so you see that I am not likely to freeze or starve to death…
>
> I have been thinking that if some of my Nebraska friends could drop down here, without the long tiresome journey, what a delightful change it would be; from the snow and ice to be fanned by the warm breezes laden with the perfume of flowers, and to drink of the spring of perpetual youth, the same that Ponce de Leon discovered many years ago, and which has made Florida famous ever since.
>
> I am trying to invent a flying machine so all of us can make a visit down here every winter without so much cost and delay. I expect to start back in a week or so, for Nebraska. I must get back in time to raise my forty acres of hogs, and fix up my flower garden. We must have our usual goody time…

The summers found him reporting the prospect of a bountiful harvest. The July 25, 1902 *Curtis Enterprise* ran an item about the prominent Medicine Creek stockman and farmer: "W. H. Miles… was in town last Saturday chatting with the town folks and discussing the bright future for Frontier County… Mr. Miles says that he has a field of 100 acres of corn that will, without doubt, average over 60 bushels per acre; stands over seven feet high and the stalks as large as a man's wrist. Miles has the garden spot of Frontier County and where crops never fail."

Nevertheless, the December 15, 1905 *Enterprise* reported that the Miles were relocating permanently: "W. H. Miles and family have finally decided on account of Mrs. Miles' health to sell out and locate in California. We are sorry to see them leave Frontier County. They are pioneers – spending the best of their years on their valuable ranch on the banks of the Medicine not far from Curtis." The portrayal of Paddy and Nellie Miles as a couple was a pretense. It was, in fact, only Nellie Miles and the three children who moved to California. Paddy Miles had moved by himself to Long Beach about two years earlier. Just when the Miles were divorced is unclear, but even though Nellie and the children also moved to Long Beach, Nellie never again lived under the same roof as Paddy Miles.[13] On January 20, 1906, the following item appeared in the *Curtis Enterprise*: "A number of Curtis lady friends of Mrs. W. H. Miles were kindly remembered by her on receiving last week, each a box of long stem roses, mailed from Long Beach, their new Pacific coast home..."

The farm sale was held January 23, 1906. The sale bill listed Nellie Miles as the owner of the property sold, which included work horses, driving horses, milk cows, one shorthorn bull and ten head of stock cows, hogs and farm equipment – and one shot gun. Nellie Miles had also held title to the Wolf's Rest real estate, which she sold before leaving Nebraska. On January 26, 1906, the *Enterprise* reported that the sale "was the largest attended public sale that has taken place in Fron-

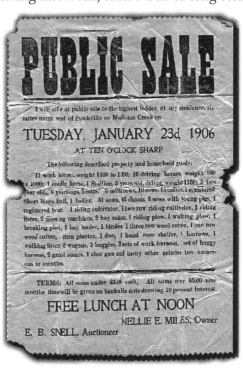

The Wolf's Rest property was in Nellie Miles' name by 1906. The bill for her sale listed 11 work horses, 10 driving horses and 1 stallion, as well as 2 yr. olds, yearlings and colts. There were also 5 milk cows, some stock cattle and hogs. Other items included haying equipment, a walking plow, 2 wagons, 2 buggies, harnesses and a shotgun. *Courtesy Norman Miles*

---

13   Edward B. Miles to Robert Van Pelt, Dec. 27, 1986.

tier County for many years. It was reported that some 400 or more were present."

On April 20, 1906, following the great San Francisco earthquake that had occurred just two days earlier, Paddy dispatched the following to the *Enterprise*:

> I thought perhaps that our friends in Nebraska would like to know that we are on top side of dirt yet, although we have had a shaking up out here by the earthquake. No doubt but what you all know by this time that San Francisco and other towns have been destroyed by earthquakes and fire, the greatest disaster of the age, so I will not enter into any of the details, only to say that I never saw so much excitement since the civil war...
>
> Will Miles is a member of the California Guards and his company has been ordered to the seat of war, and thousands of people saw them off today. They made a fine display, armed and equipped for a long siege of guarding the city from a rampant mob. The gun boats have also gone from here to the scene of disaster. It takes all the sailors and soldiers to keep back the mob of thieves and outlaws.
>
> San Francisco will be built up again. Millions of dollars has already been raised for that purpose. Cyclones, wars, earthquakes and floods can't keep the American people down and let a few grasshoppers chip in also. I am going out in the mountains and shovel up a sack of gold and get back to dear old Nebraska where I can be safe from earthquakes and the sharks and whales. I will write again if I am still on mother earth. With best wishes extended to all my old friends in Frontier, I remain yours...

This letter reflects the typical Paddy Miles in a high mood – magnanimous of spirit, extravagant with language and ever-hopeful. Twenty-year-old William Palmer Miles was serving with the Company H, 7th Infantry National Guard when he wrote his mother from Oakland, California, following the quake. Nellie Miles shared her son's letter with the *Enterprise*, which published it on May 4,

The Miles' home circa 1880s. Paddy is to the left and his daughter Laura is seated in middle. The woman to the right is probably his second wife, Nellie. Legend has it that Paddy once rode his horse through the south door (shown) and up the stairs to his second story bedroom. *Courtesy Frontier County Historical Society*

Still lived in on the Medicine Creek, the house was moved out of the flood plain about 1915. The south doorway has been removed and some of the windows have been replaced. The original turned spindles of the stairway still grace this country home after 120 years. *Photo by Gail Geis*

1906. An excerpt reflects the urgency of the situation following the earthquake:

> I have been on guard in several places, some of them I had to stop every one that came along. Other places where there were valuables, we were ordered to arrest anyone that looked like they wanted to steal, or were trying to break into any buildings. Some of the people will run right into the bayonets; others when you say "halt," will turn and run their best. The soldiers do not use as much force here as they do in Frisco. Those that went over a few days ago, if they caught anyone stealing they would shoot them down, and some that persisted in their stealing were thrown in the flames alive, but nothing of that kind was done by any of our boys...

On December 9, 1909, the *Maywood Eagle-Reporter* ran the following:

> W. H. Miles – known as Paddy Miles – died at his home in Long Beach, Cal., the last of Oct. of diabetes. Mr. Miles was a pioneer settler having taken the first homestead in the territory, now Frontier county, locating on the Medicine in 1870. Fort McPherson was the nearest town, his neighbors were Sioux Indians; the buffalo, deer and elk was the source of his supply. When this county was organized in 1872, Mr. Miles was one of the first commissioners...

William H. Miles died on October 19, 1909, at the age of sixty-three and was interred at Sunnyside Cemetery in Long Beach, California.[14] Though he had burned his candle from both ends, he died with his boots off. An unrivaled combination of faults and virtues, he made a significant contribution to the early development of the area. Certainly he abused intoxicating beverages and living with him could be the definition of terror. A dead-drunk Paddy riding horseback up the stairway to the second floor of his house makes a great

---

14 Edward B. Miles wrote that Laura C. Miles, who never married, took care of her stepmother until Nellie Miles' death in 1929. Neither of Paddy Miles' daughters had children.

story but a poor bedfellow. This singular fact remains – the legend of William Herbert (Palmer) Miles of Wolf's Rest – whether called Bert, Willie, Billie or Paddy – is essential to the history of Frontier County and southwest Nebraska.

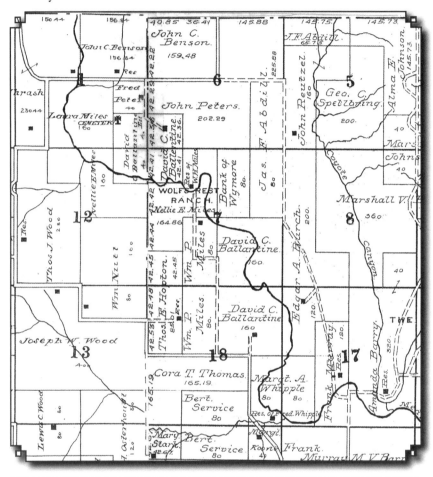

This 1905 *Standard Atlas of Frontier County, Nebraska* map of sections 1, 12 & 13 in NE Sheridan Precinct and sections 5, 6, 7, 8, 17 & 18 in NW Stockville Precinct shows Wolf's Rest Ranch. Sunset Point Cemetery is in the SE¼ of Sec.1, Sheridan Precinct. The Ballantine's sod home was located in the NE¼ of Sec.18, Stockville Precinct. Hank Clifford and the Cut-off Sioux were camped near the mouth of Coyote Canyon in the SE¼ of Sec. 17, Stockville Precinct. At that time the Medicine Creek (not labeled) took a course through the quarter section deeded to Paddy Miles' daughter, Laura Miles, in Sec. 1, Sheridan Precinct, past Wolf's Rest and exited Sec. 17, Stockville Precinct, on the Barry property.

These photos from the Miles' collection show a group of unidentified campers near Stockville, Nebraska. The ladies are dressed in their Sunday best and may have been attending a Chautauqua or old-time revival camp meeting. The number of stars on the flag (top photo) indicates the photo was taken sometime after 1889. Notice the hammocks and bicycle. *Courtesy Norman Miles*

9

Ambrose Shelley

*W*hen Ambrose S. Shelley rode into the trappers' camp on the Medicine Creek in 1871, his sole possessions besides his horse, saddle and bridle were a frying pan, a coffee pot made out of a tomato can, two blankets, a rifle, and two Colt army revolvers. That be as it may, the twenty-eight-year-old veteran had plenty of nerve and pluck. One old-timer who knew him said that Shelley was a peaceable man, "but was known to knock a big buck Indian down before his whole tribe, which scared his white partner pretty near to death – they being the only whites in hundreds of miles."[1] Of German Pennsylvania Dutch ancestry, Ambrose Shelley was born December 18, 1843, in the small village of Hereford, Berks County, on the eastern edge of Pennsylvania. (His name at that time was actually Ambrose Shultz – Shelley was his mother's maiden name.) As a young man, he worked as a millwright until the Civil War broke out. He then volunteered in the Union Army, joining Company G, 47th Pennsylvania Regiment where he served under General Nathaniel Banks and General Philip Sheridan.

The most compelling of Shelley's war stories was that of General Sheridan's victorious battle at Cedar Creek in the Shenandoah Valley of Virginia. More than a month of heavy fighting in the valley had weakened the Confederate effort to a point that General Sheridan felt safe in dispatching a number of Union troops to another front. He had, unfortunately, underestimated the fight left in the Con-

---

1 Gammill.

federate force, which had withdrawn up the valley. After receiving a letter from General Robert E. Lee exhorting him to take action against Sheridan's forces, the Confederate commander assessed the Union position, found an opening, and developed a plan of attack. In a daring move the Confederate troops made a nighttime march, catching the Union forces encamped along Cedar Creek completely off-guard. Though the Union soldiers fought a strong defensive battle, they were unable to gain the momentum needed to repel the Confederate troops.

Returning from Washington, General Sheridan was at Winchester, Virginia, fifteen or so miles away on the morning of October 19, 1864, when the sound of the artillery alerted him that the battle was in progress. Returning to his command, he was just out of Winchester when he began seeing the disorganized and defeated Union soldiers falling to the rear. General Sheridan put the spurs to his magnificent black war horse, Rienzi, and pushed on to the front of the Union line where he restored the morale of his troops, and they quashed the Confederate army. The Cedar Creek battle became famous, General Sheridan became famous, and the horse (renamed Winchester) became famous – immortalized in poetry, prose, and paintings. Ambrose Shelley was at Cedar Creek, and he put it simply: "We [were] badly demoralized and almost put to rout when he [Sheridan] rode in on his black charger, all white from frost and foam. He rallied us and we won the fight…"[2]

Following his discharge from the army on Christmas Day 1865, Shelley worked with his father for a year and a half helping rebuild some of the mills that had been destroyed during the war. He then came as far west as Council Bluffs where he worked for his mother's brother, B. Y. Shelley, who was a freighter. After a short time he struck out on his own and hired on with a crew that was contracted to supply hay for the horses and mules being used in building the Union Pacific Rail Road. He stayed with the railroad until the last rail was laid, and he was there when they drove the golden spike that joined the Union Pacific with the Central Pacific at Promontory,

2 Ambrose Shelley, (*Maywood, Nebr.) Eagle-Reporter*, Sept. 15, 1928.

Ambrose Shelley as a young soldier during the Civil War. *Courtesy Cheryl Muilenburg*

Utah Territory, on May 10, 1869. This was a watershed event in the history of the country – the last link in the great trans-continental rail line. But when the excitement of the moment was over, Ambrose Shelley turned his face to the wind and got on with his life. He was apparently working for the Union Pacific in Wyoming Territory when he had an Indian scare he never forgot:

> One day while working in the timber on one of the streams, getting out ties, I thought I would take my gun and go out on the prairie and maybe get an antelope. I was out probably a mile, when instead of an antelope, up over the hill came half a dozen mounted Indians on the war-path and headed right for me. I turned and started for "tall timber" and was holding my own pretty well as they had to detour on account of gulches, when looking to my left I saw two more cutting across to head me off. I wasn't afraid of them as there were several deep canyons that they must go around, but the Indians behind me were gaining now, mighty fast, too!

> Maybe the wind was blowing; if it wasn't, I made breeze enough to lose my cowboy hat. No, I never stopped to pick it up, but just as I dodged into the timber I saw a warrior stoop and snatch it from the ground [and] wave it like a scalp. Well, I'm glad it was my hat and not my scalp he had, and so far as I know he has it yet.[3]

The following summer found Shelley once again in Wyoming Territory. It was about this time that he joined a group of men on a gold prospecting expedition in North Park, Colorado Territory. The prospectors were attacked by a party of Ute Indians, and a man by the name of Charlie Wood was shot and killed while he and Shelley were standing on a ridge overlooking the Indian camp. After burying Wood, the prospectors sent Shelley to the nearest military post, as two of the ten fellows in the group were either too old or too sick to make a forced retreat. Shelley made it to the post in twenty-six hours and was soon on his way back with a military escort and wagon. When Shelley and the military escort returned, they found

---

3 Ibid.

five bodies and no trace of the other four prospectors. Shelley was, of course, thankful to have escaped with his life, but in the excitement of the return, he forgot to retrieve the bottle of gold nuggets he had buried before he left to get help.[4]

It was sometime after this last excursion that Shelley came back down to McPherson, and along about the same time he became Ambrose Shelley, rather than Ambrose Shultz as he had appeared in the 1870 U. S. Census, Wyoming Territory. He worked around the post, and toward the end of December, he and several other fellows took a notion to head for the Medicine Creek country where they had heard there was good hunting and trapping. They arrived on Christmas Eve of 1871 and participated in the first Christmas to be observed by white men on the Medicine Creek. Shelley spread his bed roll on the floor of Hank Clifford's lodge that first night on the Medicine. The Clifford tepee was also the site for the organization of Frontier County a few weeks later. While Paddy Miles gave the names of only seven white men as being present, Andreas' *History of the State of Nebraska* names Shelley as being one of fourteen men who took part in this historic occasion. It is said he was one of the signers of the charter, and though he was not given an office at this first meeting, when an election was held in October 1872, Shelley was elected to the position of assessor.

The legendary buffalo hunt held for Duke Alexis of Russia in present day Hayes County also occurred in January 1872. The duke was the guest of General Philip H. Sheridan, the commander Shelley had served under during the recent War Between the States. One can only wonder whether Shelley got to meet the famous general for whom he held high regard. There is little chance Sheridan would have recognized one of his foot-soldiers, and Shelley was no doubt too modest to approach his former commander. In any event, Shelley was once again on the scene while history was being made. Another oft-told tale happened along about this time:

> It was the first year after the county was organized. As one of the county officers, I had some duty to attend to

---

4 Riley. John Bratt also made this trip as two of the men were prospecting for him.

in the west part of the county, near the Colorado Line. Our county at first reached to the east line of Colorado, bounded on the north by the Platte River, and on the east side it extended to Plum Creek, now Lexington, and to Kansas on the south.

Knowing I had a long ride before me, I took food and a blanket so that I could camp whenever night overtook me. I reached a wooded stream in what is now Hayes County, just at dark. Tying my horse, I unsaddled him and made preparations for the night. I groped around and found enough sticks for a fire, broiled some buffalo meat, and after a hearty meal of juicy steak and hard bread, I placed my saddle at the foot of a large tree and rolled up in my blanket with the saddle for a pillow. I was soon sound asleep. Knowing my horse would warn me of any danger, I slept very well until daylight. Along in the middle of the night, the coyotes yipped and yelled on the edge of the prairies and toward morning I heard a horned owl hoot in a tree not far away. The only time I had a thrill, or rather a chill, was when a little screech owl let out a quavering wail that ended up in a vibrating screech, wild enough to make your hair stand on end, but I was used to them and slept on until morning.

I awoke just as it was dimly light. Lying on my back with my face up, on opening my eyes, I looked up into the branches of the tree, with some start, I tell you, for right over me hovered a dark object, outstretched limbs, ready to drop on the very spot where I lay. It looked like a black bear, but I knew there were no bears. It was too dark colored for a mountain lion that I knew had been seen in these parts.

No, I wasn't scared, but I wasn't going to take any chances with an unknown danger. By this time it was light enough for me to make out the thing above me more clearly. I saw cross sticks lying on the tree limbs and all at once it dawned on me that I had seen something like it before in my experience with the Indians... I saw at once that this was the burial place of the Indian brave. I looked around, and there, close by was the skeleton of his horse. I didn't touch the robe. A burial place is sacred to an Indian, and I always respect the tradition of any people. Of course, I wouldn't have stayed under that tree if I had known I was so close under a dead Indian.[5]

Intent on putting down roots in the new county, Ambrose Shelley was anxious to build his own home. From "Medicine Valley, Nebraska," he wrote to his father in Pennsylvania on June 15, 1872:

Dear Father,

I will drop a short note to you this evening to ask if you would be so kind as to send my chest of tools to me. I am going to build a House on towards fall… The government is also going to build a Fort here. They located their Reservation [temporary camp of Cut-off Sioux] about four miles west from my claim. That will make some lively times here. The Rail Road [is] coming [up] the Republican Valley and the Government establishing a fort here will clean the Indians out in a very short time which will induce people to settle here, [and] if I have my tools here I can pick up a good many jobs and I have to have my tools to do my own work anyhow. I inquired what it would cost me to have them sent here and the Freight Agent told me not over eight dollars by freight. I don't care if it will cost eighteen it will still be a good deal cheaper than to buy new tools in this country.

I wish you would send the chest as soon as you possibly can, as it may take a good while before she gets here. I expect to come home by next spring if I possibly can but I am going to built [*sic*] me a good House and make all the necessary improvements on my claim before I leave it. I think the old chest will stand it if the tools are well packed. I don't know whether there is any pieces on the bottom of my chest for her to set on or not. If not perhaps you had better fix [some] on the bottom and sink the key into one of the pieces and screw it well onto the bottom of the chest. That way you can also send the key. I will give

---

5 Ambrose Shelley, "When I Slept under a Dead Indian," FCHS newsletter, Vol. 14, Issue 2 (1999).

you the address. [Send the] Chest well secured and well addressed:

A. Shalley,

North Platte City, U. P. R. R.

Nebraska

In care of John Bratt

These men live at North Platte and Mr. Bratt comes here often. He has over sixteen thousand head of cattle in the country and he offered to take the chest …out for me as soon as it gets there. I am about 70 miles away from the rail road and I might not find it out in a hurry when the chest arrives there, but any of these men will take it out of the Freight House for me and then they can't charge no storage at the station. Have it well directed and she will find me.

We have a very heavy thunderstorm this evening. It is raining powerful this very moment. My Corn and Potatoes and Melons look splendid. My garden is getting along fine too. I have over three hundred hills of Melons planted. I can feed the whole state of Nebraska on Melons if nothing happens [to] them. Write me a letter with all the news in when you send the chest, and put it in the chest then I will get the letter as soon as the chest, but I have to close. It is getting late. My best respects to mother and sister and accept the same yourself.[6]

The letter was signed A. S. Shultz, although the fact he was using Shelley (spelled Shalley in this letter) as his surname in the West was no secret. Shelley set about building his log cabin on the north side of the Medicine later in 1872. There was never a government fort built on the Medicine, but it turned out the buffalo caused Shelley more problems than the Indians did. Whenever he would leave for any length of time, the buffalo rubbed against the logs until they fell to the ground. After this scenario was repeated several times, Shelley finally chose a nice little flat on the south side of the Medicine and built his cabin out of cottonwood logs there. That log cabin stood on

---

6 Ballantine MSS.

Built in 1872 of cottonwood logs and chinked with mud, Ambrose Shelley's cabin was one of the first in Frontier County. The sturdy little cabin now stands on the fairgrounds in Stockville, Nebraska. *Courtesy Frontier County Historical Society*

the same location for over fifty years, and it was the birthplace of his six children. While he was still a bachelor, Shelley went up to Fort Robinson and worked for Hank Clifford in the trading post there. During his absence, Monte Clifford and his family lived in the log cabin to protect it from the buffalo. It was there in 1877 that Julia Clifford gave birth to her daughter Rosa.

Ambrose Shelley was married to Hannah Gregory, a young widow and the daughter of neighboring homesteaders John and Ellen Lynch, in 1879. A year later, on May 5, 1880, Hannah died of complications from childbirth. Shelley then set his sights on Hannah's auburn-haired sister Nellie, to whom he was married in 1886. The Shelley family grew by five more children and providing adequate schooling for the children was, of course, always an issue. In about 1896 a session of school was held in the Shelley's rock-cellar and a year or so later it was held in a rock-cellar on the Lynch place. In

1899 the Shelleys moved into Stockville so the children could attend school there. A few years after that Ambrose made the long trip back to Pennsylvania to attend a funeral and stayed almost a year. While he was gone, Nellie and the children moved back to the farm. Times were hard, and Nellie's material assets at that time were one milk cow and the thirty-six cents she had in her pocket. For his part, young George considered the bag of kittens he carried on the five-mile-walk back to the farm to be a pretty valuable asset.[7]

In a letter written to his brother and sister on April 7, 1897, Shelley summarized his first twenty-five years in Frontier County:

> While my neighbor Ranchmen started out with plenty of money, they have clear sailing, but when I come to think [what little I started out with]... among hundreds of Indians and millions of buffalo, I sometimes think I done pretty well after all, but if I had to start out again knowing what was ahead of me, I should probably study the matter over quite a bit before starting...

> I made just two mistakes, which I very much regret in all my 25 years experience here. One was dropping the cattle business to a considerable extent and engaging in horses just about a year or so before horses commenced going out of fashion. My next bad break was to engage quite extensively in farming, which I think is an up-hill business in any country. I raised a large and splendid crop of corn last year. But I can buy 10,000 bushel of corn inside of three days for $.08 to $.10 for a bushel and if I know anything at all about addition and subtraction, then I know that the corn I raised cost me about double that money, everything considered... It is hard to make the average farmer believe that over production lowers prices or that the law of supply and demand governs prices...[8]

Ambrose Shelley experienced the usual hardships of the early settler. Drought, coupled with other factors that put the Midwest in tough times during the 1890s, undoubtedly contributed to his 1897 summation, "I may also safely say that the last five years of my

---

7 Biography of Ambrose Shelley. Author and publication information unknown, FCHS.
8 *Stockville, Then and Now*, pp. 440-441.

Ambrose Shelley's homestead on the Medicine Creek southeast of Stockville as it appeared (viewed from the south) about 1890. Shelley is standing by the side of the road, and his son John is holding the horse by the fence. Phil Black, who worked for Shelley, is on the horse to the left. R. D. Logan, the druggist, is seated to the west of the house, and his wife and mother are on the porch. The woman standing in the corral is believed to be Phil Black's sister Mary. The west end of the house is the original log cabin. *Courtesy Robert Van Pelt Estate.*

life put more screws in my coffin and more gray hairs on my head than all the rest of my years put together. But I presume such is life. I have no idea of giving up the struggle yet for a while..." By the roll of the dice, Shelley just happened to be on the scene for several events of major historic significance. And although he liked his whiskey as well as the general run of men, he managed to avoid the pitfalls of excess. The particular aspect that made him unique among that first settlement of white men on the Medicine Creek was his stick-to-itiveness. Even early-comer Paddy Miles eventually

Ambrose Shelley circa mid-1920s. *Courtesy Cheryl Muilenburg*

left, leaving Ambrose Shelley as the only member of the founding fathers of Frontier County who could say, "I came and I stayed."[9]

9 Ambrose Shelley also served as county clerk and county treasurer. He died Dec. 2, 1930. Nellie (Lynch) Shelley died Oct. 26, 1934. Both are buried in Stockville's Arbor Cemetery. Thomas Owens bought the Shelley place in 1905, and his son, Lewis, was born there in 1906. The Owens gave the log cabin to the Frontier County Fair Association, and it was moved to the fairgrounds in Stockville in the late 1920s. Other sources: Riley, Ballantine MSS; William Shelley to Arthur Carmody, May 3, 1952, Carmody MSS, NSHS; George Shelley to Robert Van Pelt, April 3, 1986, Robert Van Pelt Estate.

The first Stockville Fair was held in the alley of the block across the street west of the Courthouse. There were only two exhibits - Paddy Miles' caged bobcats and Ambrose Shelley's domestic bobtail cats. There were also penny showers, horse races and foot races. For those who wanted to put the strength and endurance of their horses to the test, there were races between teams of horses pulling sleds and wagons. The September 8, 1898 *Stockville Faber* announced: "One of the features of the coming county fair is a team-trotting race by all the county officials. They each have a team and will decide at this fair, which is the best. This race will come off Wednesday, the second day, and there is now quite a little interest worked up in this race. The contestants will be Bradbury, Wilson, Reed, Logan, Pyle, Lincoln and Nickerson."

10

Ena of Wolf's Rest

Only a few short months after she left her old home in Georgia, Ena Raymonde stood looking down at the stiffened corpse of a dead wolf on the banks of Medicine Creek in southwest Nebraska. Having been caught in the powerful jaws of a steel leg trap, the injured animal had pulled the trap loose from its anchor and drug it across miles of rough country before succumbing to death. It wasn't a pretty picture, but Ena saw a certain poetic quality in the scene and named her new home Wolf's Rest. It was this ability to adapt to the frontier with gusto that eased her transition from a southern belle to a woman of the plains, for certainly the contrasts were many. Spring had brushed the landscape with green, and the azaleas were in full bloom when Ena Raymonde and her parents left the sunny South in March of 1872. The Nebraska frontier that greeted them was a far different picture – the countryside a palate of browns, broken here and there with a lingering drift of snow at the heads of the canyons. This well-bred woman, who had lived a life of privilege in the South, spent her first night on the Medicine Creek rolled up in a buffalo robe under the stars.

Annie Eliza "Ena" Raymonde (Ena was short for Einna – Annie spelled backwards) was center stage once she arrived on the Medicine Creek. She and her mother were the only white women in the newly organized Frontier County, and Ena quickly caught the attention of every red-blooded white man in the area – and at least one Indian brave as well. Though she had been recently widowed, it seems the period of mourning had been brief; Ena no longer wore black. With someone always in the wings providing shelter and food as well as protection from the inherent dangers of the west, she was allowed a luxury seldom afforded women on the frontier – the freedom to indulge and write of her passionate emotions. A well-educated writer and published poet, Ena could handle horses, guns, and men with equal ease. She recorded many of her impressions of 1872 and 1873, although she was too caught up in the activity of her new life to keep a journal for the first few months. Her first journal entry, made on June 7, 1872, pertained to Texas Jack Omohundro's attempt to rope buffalo:

> First of all, I have been introduced to "Texas Jack" – one of our "Western Heroes" – and a fine picture of handsome, dashing, manly manhood he is. Certainly one of my beau-ideals of a hunter or a "Scout". Hope I shall see more of him and that I shall like his character as well as I do his face. He made a very graceful presentation in the way of a handsome toy-bag of China-work – its original purpose I do not know; but he used it for cartridges, and so shall I – i.e. if I keep it; for it is but the souvenir of a challenge to shoot; and after having the bravado to take up the gauntlet thus thrown down, if he does beat me (and I expect it will be "even so"!), I shall not have the courage to retain such a memento of my defeat, but [will] give it back with my pistol to boot! But enough of this hero for the present, only that he now heads a party out on about as wild an adventure as even my wild brain could devise – viz: lassoing buffalo – full grown ones – for the purpose of shipping them alive on the train. Some say it is dangerous work; some prophesy not only broken arms and legs and crippled horses, but dead men as well as dead horses! …

> Bert [Paddy Miles] is with the party, and his last words were, "I only wish you could go, Einna!" … Dick S[eymour], my very good friend, is also with the party… I saw Charlie Emmett ["Dashing Charlie"] among the party also. He was interpreter for the band of Sioux that came to our camp the second day after our arrival here – a "cut-off" band of which "Whistler" is chief.

A week later Ena wrote of the return of the "Buffalo Outfit":

> I saw the whole "Buffalo Outfit" Tuesday morning. "Texas Jack," Charlie Emmett, Andy [Barrett] "The Half Breed" or the wonderful "California Horse Tamer," and [Sidney Barnett,] the Saratoga Man. Was introduced to and shook hands with the Horse Tamer. He is a rather fine looking man, yet somewhat stolid in his appearance. Had a pleasant little chat with Texas Jack – in fact, with all the white men. Their wagon came in and the "Saratoga Man" showed me a young antelope, which he was taking East… The little creature was docile and fearless. Wish I had one.
>
> They caught seven or eight buffalo. All died save one and it was left here. I rode out with Mr. Snell to see it…[Paddy] Miles, [Richard] Seymour, [George] Dillard, [John] Fritcher, [William] Black and Mr. P[almer], brought up the rear. They got the poor beast on his legs after awhile, and he really tried to fight. An Indian and a buffalo never yields to its conqueror or succumbs to pain! But this little "animule" – what a caricature of defiance and fierceness.

Because one branch of the military road that linked Fort McPherson with points south passed near the little settlement on the Medicine, it was a convenient stopping place for the traveler to rest his horse. Consequently, Ena mentioned a number of visitors, all of whom, no doubt, appreciated the bonus attraction of the charming young newcomer at Wolf's Rest. Washington M. Hinman, a millwright, who had established a steam sawmill and blacksmith shop at Cottonwood Springs (site of Fort McPherson) in the early 1860s, was prospecting for a sawmill when he hitched his horse at Wolf's Rest. Ena wrote of his visit: "He says he has traveled north, south, east and west, but has never seen so much 'romance' or aught so 'romantic' as we of Medicine Creek!!! He did not qualify or specify the who, which or how!"

The following day Ena noted that a Lieutenant Miller had stopped by on his way to the "Post." "I found him to be a man of refinement – or rather a refined education. He quite charmed me with his graphic description of Western life, Indians, etc. He spoke of the

Ena (Palmer) Raymonde and her mother were the first white women to settle in Frontier County, Nebraska. Photo taken in Springfield, Missouri, circa 1874. *Courtesy Nebraska State Historical Society*

<u>Poets</u> – he declaims finely. I have half an idea that he tried to draw me out – i.e. to speak of myself, but had too much tact to <u>press</u> the subject." On the evening of the ninth, Ena reflected on her new life: "What a strange wild charm this new world has. My life seems half a dream… My little tent looks <u>friendly</u>. My books, pictures, pistol, <u>all</u> belong to the familiar "by-gone" – Only the buffalo robes that make my couch and the white canvas drawn above me tells that I am camping in the wilderness of the 'Far West.'" The journal entries of June 22, 1872, give a picture of the comfortable friendships Ena developed. At the time, Ena and her parents were living in tents as the ferocious March winds had driven them from Raven's Cliff, the first cabin Paddy Miles built atop a high bank overlooking the Medicine:

> My <u>tepe</u> is too warm and so I've brought my journal out here to scrawl a line or so. It will be a <u>scrawl</u>, I expect, in more than one sense; for I am by no manner of means <u>alone</u> with <u>thought</u>, <u>paper</u> and a <u>willing</u> <u>pen</u>. Wilk Snell is fishing about two rods of my seat; my irrepressible George [Dillard] is gracefully <u>reclining</u> near my side. Mr. Snell Sr., is my vis-à-vis [situated opposite]; while Bert is prone upon Mother-Earth just beyond Mr. Snell. A game at cards is on the *tapis*. I quit writing that I may play. *Tepe Chees Cheela*, Night, 11:00 o'clock:

> <u>Alone</u> for the first time since morning. Wilk, George and Bert have just left me. We have sung every song imaginable and a good many more <u>un</u>imaginable I'm inclined to think… Dick Seymour has left "Wolf's Rest" – can't say I regret it, as I think it best in more ways than one that he should go. He has gone in to the Post.

> I went to ride with Mr. Wilk [Snell] today… Wilk Snell and his father came last night. Mr. Wilkins [Wilk] was with us on our <u>first</u> introduction to the <u>Prairie</u>. He drove us out here. I think him quite handsome and very pleasant in his manner. It seems like "old times" to meet again. He taught me how to make <u>biscuit</u>, "wash dishes," [and] <u>stew</u> coffee… I shall always like Wilk Snell for the kind and

sensible manner in which he acted when I was a "Stranger in a Strange land."

On the first of July the lusty young "Lords of the Medicine" spent the day prowling the countryside:

> I've had a tramp on horseback with Bert and George way up the Medicine – caught a gopher, or what I should call a ground-squirrel, on the prairie. Carried it eight miles and then let it get away… We put up a claim-post – shot pistols – ate green grapes – declared ourselves "lords of all we surveyed" – dared the hills to dispute it – and then, well pleased with a proud knowledge of the courage we had so gallantly displayed, we turned our faces toward that haven of rest known not widely but so well as Wolf's Rest.

Two days later the "Medicinites" rode into McPherson to partake of the Fourth of July festivities. Ena, who had been suffering from bouts of ill health – most likely the lingering effects of malaria – was to remain at McPherson for the summer where she would be staying with Wilk Snell's parents. Mr. and Mrs. Snell lived in a log cabin outside the confines of the fort where Jacob Snell was the sutler or trader at the fort while Elizabeth Snell cooked for the officers. Ena's first journal entries from McPherson:

> Ft. McPherson, July 9, 1872 –

> We of the Medicine came in here the day before "the fourth." They, Bert and G[eorge] [Dillard] & J[ohn] [Fritcher] returned on yesterday. I am to remain here until I find some change in my health… I rode in! We just rushed through. I really enjoyed the ride, ill as I was…

> Went to see the horse-race fourth of July's eve. The pony I bet on beat! Washta! Some wished me to go to North Platte on the fourth – but somehow and for several reasons I could not "see it"…

> July 10, 1872 –

> Went to ride with T[exas] J[ack] this afternoon – had a good ride of it, only my Injun pony, Falcon, got *de mal*

en pis, and I don't know if I can ride him again, tho' I have made an engagement to ride tomorrow afternoon.

I've spent one night with Mrs. Cody – she took me in out of charity…with the promise that I might sleep just so late as I pleased. But I did not sleep late – I was delirious all night – talked or rather raved in my usual crazy style. Hope I said nothing *mal a propos,* as Mr. Omohundro slept in the adjoining room. Mrs. Cody is quite kind and pleasant in her manner. She has two charming little children. Kit Carson, the boy is a handsome, precocious little fellow – not more than three years old, or rather not three years – and just as keen as the little rascal can be. He gives promise of a future. [Kit Carson Cody, the only son of Wm. F. and Louisa Cody, died April 20, 1876, of scarlet fever.]

The time Ena spent at Fort McPherson was filled with variety – interesting events and people always coming and going. Though she did not feel well much of the time, Ena wrote with enthusiasm of her experiences there. She also enjoyed the pleasure of Texas Jack's company before his departure from the fort in July as the trail agent hired by the government to accompany the Pawnee Indians on their summer buffalo hunt:

July 11, 1872 –

Mr. "Texas" had quite a time lassoing my little rascal of a pony! We found it pleasant after getting out on the prairie – no mud – and my (I mean our!) <u>Western</u> <u>Hero</u> made himself just as pleasant as possible – delicate, yet <u>kind</u> and <u>manly</u> in his attentions…! In short almost everybody is just as kind to me as <u>can</u> <u>be</u>. Mrs. Snell is just as good to me as possible. So is Mr. Snell – and Wilkins and I get on famously – sometimes he humors my whims and sometimes teases me to the very extent of my amiable (?) temper!

I must not ride Falcon again; Mr. Omohundro says it is dangerous and I should not attempt it. Bert told me as much before! I wonder if I care anything for my neck? <u>Some</u> people always seem to think I <u>should</u>…

Friday, July 12 –

Texas Jack received a telegram this morning, which takes him a hundred or two miles from here. He is appointed agent for the Pawnee Indians; will have about three thousand under his charge, I believe. He came to bid me goodbye at noon. Looked <u>fine</u>, with all his hunting accoutrements about him and mounted on a good horse! …

Wednesday, July 24 –

I was introduced to "Buffalo Bill" yesterday. He has just returned from a <u>scouting expedition</u> – been away for six or [more] weeks I believe.

I, very unexpectedly, received a call from Texas Jack, evening before last, I believe it was. He remained in but a short time; had a few Pawnees with him. I do not think them as fine looking, not so <u>erect</u> as the Sioux; but they say they are better "braves" than the latter. When asking one of the Pawnees if he was not afraid to venture so far on the hunting ground of the Sioux, it was fine to see the expression of unutterable scorn that lighted up for a moment, the stolidity of his face; then instantly relapsing into the grim Stoic, he quietly crossed his throat, giving the sign of the Sioux, and said they were "heap squaws." Mr. Omohundro said the Indians were in fine spirits; plenty of buffalo, and the papooses all fat.

July 26, 1872 –

Mr. Cody has <u>invited</u> me to <u>shoot</u> with him; says he hears I am a good shot, etc. But I don't know about shooting again… When I shot with Texas Jack (it was <u>not</u> a shooting match) and acquitted myself with <u>decided</u> credit, there was such a fuss made over it, that I thought I would not shoot again while in here; not because I think any sensible person could attach any <u>blame</u> to it; but because these people, or some of them, may misconstrue my intentions and think I am trying to make myself famous as a shootest. I scorn anything like an <u>egotistical</u> <u>display</u>!

I shoot because I love it; because I know I am a good shot; and because it is my pleasure! I am no stickler for praise…

In the meantime, reports reached McPherson that flooding on the Medicine had put Wolf's Rest under from two to four feet of water. In addition to concern about the books and manuscripts she had left behind, Ena was hoping for the opportunity to finally go on a buffalo hunt. With that in mind and hiding her riding habit and saddle from Mrs. Snell's view, Wilk Snell hitched a team to the wagon and took Ena to the Medicine. The flood had, indeed, wrecked havoc on the Medicine, taking Ena's tent, *Tepe Chees Cheela*, in its sweep, and the family had taken refuge at Raven's Cliff.

A few days later Ena was back at McPherson, where she wrote of the thrilling buffalo hunt:

> [We] made a dash for the main herd, and in less than five minutes they were all on the "dead go"… What a wild grand chase it was. I could hear the steady tramp and roar of their feet as the huge creatures swept over hills and down canyons at a speed that put our horses to their best… Wilk and Bert "went for them" in good Indian style – bare headed and riding as horsemen should! They were soon in their midst, shooting right and left…

Ena's attempt to "kill her own meat" was thwarted, however, by a series of mishaps involving her unruly horse. It wasn't until near the end of the hunt that she finally got her chance. Being small of stature, however, she could not handle the heavy needle-gun while horseback, so she had to get ahead of the buffalo and dismount:

> Off I went to the ground in "good order," ready for the gun to be placed quickly in my eager, but not trembling hands! We had distanced our buffalo about ten yards, per-haps, and as the huge fellows came thundering past, it was but a breath when I had knelt and fired at the foremost bull. The dull thud that came back to us, as well as the sud-den lurching off of the bull from the lead told that I had made a home shot.

Texas Jack Omohundro was an important part of the panorama of the plains in southwest Nebraska in 1872. His endeavor to rope live buffalo involved Paddy Miles as well as several others who hung around Wolf's Rest. *Courtesy Buffalo Bill Historical Society*

The reports of the buffalo hunt reached McPherson before Ena's return: "The news that I had killed a buffalo preceded me here! … I wonder at what distance I shot that fellow? Wilk says 120 yards, I believe." Two days later she added: "This morning Mr. Lewis came to me with a peculiar smile on his face, and handing me the *North Platte Democrat*, pointed out a passage; I took it, and read among the 'personals' quite a little speech about myself. I am termed the 'Lady Shootest,' and there upon is turned a neat description of my buffalo killing together with a graceful little compliment as to my skill as a shot…" (Some writers, including Paddy Miles, have said that Ena shot a buffalo while riding horseback, but she never made such a claim.)

Ena's shooting was challenged on other fronts in August of 1872: "Bert came in from the Medicine today…[and] again asserted that he could and would beat me shooting; So Mary, he and I went to walk this afternoon to the Soldier's target and we tried the matter. I beat him, but that will not keep him from vowing the next time that the subject is mentioned that he can beat me, if he never does!" A week later: "Shot pistols with Wilk today and beat him! … When I was ill I shot a snake's head off while in bed! It came up through the floor in the next room and I shot the reptile through the door."

Ena also marveled at the ever-changing current of life along the great western trail: "I do wish I could keep a journal of the many rich things I see and hear in this great wild splendid West! … Wanderers of every kind; and waifs from every shore meeting and passing away from each other as the waves meet and pass upon a troubled Sea. I like it! This constant change…" A few days later she was equally as enthusiastic over the domestic work: "Mary and I were taken this morning with a fit for fixing… Scrubbed a room, that never had that attention before…and then we tore down beds, put them up, swept, dusted… O! I will get to be a domestic woman if I keep on with my dish-washing, sweeping, bed-making, house-scrubbing, ironing, etc. etc. Quite a 'cart-horse' in time! And I am getting well at it too!"

It was on September 9, 1872, that Ena first mentioned the arrival of the young Dr. Carver from the East. As her friendship with Carver developed, she frequently referred to his practice of dentistry, their shooting together, and his coming and going. Carver, however, at that point was just one of the young men whose company Ena enjoyed while at McPherson. One Friday in September she noted, "No man around the house today; but they will make up for it tomorrow and Sunday. 'And still them come!' is the watch-word every Saturday and Sunday!" Texas Jack returned from the hunt with the Pawnee in late September or early October. Ena noted on October 8, 1872: "I went to walk with the Dr. (i.e. my 'little bubber'). We had a good little time of it! Shot lots! I just did the finest shooting out. We shot for the champion-ship of 'Ameraky' – who beat? Ask the Dr.! … Met M[ary] and T. J. on our return. I hope I've caused no unpleasant feelings. – pshaw! I am always in trouble." Ena was with Carver, but there was a mutual attraction between her and Texas Jack – a fact that surely was not lost on either Carver or Mary Snell.

Texas Jack, for his part, still had to deal with Indian skirmishes as Ena also mentioned: "They say 'Whistler' and some of the Pawnees are apt to have a little unpleasantness 'over on the River' tonight. Believe Texas Jack has gone over to see something about it." Autumn of 1872 saw a number of changes – not only in Ena's life but in the lives of Doc Carver and the frontiersmen he would seek to imitate. Buffalo Bill and Texas Jack served as guides on a hunt with the Earl of Dunraven, an English sports hunter, and then traveled to the East to appear in dramatic interpretations of their life on the frontier. In November Carver would move to Wolf's Rest with Ena, but in the meantime there was still October at Fort McPherson:

> October 9, 1872 –
>
> The Dr. has been teasing me – I begged him to stop – telling him I had written but a half sentence. The scamp got off a piece of his wit at my expense in reply. Telling me my life was made up of half-sentences and that it would "end in a broken sentence if I did not take care!" We have lots of fun, the Dr. and I…
>
> Thursday, October 10, 1872 –
>
> The Ball at North Platte comes off tonight. I should not be surprised if somebody will be quite disappointed at our not going. I hear that Texas Jack has gone away with the Pawnees that came into the Fort day before yesterday. I hear that the tooth I hammered for him has given him trouble…
>
> Thursday night –
>
> How still it has been today! We miss the Doctor. Mary looks blue and her little black orbs have a far-off wistful look, really sorrowful to see. "I love thee fondly dearest"

has been the burden of her song today.

We "might have been" dancing tonight – when I was younger and less <u>wise</u>, how I would have chafed under the bane of "staying at home" away from any scene of festivity...

Friday, October 11, 1872 –

Dr. Carver brought Mrs. Snell down at noon. Mr. James [Snell] came in the morning. They report having a delightful time at the ball – i.e. Mr. Jamie [Snell]. The Dr. looked sick and half out of sorts. The gentleman returned this evening.

Monday, October 14, 1872 –

I have just been out in the moonlight. Oh! The soft haze of this gorgeous autumnal weather. I am entirely charmed with this <u>western fall</u>... I have just got a funny letter from Eny's "Little Bubber" [Carver]. I must write him tonight and send the letter up by Mr. Jamie, who returns in the morning.

Wilk took me to ride yesterday afternoon. We had a most delightful time. The horses were willing – the weather perfect – and my handsome cavalier in the best possible humor; of course we had a rapid, pleasant ride. I have but one unpleasant memento of it!!!

And then it was back to the Medicine. Ena was ready as she wrote from Fort McPherson on Sunday, November 3, 1872: "I write a <u>farewell</u> to this place and its 'peoples.' Hurrah! For the Medicine! They can't winter me in here. I start out with Bert and Dr. Carver tomorrow. 'You bet.' I am glad to go! I am going to 'trap'; have got all my tricks ready..." Just as she had thrived on the activity at the fort, Ena was now ready for a quieter life. She wrote from Wolf's Rest, Medicine Valley:

November 6, 1872 –

Calm and beautiful as a summer's dream the sun steals to rest behind the looming hills of the Medicine. How delightful I find the restful <u>freedom</u> and <u>splendid</u> quiet of today!

Evening before last the Dr., Bert and I arrived here. Yesterday was passed amid a rush and tumble of men, horses, guns and shooting. Today they all went on a big camp hunt except Mr. P., a workman and Wilk Snell, who arrived yesterday, on his way to the "Muddy" but was too ill with his teeth to proceed further today.

Thursday, November 7, 1872 –

The weather has grown much warmer; I am glad for the hunters – our boys, I mean. They will be back today – tired and hungry. We must get something for them to eat.

Wilk and I went to walk last evening. The weather was perfect! I went the paths, or <u>some</u> of <u>them</u>, that I used to go, but did not feel the way I used to feel. I trust I shall get entirely strong this winter.

Friday, November 8, 1872 –

I have just had a big play and quarrel with my "<u>little bubber</u>." He has gone to sleep, and I turn to my journal for a moments chat! We had a visit from some Sioux today – Long Man, his squaw and a girl he has for sale. Four horses is the price. I shot with Long Man and beat him. He seemed very much amused at my shooting. I gave the young squaw all sorts of colored corn.

We are going to commence to trap tomorrow.

Saturday, November 9, 1872 –

Today I have really commenced to trap. O! and I am so <u>tired</u>! Poor little Einna, how she did plod through the tall grass after Mr. P. and the Doctor. We saw two deer. If I had had my gun I would have "knocked one down." I am going to hunt soon.

I must go to Sioux City to see my Indian visitors tomorrow. I like the papoose and squaw. I must cultivate her acquaintance.

The initial exhilaration Ena experienced on her return to the
Medicine was soon tempered, however, with a severe attack of rheu-
matism as well as emotional turmoil. She neglected her journal until
December 8, 1872: "One month since I have traced a line within
this book – or anywhere else scarcely. One month, and nothing to
tell what has been written within the mystic pages of Life's strange
book! And why has it been thus? And do I dare call myself *in foro
conscientiae?*" With no further explanation from Ena, it can be assumed there was a troubling undercurrent to her relationship with
Doc Carver. They were by all appearances sharing a room at Wolf's
Rest and given the moral code of the time, the issue of their intimacy
– however it played out – undoubtedly created tension. Ena's journal
entries for the balance of 1872 covered a mix of the events of her
everyday life (including her obvious relief at Long Man's departure),
deep soul-searching, and poetic observations:

> Wolf's Rest, December 23, 1872 –
>
> Tomorrow is <u>Christmas eve</u>! The night wanes, yet I can-
> not sleep…The changes of a few short weeks come troop-
> ing upon my half-confused memory in troubled haste…
>
> I am better of my rheumatism, but far from being
> well…The Dr. is still with us. In fact Mr. P., Madame, the
> Dr. and I are the sole occupants of Wolf's Rest at present.
> Bert looks in on us every three or four days. He is about
> Medicine Lake just now, I expect. He will try trapping
> and hunting up there for a while…
>
> I have seen Texas Jack <u>once</u> since my return to the Med-
> icine. He made a dash call one evening while out here
> with the Earl of Dunraven. Jack was guide, etc., for the
> Lord and his party. He told me then that he and Buffalo
> Bill expected to go east on quite a tour. They have been
> gone some time now. Of course the papers are full of their
> sayings and doings…
>
> Dick S[eymour] told me "good bye" until Spring some
> days ago. He will "<u>winter it</u>" among the Indians with the
> "Clifford outfit" hunting and trapping.

I have had quite a number of Indian guests… Suffice it to say that I was not sorry when "Long Man" took down his lodge poles and started for "<u>heap</u> <u>Sioux</u>." He gave me a gift before leaving in the shape of two <u>huge</u> (without the h!) lumps of *cha-hum-pee* [sugar], which looked rather the worse for wear, as he gravely drew them from the darkened recesses of his calico shirt! In a moment of necessity I magnanimously used some of this gift for the Dr.'s coffee; but strange to say he seemed highly incensed when my generosity came to his knowledge, nor could I reconcile that ungrateful fellow even after telling him <u>how</u> carefully I had "<u>scraped</u> <u>the</u> <u>outside!</u>"

December 25, 1872 –

<u>Christmas</u> <u>night</u>! Why has this dim indifference settled upon my spirit? Where is the old impatient longing? …

December 26, 1872 –

I have been sitting up by the stove <u>thinking</u>? Trying to decide for myself the <u>worth</u> of living! Trying to <u>weigh</u> the <u>question</u> calmly and in all justice to <u>others</u>…

December 27, 1872 –

The Dr. left at noon today. There was a snow-storm in the morning; and a fall of about from 8 to 10 inches. It was the first snow-storm I had ever seen. What a misapplication, when we term the noiseless drift of misty snow wreaths, a "storm." I was charmed and felt the spotless robe that… cast a mist of its pureness upon my own life…

How very <u>quiet</u>! My little cabin looks familiar and cheerful. Half an author's den, and half a hunter's lodge, with its strange, yet picturesque commingling of books and pistols; manuscripts and cartridges; guns and pictures; book-casings and horns of every description: Elk horns, buffalo horns, deer horns, etc., from which are suspended walking boots, over-shoes, cartridge-belts, etc., etc. while on the floor are spread buffalo robes, <u>gunny</u> <u>sacks</u> and "such like." My bed fills one corner; my writing table another; there is a crimson curtain before my single window; a couch of wolf-skins at my feet, and a warm fire in a grateful stove.

A little clock ticks cheerily away by my book case, and the friendly light of my solitary lamp gleams with a softening radiance as I look around upon the contents of this rude log cabin, yet feel my heart swell beneath a gentle influence as I realize that this is home – my home, untrammeled, <u>free</u> and <u>mine</u>… I hunt and shoot – sew and read – play or work – write or talk, whenever I feel like it…

Friday night, December 28, 1872 –

Mr. Fergu[son] has just called to deliver me a note from Dick S[eymour]. They were at Frenchman's Fork when he wrote. Quite a lot of news in a "nut-shell": Pawnee and Sioux fighting; quite a little engagement (for Indians) on Christmas day, and the chief <u>Whistler</u>, reported killed…[1]

Saturday, December 29, 1872 –

The red glow of the setting sun streams through my little window and falling like liquid gold upon the open leaves of my journal, invites me to the pleasant task of having a pen-chat with myself; so I have laid away my sewing – which is a scarlet hunting suit – although I know I ought to work for at least two hours yet. But I am tired; have been out all the afternoon with pa, hunting. Walked seven or eight miles and saw nothing to shoot at but *Shea-ahs* [beaver?]; would not waste my cartridges on them.

Saw lots of coyote tracks; followed the trail of a wounded one some distance. I shot one over a day or two ago, at the distance of 500 yards. Expect it was the same one. The wolves make the night wild with their dismal howls; I sometimes go out and listen to them – over the desolate hills in every direction you can hear the shrill scream of the coyote making strange concord with the deeper howl of the large gray wolf…

We have just had our cozy little supper…around my stove. Pa and Ma go to the kitchen, or cook room and "yanks" out the "grub"; then we "warm it over" on my stove. When that is done each one gets his or her plate

---

1 Whistler's death was not a result of the Pawnee and Sioux fighting or the Christmas Day skirmish.

and cup and we "tackle" the "grub-pile" in good earnest! The excitement of eating over, each returns to their work or amusement, as the case may be, and quiet is restored to the camp. At present Mr. Palmer is busily engaged in roasting a coon before the fire in his room; he has the unfortunate quadruped tied in midair by a string with a dish underneath to catch the drops of grease that ooze slowly out. Every now and then he calls out to me to say that the "coon is roasting brown."

Monday, December 30, 1872 –

I got papers from Texas Jack – If sensation is a mark of success, he and Cody certainly have not failed in the object of their visit. The last intelligence, they were in Chicago – drawing thousands to Nixon's Amphitheater. "Ned Buntline" takes the character of Cale Durg. He writes the play, which they are presented under. It is a dramatization of some of "Ned's" stories of the "far West," called *Scouts of the Prairie*, etc., etc.

The Daily Report of the 17th says: "The first appearance of Buffalo Bill last evening was a signal for such a shout as never before welcomed an actor in Chicago." *The Inter Ocean* gives the author, play and actors a somewhat more questionable praise – for instance in speaking of the audience it says, "The audience was not what the ordinary critic would stigmatize as select and cultivated; but it was appreciative, yes, enthusiastic. It was a "Dime Novel" audience – etc. etc. It was worth more than all the play to watch this audience…

Again, in speaking of Buffalo Bill, he is termed a "tall, handsome-looking fellow" but ill at ease and "quite at a loss what to do with his hands."… Poor Cody! The idea of looking "ill at ease." He is out of his sphere. I have seen him the very personification of graceful ease and manly beauty; but it was not in a crowded city, before the glare of the footlights, and amid the crash of orchestra, and flash of stage-gewgaws: but dashing over the free, wild prairie, and riding his horse as though he and the noble animal were bounding with one life and one motion!

By the end of 1872, Ena Raymonde was truly a woman of the plains; southwest Nebraska was firmly woven into the fabric of her life. Likewise, threads of her life run through the stories of those with whom she associated. The name *Pa-he-minny- minnish* or "Little Curly Hair" that Carver bestowed on Ena surfaced, for instance, in later writings by and about Carver. Discerning just who pulled her heartstrings at any particular time is difficult. Wm. Frank "Doc" Carver was certainly front-and-center in Ena's life during the latter part of 1872 and into 1873. On the other hand, Texas Jack Omohundro, with his laughing dark eyes and magnetic personality, had struck all the right chords in the time he spent with her earlier in 1872. Just when Ena's friendship with Texas Jack changed course is hard to determine, but certainly her attention to Doc Carver was of no small consequence. Ena's journal entries for July of 1873 were fraught with despair as she looked back on the events of the previous year. On July 10, 1873, (one year following a horseback ride with Texas Jack) she wrote: "One year ago I fancied I had found that which would make me count the hours of Life jealously – perhaps I had – but it has slipped from my grasp – or has been thrown away in madness – God only knows which."

One year in the life of Ena Raymonde – the woman who might have several gentleman callers and yet write in her journal "Nothing of him-portance today!" If she let a possible future with Texas Jack slip away, she apparently made the deliberate decision not to follow Carver when he left the Medicine Valley. Ena eventually found the love for which she yearned, and she experienced a full measure of life's pleasures and heartaches before her own untimely death. She wrote from Fort McPherson on July 21, 1872: "Ah! I think I shall love this wild new world! I wonder if the passion of its spell will be strong enough to chain my restless Spirit?" In retrospect it can be said, the new life Ena Raymonde found in Nebraska did chain her restless spirit.

11

Carver in the Crosshairs

*I*f brute strength, nerves of steel, and the tenacity of a bull dog were attributes to the early dentist, then Dr. Wm. Frank Carver was the man for the job. Over six-feet tall and weighing around two-hundred pounds, he could most likely put his knee in the chest of a patient, hold the hands down with one hand, and pull the offending tooth with the other. Beyond strength, the requirements for being a dentist in the 1870s were few. Bartenders, barbers, and blacksmiths might double as part-time dentists. Carver's strong arm and steady hands were bonus qualifications and would serve him well when he went on to become a champion rifleman. Although he later denied having been a dentist, Doc Carver hung his shingle in North Platte. Beginning with the week of Sept. 4, 1872, the following advertisement appeared in the *Lincoln County (Nebr.) Advertiser*:[1]

DR. W. F. CARVER
DENTIST
Office at RAY'S DRUGSTORE

Carver's precise reasons for coming west aren't known, but he was quickly seduced by firearms and gun powder – and smitten with Ena Raymonde. A southern belle, who had just recently set her

---

1 Paul D. Riley noted that five issues, Aug. 14, 1872 – Oct.12, 1872, of the *Lincoln County Advertiser* are on microfilm at the NSHS, Carver Collection, NSHS (hereafter cited as Carver MSS).

The photo of Doc Carver in plainsman's attire was taken in Omaha in 1880. A monument marking the site of Carver's homestead on the Medicine Creek in southwest Nebraska reads: Memoriam: Doc F. W. Carver, Champion Rifle Shot of the World. His cabin home was here in 1872-73-74. He was proud of his Indian title, Evil Spirits of the Plains. His cabbin [sic] 50 rod south. *Photo of Carver courtesy Denver Public Library; photo of monument courtesy Frontier County Historical Society*

dainty foot on the Nebraska frontier, Ena spent most of the summer at Fort McPherson. She mentioned the arrival of the young doctor from the East in a journal entry on September 9, 1872. That Carver was not yet an expert shot is evident:

> Sunday afternoon we all – i.e. Bert and George, Mary and I, in a wagon; James Snell, the Doctor and Curt in a buggy; and Wilk on horseback – went to see a prairie-dog town! We went at half-speed or better all the way. Shot about 200 rounds; The Dr. doing the most of the business of shooting if not killing; got buffalo berries and grapes after which we started back at the same "rattling" rate we had come. Saw a wolf – Wilk gave it chase – had a fine run…

In the weeks to follow, Ena continued to refer to "the Dr." and his dentistry. By October she had become one of the doctor's patients – and occasionally his assistant. From Fort McPherson on October 8, 1872, she wrote: "I've had a lot of work done in my mouth – it looks like a flash of sunlight – my mouth I mean. I am learning to be a dentist – I hammer everybody's teeth for the doctor!" The same journal entry reveals the fact that Ena Raymonde, an expert shot herself, was still outshooting the doctor. Carver was in North Platte practicing dentistry for a good part of October, and he and Ena wrote letters back and forth. In Ena's company, Doctor Carver took up residence at Wolf's Rest on the Medicine Creek in early November. Following their arrival on the Medicine, there was "a rush and tumble of men, horses, guns and shooting" before the men left on a "big camp hunt." Over the next few months Carver was back and forth between North Platte and Wolf's Rest. On December 30, 1872, Paddy Miles, W. L. McClary, a fellow by the name of Bruster, and several others rode into Wolf's Rest from McPherson. Along with a message to Ena from Carver, Miles delivered a bundle of newspapers from Texas Jack, telling of the acclaim he and Buffalo Bill were receiving.

While Buffalo Bill Cody and Texas Jack Omohundro were exploiting their frontier experience for profit in the East, Carver was just breaking in his buckskins. That be as it may, he was learning to shoot. As Paddy Miles put it, "To be a good shot was considered the highest accomplishment, and Dr. W. F. Carver's ambition ran that way, so he did nothing but hunt and shoot until he became the greatest shot in the world."[2] While she never said so herself, the old-timers on the Medicine maintained it was Ena who taught Carver to shoot. Carver staked a claim on the Medicine, and though he established a residence – a dugout or cabin of some type – it is hard to determine when he lived there. From Ena's journals, it appears "the Dr." took his boots off at Wolf's Rest when he wasn't in North Platte or off on other travels.

In February Ena mentioned that the Doctor was on his way to Chicago, and then on March 7, 1873, she wrote: "The Doctor will be gone a month tomorrow. I think he left on Saturday – the 8th of February. This is the longest period by over two weeks, since we met at Fort McPherson…just six months ago today, that we have been apart!" The next day she indicated she had heard the Doctor was in Chicago, "I am sorry for [him] – I think I know the cause! Those who sow the wind must expect to reap the whirl-wind!" There is no explanation of the business Carver was attending to in Chicago, but Ena believed he was responsible for the outcome. Her journal entry two weeks later deepens the mystery: "The Doctor arrived this evening at sunset. I was standing at my little window watching the fading brilliance of the tinted clouds when a passing form darkened the view. I scarcely could recognize in the pale, agitated man before me, the ruddy face and wild hilarity of the one that had left me about six weeks ago!"

The reference to Carver's wild hilarity portrays the energy and unbridled enthusiasm of youth and, indeed, at twenty-one years of age, Carver was a relatively young man when he came to Nebraska. Later, as he gained national acclaim as a sharpshooter, he was questioned by admiring audiences about his life on the frontier, and the yarns he spun required a greater span of years. Consequently, Carver added better than ten years to his age. Although he gave his date of birth as being May 7, 1840, a reliable source gives Carver's birth year

---

2 Miles and Bratt, pp. 20-21.

as being 1851.[3] His mother was born in 1829, which further under-
mines any possibility of the 1840 birth year being accurate.

A cock-and-bull tale of his early life along with extracts from
actual press releases covering his first year of exhibition shooting appeared in *Life of Dr. Wm. F. Carver of California: Champion Rifle Shot
of the World*, a book Carver published in 1878. Romanticized stories
of white captives living with the Indians were especially popular in
the "civilized" East in the 1800s. It was this genre that influenced the
spin Carver put on his fabrication. Carver claimed he witnessed the
brutal murder and scalping of his mother and little sister by Indians
in 1844 when he was only four years old. By some miracle his life
was spared:

> Meantime, the bright-faced, sturdy little boy, who never
> knew whether it was by some sudden relenting of the sav-
> age heart or a fancy they might have conceived for the
> beautiful, brave child, that he escaped the terrible fate of
> his mother and little sister, was taken, a horror-stricken,
> shuddering captive of their train. Walking with tender
> baby feet along the rough trail that was sometimes trying
> even to the accustomed feet of his savage captors, as if the
> grief and terror and hardships were not enough torture for
> the carefully nurtured child, he was compelled to carry in
> his hand the scalp of his baby-sister, whose shining tresses
> it had been his delight to fondle in happier days…[4]

Carver did have a little sister May who died at just under two
years of age. She wasn't born, however, until May 5, 1856, and died
January 1, 1858. And his mother, who actually resided with her son
on the Medicine Creek for a short while, lived until 1907.[5] While
on the Medicine Creek, Carver had christened Ena Raymonde *Pa-*

---

3 Don Russell, *A History of the Wild West Shows*, (Fort Worth: Anon Carter Museum of
Western Art, 1970) p. 10. William Frank Carver was born in Winslow, Ill., to William
Daniel Carver, a practicing physician, and Deborah Tohapenes (Peters) Carver. Russell
drew on several sources for his summary of Carver, but credited Paul D. Riley for information on Carver's early years.
4 Wm. F. Carver, *Life of Dr. Wm. F. Carver of California: Champion Rifle Shot of the World*,
1878, <http://books.google.com.> p. 19.
5 When Wm. F. Carver died in 1927 he was buried near his mother and sister in Winslow,
Illinois.

The excerpt (above) from Ena Raymonde's December 23, 1872 journal mentions Doc Carver's presence at Wolf's Rest. Mr. P. and Madame were her parents. Ena also indicated Bert (Paddy Miles) was trapping and hunting on the Medicine Lake near present day Wellfleet, Nebraska. The drawing, titled "Long Man," was found on the pages of Ena's journal. *Courtesy Nebraska State Historical Society.*

he-minny- minnish or "Little Curly Hair." That the memory of Ena pulled on Carver's heartstrings long after he left the Medicine is evident in a tale purportedly told from the point of view of another captive. By this time the fictitious Frank Carver had been adopted into the tribe and spent carefree days in the company of a beautiful little Indian girl who had long, curly hair.

> Frank [Carver] was flying around on his pony, his long golden hair shining in the sun. He rode without a saddle, and guided his horse with a rawhide thong tied around its jaw. Pa-he-minnie-minnish, or Pa-he, as they generally called her, rode with him, and a prettier picture I never saw than the two children made as they travelled along… They seemed very happy together, and I wondered many times during the day whether they would grow up together, and whether Frank would ever be happy among his own people if he should some time be allowed to return to them. The little girl, whose Indian name meant "Little curly-hair," which was given her because of that peculiarity, was a famous rider, and the pet of the camp.[6]

Carver commandeered the essential elements of several southwest Nebraska events of 1872 – at which he wasn't present – to embellish his frontier credentials. Apparently it took some years to polish these stories as they appear in Raymond Thorp's 1957 biography of Carver but not in Carver's 1878 book. (The story of being captured by the Indians had evolved into running away from home and joining an Indian tribe by the time Thorp wrote Carver's biography.)

The buffalo hunt staged for the Grand Duke Alexis of Russia occurred in January of 1872, eight months before Carver came to Nebraska. Several of the fellows from the Medicine rode over to the Red Willow in present day Hayes County to partake in this grand adventure. Hosted by General Phil Sheridan and two months in the planning, every accommodation was provided for the physical comfort of the twenty-one-year-old son of Alexander II, the czar of Rus-

6 Carver, p. 19.

sia. There were troops on hand to guarantee the safety of the duke and his entourage in case of an Indian attack. As a certain amount of wild west flavor was desired, Buffalo Bill Cody was recruited to secure Spotted Tail and a body of his warriors to be present.

Accounts vary as to whether or not Duke Alexis actually killed his own buffalo. Buffalo Bill Cody wrote that the duke at first insisted on using a pistol but emptied both his and Cody's pistols without felling a buffalo. Cody claimed he then handed his rifle to the duke. The duke was riding Cody's good buffalo horse, Buckskin Joe, and Cody told the duke to urge his horse close to the buffaloes and shoot when Cody gave the word. Cody then gave the horse a good whack across the rump with his whip, and with a couple of jumps, the horse carried Duke Alexis to within a few feet of a big buffalo bull. The duke fired, the buffalo went down, and the "Grand Duke stopped his horse, dropped his gun on the ground, and commenced waving his hat."[7]

Although he was not there, Carver wrote himself into the event by reworking a Paddy Miles' story. The way Paddy told it: "The duke could not ride over the rough country fast enough to kill a buffalo; he did not want to return to Russia before killing one. So Bill Reed ran down a buffalo calf and held it until the grand duke came up and shot it."[8] Carver's version also involves Bill Reed (sometimes spelled Reid), but it has Carver driving a buffalo into camp and then shooting it in the spine so the Grand Duke Alexis could make the killing shot. Supposedly the injured beast – still standing on its front legs – was moving in a circle so fast the duke couldn't take aim. Carver claimed Bill Reed then seized the tail and slowed the angry buffalo enough to allow Duke Alexis to make the killing shot.[9]

Carver also injected himself into the great adventure of roping live buffalo. Later in the summer of 1872 following Texas Jack's failed attempt, Colonel Sidney Barnett, an east coast promoter, was successful in his endeavor to have a few buffalo captured and shipped

---

7 Cody, pp. 295-301.
8 Miles and Bratt, p. 22.
9 Raymond W. Thorp, *"Wild West" Doc Carver: Spirit Gun of the West,* (London: W. Foulsham & Co. Ltd., 1957), p. 60.

east. Titled as the "Grand Buffalo Hunt," the exhibition took place at Niagara Falls on August 28 and 30, 1872. Billed as the most celebrated scout and hunter of the plains, Wild Bill Hickok was in charge of the event.[10] It was a combination of Barnett's unsuccessful attempt to have buffalo roped in June and the later event featuring Wild Bill Hickok that Doc Carver appropriated for his version – only he had it occurring five years earlier. As Carver told the story, he and Hickok came to the Medicine in 1867 and successfully filled a contract for one hundred live buffalo with the assistance of John Y. Nelson and the Clifford brothers. Of course, neither Nelson nor the Cliffords were on the Medicine yet in 1867. No matter, by the time Carver started building his repertoire of frontier stories, Hickok was dead, the Cliffords had other concerns, and John Y. Nelson never objected to being spun into any man's tall tale.

In December of 1872, Ena Raymonde wrote that Texas Jack had made her a "dash call" several weeks earlier while hunting with the Earl of Dunraven. An English sports hunter, the Earl of Dunraven had seen the mounted head of an elk while visiting with General Phil Sheridan in Chicago. Upon Dunraven's expressing a desire to hunt in the country that produced such a fine specimen, Sheridan arranged to have Buffalo Bill Cody and Texas Jack Omohundro accompany him on a hunt. Toward the end of the hunt, Cody was called away to guide some other friends of General Sheridan's, and Texas Jack finished the hunt with Dunraven. Although Carver claimed he hunted with Texas Jack and the Earl of Dunraven in 1872 and again in 1873, it is doubtful he was on the 1872 hunt.[11] Carver related one credible anecdote that never appeared in the biography, probably because Thorp adhered to Carver's desire to be portrayed as a non-drinker:

> They [Dunraven, Kingsley – the earl's physician – and Texas Jack] came out to my country and pitched their tents at the mouth of the Mitchell, a little stream run-

---

10 Joseph G. Rosa. *They Called Him Wild Bill,* (Norman, Oklahoma: University of Oklahoma Press, 1964), pp. 114-115.
11 Yost, 1979, noted that there is dispute among historians over which years Dunraven hunted in Nebraska – 1871 & 1872, or 1872 & 1873.

ning into the Medicine about a quarter of a mile [actually several miles] from my shack. Early in the evening, a good old-fashioned Nebraska twister came along, blew their tents down, turned the wagons over, and scattered everything they had all over ten acres. Soaking wet, he [Dunraven], Kingsley, and Jack came up to my little shack and spent the night. Of course, on all hunting trips there is always a supply of whiskey, which seldom gets lost, so the night was spent, not in sleep, but in drinking whiskey and drying clothes – and it was mostly Scotch highballs. And it took three days to gather up the mules, tents, bedding, food, etc. and get ready to continue the hunt.[12]

Sometime in November 1872, the old war chief, Whistler, and two other members of the Cut-off band of Oglala Sioux were killed. Suspicion was at first cast on the Pawnee, but the evidence soon pointed to white trappers. Although the three murdered Indians had been hunting somewhere near the forks of the Republican, their temporary reservation was several miles east of Wolf's Rest on the Medicine. Whistler had been guilty of depredations against the whites in years past, and though still capable of assuming a threatening stance, he was considered a peaceful Indian. The general consensus is that the three Indians approached a trapper's camp in search of food; a movement or signal was perhaps misread, and the white men killed them. Regardless of how it happened, the incident presented a very real and imminent danger for the whites. Carver's contention that he killed Whistler was obviously another attempt to puff up his plainsman's, or in this case, his Evil Spirit image. He had *just* arrived on the Medicine when the Indians were killed, and Ena's journals clearly indicate he was traveling back and forth between Wolf's Rest and North Platte where he was practicing dentistry.

On March 31, 1873, nine days after his return from the trip to Chicago, Ena noted that Carver had again bid her goodbye. The wind was throwing a typical March tantrum: "I am sorry the Dr. went today – this sand or dust storm is fearful – the whole earth is darkened. Poor fellow, how he dreaded to start!" While at Wolf's

---

12 W. F. Carver to R. W. Thorp, March 11, 1927, Carver MSS.

Rest, Carver had gone on a camp hunt with Ena, Paddy Miles, Mr. Palmer and Jack Fritcher. They took a wagon, tent, and camp equipment, and headed out toward Plum Creek. Ena wrote that the following morning, "Pa, Bert and I started back in the wagon, having found no water for the horses, and the Dr. and Fritcher 'took to the hills.' We saw them when they struck a band of elk, about two miles off. They did not get in until near night. The Dr. killed four elk..." It was in the same journal entry that Ena related the incident that shows the unvarnished human side of Carver:

> But I came very near having all my aches and fears ended last Wednesday! I was sitting reading by my table when the Doctor accidentally discharged his pistol. The ball just passing my side and entering the wall [and] went into Madame's room, raising a cloud of dust! The muzzle of the pistol was in about a foot and a half of my face – I only remember a flash, fog and crash! I suppose I must have fainted, as I did not speak.
>
> The Doctor says he cried out, "Oh, my God! Baby have I shot you?" and when I did not answer, he rushed to the eating room and called Bert! No one asked what was the matter; they had heard the pistol and one look at the Doctor's white, horror stricken face told the rest! Ena was killed! Ma says the Doctor passed her door like a shadow – then Bert – then Pa, Black, Fritcher and Oscar [Curtis]! And then she came out, the great horror dawning upon her too, and growing a fearful certainty before she reached my door. And now I remember raising my head from the table, looked half-bewildered on the forms crowded before me!
>
> With this first movement, Bert sinks into a chair and covering his white face with his hands exclaimed, "My God! I thought she was killed!" Ma had fallen down at the door, and mingled with her wild words was the Doctor's

voice, laughing a poor, trembling, hysterical laugh, when he sees me stand up and say, "I don't believe I am shot!"

No not shot – yet very near it, and every one goes away with faces, from with not all of the horror gone as they think how very near the truth it had been. And the Doctor looks at me, and seems only half credulous as he says over and over again, "And did I most kill you, little Baby?" I trust it will be a lesson for him – he is too careless with firearms.

Tracking Carver's movements through Ena Raymonde's journal comes to a near dead-end after April 1873, as their relationship seems to have hit the rocks. On the seventh of April, she mentioned that he was to have started for the East the previous Saturday. She then made a brief reference on May 4 to having received an ultimatum from Carver on the twenty-second of April, and indicating she had not answered his letter, she continued, "nor do I intend to." With Carver apparently still in the East, Ena wrote on July 2, 1873, that she had expected "to go West to my friend. It was a mistake. I will not go at all now." Texas Jack Omohundro was still on Ena's mind and perhaps someone else as well; Carver was not the only man pulling her heartstrings. On October 26, 1873, Ena's life became "a sealed book," as "weary of the weakness of [her] own words" to express what was in her heart, she quit writing in her journal.

As for Carver, he returned to the Medicine with his mother and younger brother William Pitt Carver in early July of 1873. As Carver's "shack" or dugout was not suitable lodging, Mrs. Carver and her younger son took up residence at Raven's Cliff (the cabin on the hill that had been vacated because of the howling March winds). Mrs. Carver's arrival on the Medicine had, in fact, created quite a stir. Not only did she bring the first fine poultry and a collection of choice flowers, but she brought the first piano. Paddy Miles wrote that these things were all a great curiosity to the Indians and frontiersmen. In bringing the piano down in a wagon from the Union Pacific Station on the Platte, they got stuck in the swampy lowland. They couldn't get enough horses hitched to the wagon to pull it out, so the piano was covered with buffalo robes, and there it stood until the ground dried out – a period of several weeks.

Sinking a pile of lead in the process, Doc Carver continued to hunt and shoot. In the summer of 1874, after closing out their second season on stage, Buffalo Bill and Texas Jack returned to Nebraska for some hunting and adventure. While still in the East, Cody had met an Englishman by the name of Thomas P. Medley, who engaged him as a hunting guide. And while it is always difficult to ascertain just which of Carver's claims to believe, he did, in fact, participate in the hunt with Medley – though it is doubtful he shot as many elk as he later boasted. From Cody's 1879 autobiography: "Dr. W. F. Carver, who then resided at North Platte, and who has recently acquired considerable notoriety as a rifle-shot, hunted with us for a few days…"

If there was more than one man vying for Ena's heart, there were most assuredly other women waiting in the wings of Carver's life. From a noted southwest Nebraska historian, E. S. Sutton, comes the following: "For several weeks the *North Platte Western Nebraskan* ran items that Doc Carver planned to winter in California, then suddenly flashed the announcement of the 'wedding of Dr. W.F. Carver and his bride, a Miss Lizzie Moore.' They left that night for Sidney and Cheyenne to set up a dental office." It seems Carver spent several weeks doing dental work at Fort Sidney and then set up a practice in Cheyenne in November of 1874 where he remained until the following year.

By 1875 Carver was practicing dentistry in California. Ena returned to the Medicine and wrote from Wolf's Rest on February 24, 1875, that she had broken her "seal of silence." On March 9, 1875, she made one entry that can be construed as referring to Carver: "Sometimes I have half a mind to 'pull up stakes' and go to C [   ], as I've promised." The letter "C" could stand for either Carver or California. At any rate, Ena never again mentioned Carver in her journal and on October 5, 1875, she was married to D. C. Ballantine.

Carver's marital status at the time is unknown, for no further reference has been found to his marriage to Lizzie Moore.

It was an inauspicious entrance and exit to the Wild West for the man who later regaled the audiences who came to see him shoot with stories of his frontier adventures. He laid claim to having killed 30,000 buffalo in his years on the plains; it is doubtful he killed more than a few hundred. By the time Carver became a seasoned hunter, the great herds of buffalo had been severely depleted. There was certainly no "vast herd of buffalo, which covered the plains as far as the eye could see." Just as *Pa-he-minny-minnish*, "Little Curly Hair" of the Medicine, appeared in Carver's 1878 book, so she appeared in later writings related to Carver. An article referring to a buffalo hunt that may or may not have happened gave a vivid description:

> Far away, soldiers, Indians and hunters were coming. Singled out from the rest of the party were two ladies riding like a whirlwind. They seemed to fly over the plain, while cheers from the soldiers urged them to do their best. It was a race between a thoroughbred racer and "Red Lips", Carver's Indian pony. "Red Lips" never had an equal in a long race. After about two miles run between the two most beautiful girls who ever rode a saddle on the plains – Wild West against Tame East – "Red Lips" and her rider continued to race alone, the lady's red dress moving like a red flame over the plain. This was Eva Raymond [*sic*], "Pa-heminnieminsh", "Little Curly Hair" of the Medicine. She and "Red Lips" were the first to congratulate Dr. Carver on his victory.

Carver claimed a close association with Wild Bill Hickok, dating as far back as the 1860s but that, too, is unlikely. He may have made the acquaintance of Hickok in Cheyenne in 1874 or 1875. The only well-known plainsmen mentioned in Carver's book are Buffalo Bill and Texas Jack though, once again, in improbable references. The moniker "Evil Spirit," which he claimed the Indians gave him, was almost certainly his own invention. Carver's shooting records are documented, and they stand on their own. He certainly was not the only person of his time to get caught up in an elaborate web of storytelling. What sets Carver apart is that in the process of reinventing his past, he inserted a full decade of experiences that existed only in his fertile imagination. He could never have foreseen that Ena Raymonde, the woman he had once – and perhaps always – loved, would unwittingly contribute to the unraveling of his fantastic stories.

12

Doc Carver the Crack Shot

By 1878 the rowdy little cow-town of Cheyenne in Wyoming Territory had grown to a city of over 5000 with amenities that equaled those in many of the cities of similar size in the East. The most noticeable aspect of Cheyenne on April 16, 1878, however, was the unrelenting wind. Nonetheless, an enthusiastic crowd hung on to their hats and braved the gusts when the great rifleman Dr. W. F. Carver, "Spirit Gun of the West," demonstrated his skill:

> Notwithstanding the high wind which prevailed yesterday afternoon, Dr. W. F. Carver gave an exhibition of his shooting at Sloan's Lake…Imagine if you please, the breaking of fifteen balls in fifteen consecutive shots, thrown at least thirty-five feet in the air, in the very teeth of a wind blowing at the velocity of *sixty miles* an hour. His fancy shots were all perfect. Shooting at a glass ball fifty feet from the gun, the shooter standing with his back towards the ball, and sighting with gun upside down, resting across his shoulder, and holding a small hand-mirror in his left hand, thereby gaining the only sight of the object aimed at. The shots from the hip were all perfect… We have never seen, and never expect to see again, such a remarkable exhibition of skill in rifle-shooting from anyone. A few incidents occurred to relieve the monotony of the shooting, such as punching holes through silver half dollars thrown in the air. Harry Conley and George Simpson were among the favored ones. They both carried home

souvenirs of the skill of Dr. Carver, that is, they will if ever the lake dries up so they can find them; the money having been struck fairly by the balls, was driven at least fifty feet from the shore into the water. When we left Harry was making ready for a dive after his money...[1]

Carver had embarked on a new chapter of his life. He began to shoot at flying targets in small exhibitions and on December 13, 1877, he issued his first challenge to the world. Following a match in San Francisco in February of 1878, he was awarded a plaque proclaiming him "Champion Rifle Shot of the Word" for having broken 885 out of 1000 flying glass balls. For another seventeen years he won awards across the nation and around the world. Because he was virtually unknown in the field of competition shooting when his first challenge was published, there was a flurry of responses and counter-challenges from both "fireside shooters" and established sportsmen who thought it was a joke. This apparently caused a knee-jerk reaction from Carver's friends on the Medicine. On February 21, 1878, the *Oakland (Calif.) Times* published a letter from one Charles J. Bruster who was writing from Wolf's Rest, Frontier County, Nebraska. Some of Carver's hunting successes may have happened as Bruster described – if Bruster actually wrote the letter – but the following excerpt was most likely the result of a bottle of whiskey along with the combined story-telling capabilities of Bruster and the group of like-minded fellows who hung around Wolf's Rest:

> On our way home from this hunt he had a very narrow escape. I saw an old bull standing on a divide; I asked the Doctor to shoot him for me... At the time, he was riding a big American horse [domesticated rather than an Indian pony] that had never had a gun fired from his back and was very ugly... The bull saw him coming and started, but he [Carver] caught him in a short run. The moment the rifle cracked, the bull charged him. The Doctor's horse turning suddenly to the right, the cinch gave way, throwing him on the ground; he grabbed the horse and caught him by the tail. Away they went, the horse bucking and

---

1 Carver, pp. 95-96.

Wm. F. "Buffalo Bill" Cody in full plainsman's regalia. Buffalo Bill and Doc Carver became bitter enemies following the breakup of their "Wild West: Hon. W. F. Cody and Dr. W. F. Carver's Rocky Mountain and Prairie Exhibition". *Courtesy Robert Van Pelt Estate.*

kicking, the Doctor hanging by his tail. The bull charged and tried to jump on him, the blood flying from his nose and mouth all over the Doctor at every jump. The race lasted for perhaps one hundred and fifty yards, when the bull stopped; the next instant the Doctor let go; the bull saw him, charged again, and fell dead on him.[2]

Bruster also claimed he had seen Carver kill two buffalo at one shot "going at full speed, the ball passing through the first, and killing one on the other side." Just who Charley Bruster was is open for speculation. Ena mentioned him several times as fellows came into or left Wolf's Rest late in 1872 and early 1873. Charley Bruster and Doc Carver apparently hit it off, for Carver incorporates Bruster into a number of stories. Bruster also wrote that Carver killed thirty-three elk in one run on his hunting trip with Medley, "and his horse dropped dead at the last shot…" Cody, however, did not mention Carver's dropping thirty-three elk in his description of the hunt with Medley.

With a pair of rifles made expressly for him by the Winchester Company, Doc Carver set out on a shooting tour across the country. The newspapers followed his progress and frequently lavished the praise Carver sought. From the April 21, 1878 *Omaha Herald*: "Dr. Carver is without dispute the most perfect master of the rifle that has ever been seen in Omaha. His marksmanship is beyond anything that can come from mere practice. The steady nerve, the keen eye, and the celerity [rapidity] of motion, are either of them faculties rarely to be found in any individual."[3] Eight days later the *Des Moines Register* was equally as enthusiastic: "Dr. Carver is the most wonderful rifle shot in the world." And from the May 19, 1878 *Pittsburg Leader*: "The Doctor used a Spencer rifle. He shot at balls laid on the ground, holding his rifle upside down and sideways, and over his shoulder, using a looking-glass, and concluding with the wonderful 'Hip-shot', where the butt of the gun is held against the hip and the aim taken by gauging the relative positions of the mark

---

2 Ibid., p. 66. Some corrections in punctuation have been made for clarification.
3 Ibid., p. 98.

aimed at and the gun, from above…"[4] The following news item from the *New York Times* is an example of the descriptive prose Carver elicited from the New York City newspapers:

> Dr. W. F. Carver, the man who can put a bullet through a silver quarter while the coin is flying through the air, is an enlarged and revised edition of Buffalo Bill and Texas Jack. Being fresh from the broad plains of the untrammeled West, he has that delightful air of unconventionality to be found only in the land of the setting sun. A paleface, to him, is an object of pity. The aboriginal inhabitant of the primeval forest is his prey. He must dote on blood; and he can bring it out of a wasp's wing at 40 yards…
>
> Dr. Carver is, no doubt, the best short-range marksman in the world. He gave his second exhibition at Deerfoot Park yesterday, and astonished everybody who saw him. He is as fine a specimen of fully developed manhood as ever walked on Manhattan Island. More than six feet high, every part of his body is built to correspond. His chest is so deep that it would take a powerful rifle to send a bullet through it. His shoulders are broad and high, and, altogether, he is exactly the man that ordinary people wouldn't put themselves out of the way to pick a quarrel with.[5]

Though he only stayed with Carver a few months, Texas Jack joined the troop as a gun-handler while they were in Boston. The July 15, 1878 *New York Sun* described the two plainsmen as they worked together:

> The Doctor picked up a rifle, and took a position near the table. The spectators spread out in two long wings on each side. Carver's long auburn hair was thrown behind his ears. He wore dark pantaloons, lapped over his boots, a soft, white flannel shirt, his light-colored sombrero, and a glazed belt with a gold buckle, nearly as large as a railroad frog. His right hand was covered with a grimy buckskin glove… A white silk scarf encircled his neck, and was fastened to his bosom by the diamond-eyed and

---

4 Thorp, p. 89.
5 *New York Times*, July 6, 1878, Internet digital image.

ruby-nostrilled gold horse's head presented to him after breaking fifty successive glass balls while riding a horse at full speed in California. The magnificent badge given him by his friends in San Francisco, on Washington's birthday, after breaking eight hundred and eighty-five balls out of a possible one thousand, swung from his left breast…

At the Doctor's request Col. Fletcher tossed several glass balls in the air, for the purpose of putting him in trim. There were four or five misses, but from twenty to thirty were broken before the Doctor stopped shooting… Each ball was filled with feathers, and as the glass was shattered the feathers floated off on the wind. The Doctor then tried to shoot thrice, reloading his gun twice while a ball was in the air, and break it at the third shot. He did it on the third trial. Half of the ball fell among the spectators behind him. Texas Jack said, "Dead bird, but fell out of bounds." This drew a laugh from the usually saturnine [sullen] Doctor…

One hundred balls were thrown into the air alternately, and they melted away like magic. The Doctor shattered ninety-one out of the hundred. As fast as each rifle was emptied of its score of balls he laid it upon the table and seized a fresh gun. He shot faster than Texas Jack could load. The hot rifles were handed to an attendant, who sat them in a tub of water and sponged them off like horses. They were then wiped out and handed to Texas Jack, who reloaded them…[6]

T. C. Banks, the editor of *Forest & Stream*, also described the duo in the July 11, 1878 issue of that publication: "Our Western rifleman was ably assisted by Texas Jack, the well-known scout and guide of the prairies, who is apparently as much delighted with Dr. Carver's skill as if he himself were accomplishing the feats we have just described."

On August 20, 1878, Carver was married to Miss Josephine Dailey in New Haven, Connecticut. When the shooting tour was finished, Doc took Josephine on a visit to California. As they traveled

---

6 Carver, pp. 132-133.

Dr. Wm. F. "Doc" Carver moved to the Medicine Creek in the company of Ena Raymonde in 1872. He is pictured here wearing some of the medals won after he began shooting in competitions in 1878. He sent autographed photos to Ena's children throughout his lifetime. *Courtesy Nebraska State Historic Society.*

by rail across Nebraska, they made a side trip to Frontier County where Carver wanted to show his bride his old home on the Medicine. Carver never said whether he had the opportunity to introduce his new wife to D. C. Ballantine's wife, the former Ena Raymonde. The dynamics of that encounter – if it happened – are left to the reader's imagination.

Early in 1879 Carver set sail for Europe. There he shot in various exhibitions and matches using rifles, shotguns, and pistols. He shot on foot and from horseback; he shot at the newly invented glass balls and at live pigeons sprung from traps; he shot at coins or most anything a challenger tossed in the air. Although he was apparently in the British Isles for most of the tour, he also shot in France, Belgium, Germany, and Austria. In London spectators flocked to the wealthy Sydenham Hill district to see him during a long-term engagement at the magnificent Crystal Palace. America's wonderful marksman shot before titled society and commoners and was feted in many a grand dining hall. And, of course, he participated in European style hunts for such prey as chamois (a small goat-like antelope) and wild boars. By the fall of 1882 Doc Carver was back in America, and the plans for a Wild West show with Buffalo Bill Cody were set into motion.

While the Wild West show was being put together, Carver finally had the opportunity for which he had been waiting – a match with his nemeses, Captain Adam H. Bogardus, who had established himself as a champion long before Carver arrived on the scene. Carver had wanted to shoot against Bogardus for years, but "the old fox" hadn't felt compelled to respond to the challenge. The tour began with a match on February 21, 1883, at Louisville, Kentucky. Though Carver was claiming to be only seven years younger than Bogardus, the actual eighteen years age difference is implied in a report printed in the February 21, 1883 *Louisville Commercial*:

> Captain A. H. Bogardus, the champion shot, arrived in the city yesterday morning, and immediately repaired to the Louisville Hotel, where his rival, Dr. Carver is stopping. Neither of them "recognized" the other, although they met several times during the morning and dined at

adjoining tables. Captain Bogardus remarked to a friend in a fatherly way that the "young 'un" seemed to be in fine form, and Dr. Carver was overheard saying as he blushed before a plate of potato salad, that "the old man was looking pretty well himself." Once or twice they glared politely at each other, and the scene was rather amusing. Captain Bogardus would transfix a baked apple with his fork, and then cast a quick glance at Carver, who at that moment was sipping his ox-tail soup, timidly eyeing the Captain over the rim of the bowl.[7]

Doc Carver won the match in Louisville and another in Chicago, live pigeons being used at both. From there they went to St. Louis where they accepted a lucrative offer from the Ligowsky Clay Pigeon Company to go on a twenty-five-match tour for the purpose of introducing the clay pigeon to the shooting public. Counting the match they shot in Chicago, the competition took the two champions to twenty-four cities. By the time the tour finished the middle of April, there had been three ties, and Carver had won nineteen of the remaining twenty-two matches. With the competition behind them, Carver and Bogardus made their way to Omaha, where Bogardus was to join Carver and Cody. The "Wild West: Hon. W. F. Cody and Dr. W. F. Carver's Rocky Mountain and Prairie Exhibition" opened in Omaha on May 17, 1883. The show in Omaha fulfilled the great expectations. Excerpts from a report published in a May 20, 1883 Omaha newspaper:

> Great interest was taken in the representation of the attack of a stage coach, and it was a thrilling scene... The coach started out with its load of passengers; the stage agent warned the driver against his dangers, and the six mules sent the vehicle rolling down the track. As the coach reached the last quarter, a band of fifty Indians emerged from a hiding place and set out in pursuit, yelling like demons. The driver whipped up his mules and the dust flew, but the Indians closed around the coach and the interchange of revolver shots made the scene exciting. Just as it seemed that the coach was captured "Buffalo Bill" and

7 Thorp, p. 131.

Dr. Carver, leading a party of scouts, came to its rescue, driving the Indians back, shooting and scalping them… The audience went wild with excitement, stood upon their seats and cheered…

Feats of shooting were the next acts. Captain Bogardus opened with a marvelous exhibition in breaking glass balls and [clay] pigeons after the English and American rules. "Buffalo Bill" and Dr. Carver followed in feats with the shotgun and rifle, concluding with shots [made] while riding at full speed. These exhibitions are beyond all rivalry, for the three best shots in the United States and the champion shot [Carver] of the world were engaged in them…[8]

The show met with enthusiastic audiences as it toured a number of major cities from Omaha to the East coast. Nevertheless, there was friction between Carver and Cody almost from the beginning, with Carver breaking into violent rages when things rubbed him the wrong way. The enormous amount of stress and strain involved in managing a show of this magnitude no doubt took a toll on both men. The logistics of transporting, boarding, and feeding the livestock, production crew, and cast members as well as controlling the "blanket" Indians proved to be a constant challenge. And then, of course, there was the matter of Cody and Carver and their egos. They each brought a set of attributes, hopes and expectations along with personal baggage to the show. Although Carver went to his deathbed saying that Cody's drinking broke up their partnership, the evidence suggests that Carver also was tipping the bottle. Jealousy on Carver's part undoubtedly had as much to do with the break-up as Cody's drinking. An item that appeared in the (*Hartford, Conn.*) *Courant* cuts to the heart of the issue:

The real sight of the whole thing is after all, Buffalo Bill, a perfect model of manly beauty. Mounted on his blooded horse, he rode around the grounds, the observed of all observers. Cody was an extraordinary figure, and sits on a horse as if he were born in the saddle. His feats of

8 Yost, 1979, pp. 133-135.

Doc Carver in an etching that appeared in the *Harper's Weekly*. A slightly different version was used on the cover of Carver's book, *Life of Dr. W. F. Carver of California: Champion Rifle Shot of the World*, which he published in 1878. *Courtesy Denver Public Library*

shooting are perfectly wonderful…He has in this exhibition, out-Barnumed Barnum.[9]

W. F. "Doc" Carver could shoot, and he was a fine horseman. W. F. "Buffalo Bill" Cody was also a good shot and a fine horseman, but he had something else. Buffalo Bill had a showman's charisma; he connected with his audience. Then too, the audiences were already in Cody's court through the "dime novels" featuring his wondrous (albeit usually imaginary) western exploits. These largely fictional concoctions were often serialized in the newspapers and reached a number of readers. Although both men had autobiographies out, for the reader in search of western adventure, Carver's paled in comparison to Cody's. The Wild West broke up in October of 1883, and Carver and Cody divided the show in lots by a toss of the coin. Until the end of his life, Carver was filled with a venomous bitterness towards Cody. If the Honorable Wm. F. Cody was not entirely deserving of the acclaim he received, it became irrelevant. Buffalo Bill's persona took on a life of its own, and Carver's best shots weren't going to bring it down.

Carver reorganized the Wild West show with the poet-scout Captain Jack Crawford as manager. Cody went into partnership with Nate Salsbury, an old-time showman with plenty of money, and put his own show on the road. The two shows hop-scotched across the country for the next few years, although they eventually reached some sort of agreement to keep from appearing in the same city at the same time. Plenty of other issues fueled the simmering feud between Carver and Cody. There was the matter of the right to use "Wild West" in the show's name, Carver's claim that Cody owed him $29,000 from their original show, and Cody's protest that by cutting admission fees, Carver was trying to drive him out of business. In addition, both men published and distributed circulars attacking the other as a fraud. By July of 1885 with both outfits in Connecticut, the whole festering issue came to a head. In a dispatch from New Haven, Connecticut, the *New York Times* reported:

---

9 Ibid., pp. 141-142.

An interminable row has broken out in this State be-tween Dr. Carver, the marksman, and Buffalo Bill. They have been running rival shows under the same title of "Wild West." Carver is a New-Haven pet. He married his wife here, and calls this his home, and when he came along a couple weeks ago he distributed packs of circulars in which assaults in rhetoric more or less fiery were made upon Buffalo Bill. That distinguished gentleman, who also rejoices in the name of Cody, sent a representative along to watch Carver. The representative hired two or three law-yers, and while Carver and his wild Indians were disport-ing over at Willimantic they swooped down on his show and broke it all to pieces with libel suits and other little instruments of torture. Poor Carver was locked up and his Sioux defendants hurried away for their native West.

But Carver has sympathizers here. They hired other lawyers and waited. Buffalo Bill brought his "Wild West" from New-York State up to South Norwalk a day or two ago. A choice assortment of legal proceedings were wait-ing his appearance by way of retaliation in the interest of Carver. He tried a sharp game, and gave his lawyers $10,000 in cash to offset possible attachments. Carver's people attached it promptly, but they didn't stop at the $10,000…

This story will have some further remarkable features before the end comes. Both Carver and Cody profess to be ready to sacrifice all their money in fighting out their mutual grievances.[10]

The suits, countersuits, and attachments of property culminated in a trial set for July 20, 1885. When Cody failed to appear, Carver agreed to dismiss his suit for $10,000 cash and Nate Salsbury's offer to pay all court costs. Carver construed this to be "an admission by Cody that all Carver said about him was true."[11] Carver's show was broken up, and he did not have the financial resources to reorga-

---

10 *New York Times*, July 16, 1885, Internet digital image.
11 (*New Haven*) *Evening Register*, Aug. 23, 1885, cited by Sandra K. Sagala, "Buffalo Bill V. Doc Carver: The Battle over the Wild West," *Nebraska History*, Vol. 85, No. 1 (2004), p. 14.

nize. Consequently, he appeared as a feature act in similar outdoor shows over the next few years. By 1889 Carver had secured financial partners, organized a show billed as "Wild America" and launched a world-wide tour. Cody was in Europe at the same time as Carver, but the two shows managed to avoid each other with the exception of their appearances in Hamburg, Germany. A dispatch from Hamburg, which was published in the August 26, 1890 *New York World* sums up the resulting uproar:

> There is intense excitement here over a fierce row which has occurred between Doctor Carver and Buffalo Bill. The people are afraid to come out of doors after dark and the city is in a state of siege. The members of each troupe have openly declared their intention of fighting for their respective masters, even if the quarrel ends in a general battle… Carver has been following Cody all through the latter's tour of the cities of the continent, and his performances have been so much better patronized that Buffalo Bill's jealousy was aroused…
>
> [Carver] arrived in Hamburg three days ahead and opened his Wild West show in fine style. When Cody got here he found he was obliged to pitch his tent within a few feet of Carver's show. Carver had made arrangements for an exclusive supply of electric lights and this left Cody's place in the dark. Then the members of both companies took up the matter, and it is only through the strenuous efforts of the police that a fearful fight has been prevented. Hamburg is filled with a howling mob of Indians and cowboys who are awaiting the chance to scalp each other…
>
> It is an open secret that Carver did an enormous business in Berlin and Vienna, while Cody fell flat, and Carver's men are going around spreading this fact…12

Carver's success in Germany was attributed in part to his visit there ten years earlier as a champion rifle shot. In December the

---

[12] Thorp, pp. 190-191.

For the last thirty years of his life, Doc Carver entertained crowds at fairs and other outdoor shows with his diving horse act. Sonora (Webster) Carver rode the diving horses for eighteen years. Seven years into her career (and soon after her marriage to Carver's son), a diving accident left her blind. Sonora Carver continued to ride the diving horses for eleven years after she lost her sight. In the photo above, she is riding Klatawah in a dive known as the extreme plunge. *Courtesy Nebraska State Historical Society.*

entire troupe disembarked in Australia where they were once again well received. From the *New York Times* of the following July:

> F. C. Whitney, manager of "Wild America," and C. E. Blanchett, also of the organization, are in New York. Mr. Whitney goes to Washington today to take steps for patenting a number of stage novelties, and after attending to this work will start for Australia, to rejoin the show. He says that the business of "Wild America" on its tour around the world has been simply phenomenal.
>
> The big show, consisting of eighty Indians and cowboys, with Dr. Carver, the famous marksman, at the head, was organized in Detroit, July 4, 1889, and now has been over two years on the road. "During that time," said Mr. Whitney, "we have made the circuit of the globe, or we shall have done so when we reach San Francisco. We opened our season first in Berlin, intending to remain there three weeks; we staid [*sic*] there thirteen weeks. Then we went to Vienna, Hungary, Poland, Russia, Finland, Norway, Sweden, Denmark, and back to Germany, where we played a second engagement in Berlin. From there we shipped the company and stock direct to Australia, where we have arranged for an eight weeks' season. We have already played there eight months, in Sydney and Melbourne, and our welcome has not been worn out yet. We shall take in New Zealand and Honolulu, and then sail for San Francisco. 'Wild America' is the only combination that has ever made a tour of the world.
>
> "We are giving a regular dramatic performance in Melbourne," continued Mr. Whitney. "Dr. Carver has developed into a really good actor, and our Indians, cowboys, and bronchos are as much at home on the stage as in the tents and on the prairies. We have had a play written for the company, and it is now running at the Alexandria Theatre, Melbourne. It is called 'The Scout,' is of the spectacular kind, and has seventeen different sensational scenes and episodes…"[13]

---

13 *New York Times*, July 30, 1891, Internet digital image.

By 1892 Carver was back on terra firma in the United States. If his success was, indeed, as great as these newspaper excerpts imply, Carver's ego should have been sufficiently bolstered. After running both the Wild America show and the play in San Francisco, a tour of America was launched. Any number of old plainsmen had similar shows on the road by then, and the concept was no longer a novelty. In addition, an economic depression had spread across the entire nation. His biographer does not say when or why Carver shut down his Wild America, but a dispatch from Newark, New Jersey, published in the *New York Times* in 1893 indicates the show went on the rocks: "Constable Whalen today sold at auction the wagons, tents, seats, and other paraphernalia belonging to Dr. Carver, the scout actor. Peter Conklin of St. Louis, who held a chattel mortgage on the goods, purchased the entire lot for $210. Conklin was formerly a clown in the Barnum & Bailey circus."[14]

Not a man to go down easily, Carver apparently put together a scaled down show featuring his shooting exhibitions and traveled for a few more years. Thorp wrote that it was at a performance in Kansas City in 1894 that he added a diving horse to the show. Those who knew him on the Medicine remembered that Carver first dived a horse off a cliff into a deep hole in the Medicine Creek. Carver's creative spin on the story involves a pursuit by a gang of outlaws, a collapsing bridge, and a plunge by Carver and his horse into the river below with horse and rider emerging unhurt.[15] Regardless of where Carver got the idea for the act, it served him well, for he was about ready to hang up his guns.

A year later, in transitioning from one chapter in his life to another, Carver took his diving horses and his guns and began his last tour of the country. He shot a few more matches and then retired from active competition. For a while he gave shooting exhibitions along with the diving horse act, which became his primary endeavor for the next thirty years. Carver continued to live under the pretense of being eleven years older than he actually was. *The (Lincoln, Nebr.) State Journal* of August 29, 1896, said: "The Doctor is a superb speci-

---

14 *New York Times*, Nov. 19, 1893, Internet digital image.
15 *Omaha World Herald*, circa 1966.

men of physical manhood and has taken such excellent care of himself that he looks at least fifteen years under his real age. He refuses to tell his age..." The *Journal* went on to lavish praise on the man who had been impressing audiences for close to twenty years:

> Dr. W. F. Carver, the champion shot of the world, has been giving exhibitions of his wonderful skill in rifle, shotgun and horseback shooting this week at Lincoln park that mystified, surprised and astonished the audience present...
>
> The masterly manner in which Mr. Carver handles his guns while shooting is a picture hard to describe. The flashes of fire leave his gun in such rapid succession that he seems enveloped in a cloud of fire and smoke. The whizz of bullets through the air, the sharp ring of the leaden messenger as it comes in contact with the brick and turns half of it in a cloud of red dust, makes a picture to be remembered. Quicker than a flash of lightning comes a second shot, and the broken piece of brick is a ring of red dust inside of the ring made by the first shot, and both shots made so quickly... While the whistle of bullets die away in the distance the smoke and the dust settle down over the shooter and form a beautiful picture of Dante's Inferno.
>
> No wonder the savages of the plains thought him possessed of a devil and called him the evil spirit. As soon as the audience recovered from their surprise, he is given a rousing reception, for was it not the most wild and beautiful shooting picture ever looked upon by human eyes?
>
> In addition to being the champion rifle, pigeon, horseback and endurance shot of the world, Dr. Carver is also the champion live-bird shot of America, this last title having been won January 24, of this year...[16]

Doc Carver spent no more than a few years on the Medicine Creek in southwest Nebraska, but he remains inextricably linked

---

16 Carver MSS. The date and name of publication handwritten to the side are assumed to be correct.

Doc Carver in the showman's attire he might have worn during the years he pre-sented his diving horse act at fairs and other outdoor shows. *Courtesy Nebraska State Historical Society.*

with the early history of the area. His name evoked various reactions from different people. W. L. McClary was on the Medicine at the same time as Carver and also a contender for Ena Raymonde's affection. That be as it may, McClary held Carver in high esteem in later years and never believed Cody worthy of the acclaim he received. While some on the Medicine never took Carver seriously, Paddy Miles recalled that it was here that Carver "learned and practiced the art that made him the wonder of the world…"[17] Ena's son Coulter Ballantine Jr., in pointing out the spot where Carver and his horse dived into the Medicine Creek, concluded that Doc was "the craziest son-of-a-bitch you ever saw!"[18]

For his part, Carver held close the recollection of his years on the Medicine Creek. Although Ena Raymonde, *Pa-he-minny-minnish*, "Little Curley Hair" of the Medicine, died in 1884, Carver never lost track of her children. Coulter Ballantine Jr. and Anna Ena Ballantine (later Adams) were adults when, near the end of his life, Carver visited with them in Omaha, Nebraska. Anna later recalled that at the end of the visit, Doc Carver put his arms around them and said, "You should have been my children."[19]

Although Carver realized a full measure of success in his journey through life, he gave his distracters plenty of ammunition. In addition to the elaborate web of fabricated stories he spun, it seems he was often difficult to deal with on both a personal and professional level. He let his animosity toward Cody permeate his very soul. Because some of his devotees took everything he said at face value, many of the untruths he told have for the most part managed to dodge the bullet. Unfortunately, his admirers will never know the true story of Doc Carver's early life. The only one who could tell what was surely a fascinating tale died on August 31, 1927. In this respect, Wm. F. "Doc" Carver shot himself in the foot.

---

17 Miles and Bratt, p. 20.
18 William Shelley to Art Carmody, May 3, 1952. Shelley Collection, NSHS (hereafter cited as Shelley MSS).
19 Anna E. (Ballantine) Adams was interviewed in 1962 by Dr. Donald F. Danker, archivist at the NSHS.

Located at the mouth of Cottonwood Canyon in Lincoln County, the monument in the photo above (see following page) recognizes John Y. Nelson, Paddy Miles, and Doc Carver as well as other plainsmen. The monument (left) recognizing the Old Texas-Ogallala is located near Trenton, Nebraska. *Courtesy Frontier County Historical Society and www.waymarking.com*

The Neiswanger Monuments

In the late 1920s and early 1930s, D. F. Neiswanger, who had a monument business in Cambridge, Nebraska, crafted and erected a number of historical markers in southwest Nebraska. The red Colorado granite monument at the mouth of Cottonwood Canyon (opposite page) about nineteen miles north of Curtis, Nebraska, in Lincoln County recognizes the "Fort McPherson Trail from 1868 to 1880" and pays tribute to the following pioneer scouts and plainsmen: Buffalo Bill Cody, General Sheridan, General Custer, General Carr, Dr. Asch, Lute & Major North, John Y. Nelson, John Bratt, Doc Carver, Paddy Miles and Grand Duke Alexis. Additional settlers, including Charles McDonald who operated the first store at Cottonwood Springs (later Fort McPherson) and John Burke Sr., who built the first bridge across the Platte River, are named on the back. (The base and about a fourth of this monument are now below ground level.)

Neiswanger also placed a McPherson Trail monument just west of Holbrook in Furnas County (where the trail left the Republican River Valley and headed north), another twelve miles north of Cambridge and a fourth just east of Stockville. Among other Neiswanger monuments are those located at the following sites: Sky Chief Springs east of Cambridge in Furnas County; the first homestead in Furnas County; McKinley Park in Cambridge; the location where Frontier County was organized in Hank Clifford's tepee; Doc W. F. Carver's homestead on Medicine Creek; the grave of Eena Teglaka in Stockville's Arbor Cemetery; Frontier County Courthouse; the Duke Alexis Hunt on Red Willow Creek in Hayes County; the Nelson Buck Massacre near Danbury in Red Willow County; the Texas-Ogallala Trail near Trenton in Hitchcock County; Bur Oak Canyon in Hitchcock County. A Neiswanger monument west of Cambridge honors the memory of six Bohemian emigrants who drowned in a flash flood in 1885.

Although Neiswanger was commissioned to cut the stone for some of these monuments and accepted donations for others, he bore much of the expense himself. Certainly it was a labor born of deep respect for history. The photo at the top of the opposite page was taken in June 1930 during a tour of historical sights in the area. D. F. Neiswanger is to the immediate left of the marker. Others, including the man behind the camera, and in no particular order: W. H. Faling, E. R. Keyes, A. E. Thorndike, R. H. Rankin, Dr. B. F. Stewart, Charles Alberti and F. E. Holmes.

13

Cheyenne Outbreak

O n September 17, 1878, a horseman rode down the valley of Medicine Lodge Creek in southern Kansas with the news that there had been an Indian attack on settlers of the Salt Fork area of the Cimarron River in Comanche County, Kansas. Two persons had been killed and several more wounded, including a baby who was shot through the breast. The depredations against the white settlers and the corresponding alarm among the settlers continued as the band of Indians moved north through Kansas and towards the Nebraska border. The Indians were a band of nearly 400 Cheyenne under the leadership of a daring young chief called Dull Knife. The Northern Cheyenne had been escorted by government troops to Indian Territory in what is now Oklahoma the previous year. They, along with the Sioux or Lakota and a small band of Arapaho – a force of approximately 10,000 – had annihilated General George Armstrong Custer and his 7th Calvary contingent of U. S. Army soldiers in June of 1876. The young warriors chafed at the restrictions of reservation life; they had not acclimated to the climate, the water was bad, and the rations insufficient. With these and other resentments festering like an imbedded thorn, they made their escape from the reservation. The destination was their old northern hunting grounds, and although they were not a war party, pent up anger fueled hostilities against settlers they encountered along the way.

It was this same September that John Dunning along with his mother and siblings, who had only recently settled near Indianola on the Republican River in southwest Nebraska, went to visit their old home in southeast Nebraska. On the return trip they stopped at a campground in the bend of the Little Blue east of Hebron, where they ran into a couple of well-drillers working their way west to look for land. The Dunnings told them of the good land they had found in Red Willow County, but the well-drillers said there were marauding bands of Indians out that direction. The Dunnings countered that, although north of the Platte there were always Indians, there were no Indians south of the Platte. They traveled on to the west without concern for the next hundred or so miles until they saw a rapidly approaching team and wagon. As John Dunning described the encounter:

> East of Orleans Sunday morning we see a big gray team coming pretty fast and a covered wagon with a man carrying a gun. As we pass them there was a man and a woman in the wagon. They say we had better turn back because we may run into Indians. They would not stay. I overtook them and kept up with them for half a mile. They said they had run into a big band of Indians on the way, but had outrun them and got away. They did not know where they were going.[1]

The townsfolk at Orleans had not heard anything about Indians and poked a little fun at the Dunnings for even asking. As they rode out of town, someone yelled after them, saying they had better turn back so they wouldn't run into any Indians – and then laughed mockingly. The merchant at the Arapahoe trading post had no news of Indians and supposed the fleeing man driving the gray team was just chicken-hearted. The Dunning family arrived home that night, uncertain of what morning would bring. The next morning a fellow rode up near the Dunning home yelling that there were Indians on

---

1 John Dunning, "Why We Went West," circa 1930, publication information unknown. All quotes attributed to John Dunning are from this source.

the Beaver, which crosses the border from Kansas into Nebraska less than twenty miles from Indianola. Mrs. Dunning, especially, was uneasy with the situation, so they harnessed the horses and headed into town, taking a neighbor lady and her children with them. There was a perceived safety in numbers, and even though the population of Indianola was small, quite a few settlers had come into town by the time the Dunnings arrived.

The settlers who gathered in Indianola conferred and decided to send scouts down to the Beaver Creek area. The waiting settlers entertained their own thoughts and apprehensions. One woman, a Mrs. Colling, walked the streets all the time the scouts were gone, and seventeen-year-old John Dunning, who was rather keen on the excitement, wondered why she was so worried. Although she did not speak out until the scouts returned safely, her agitation was influenced by the Minnesota Massacre, which had occurred some years earlier. She told the story of how the Indians had surrounded the fort and tried to starve them out. Finally, the women had to go hungry so the men could have what little food there was in order to maintain the strength to stand by their guns.

It was late evening when the returning scouts came into the hotel waiting room with no news other than that a trail drive of Texas cattle had taken a different route to avoid the Indians. There was another report that some people thought they saw Indians coming down the "Beaver slope" at sundown, and some had been killed farther up the Beaver. Finally they heard a wagon and team coming down the road at high speed, and everyone pushed out into the street to get the news. The driver of the wagon said there were 2500 Indians coming down the valley from the west above Culbertson. He said these Indians had killed a bunch of cattle and were killing anything they came to. The people asked this news-bearer what kind of defensive action Culbertson was going to take, and he informed them that all of the towns were going to fortify themselves against the Indians.

The townspeople and settlers of the area surrounding Indianola went into war mode. William Hotze was only six years old at the time, but his memories of the battle preparations were vivid. He recalled the men going around "pants in boots," with guns of every description, revolvers or pistols in belts, and swords at side. Here and there a man sported a remnant of his blue Union uniform. Hotze remembered in particular the "swarthy six-footer with a brace of 'Colts' tucked in [his] belt and a heavy sword dangling at his legs. His rough voice and fierce visage struck terror as he strode. 'No, I didn't carry this sword in the Union Army, nor get these scars fighting the south, and I'm not answering any more questions.'" [2] John Dunning further described the preparations:

> They elected a captain and pulled a wagon up in the main square. R. H. Creswell got in the wagon and made a war speech. That was the first and only one that I ever heard. I thought it was extra good. They fortified the best they could and waited for the Indians. The older ones were figuring out how long it would take the Indians to get here so they could be ready when they came. I was only seventeen, so they hardly figured me in.
>
> After midnight I was asleep in the wagon, and the captain called every man on the main street with his gun. He called three times. I thought sure the Indians were here. Well, I decided I might as well be there as here, so I took the shotgun and went out. The captain told everyone to fall in line and report on how many rounds of ammunition each had. Then they waited for the Indians. Morning came and not the Indians…

There was no way of getting news, and the last stagecoach coming through would not stop for fear of the Indians. About ten o'clock they saw a horse come loping down the trail from the west without a rider. As the horse came closer, they saw a board strapped to its back and a letter fastened to the board. The horse, a small roan mare, spooked and ran as the eager crowd gathered in the road. She ran to the north part of Indianola, but some of the men were able to corral her and led her out into the street where the crowd had gathered to hear the news. The letter had been sent from near present day Tren-

---

2 William H. Hotze, "Indian Scares and Massacres Marked Early Settlement in Red Willow County," *Nebraska State Journal* (*Lincoln Journal Star*), Oct. 9, 1933.

ton, and according to John Dunning it said, "The Indians crossed the divide on the old trail to the Stinking Water and [have] gone north on the Ogallala trail, so people are safe." There may have been more than one horse involved in delivering the "all's clear" message, for William Hotze told a different story. As he remembered it, Mr. Doyle, a rancher living on the upper Red Willow decided to venture home. "He agreed to scout the country north and send word back by night. He led away a mare, leaving her sucking colt. About 4 o'clock the mare returned with the message attached: 'No Indians in sight.'"[3]

Much the same scene was repeated up and down the valley. Those who lived around Medicine Creek Post Office, the present location of Cambridge, had gathered on the Republican near the mouth of Medicine Creek and elected J. W. Pickle as captain. They circled the wagons, and while the families and stock gathered inside, scouting parties were sent out to watch for Indians. They, too, brought out muskets, shotguns, rifles, and revolvers, most of which had not been used since the last buffalo was shot. Ten-year-old Mae Griffith, whose parents had located northwest of the present town of Cambridge, was with her father in the Beaver City vicinity when they got word:

> All the people from around Wilsonville and Hendley had left their homes and gone to Beaver City, as they expected the Indians to come through at any time. As my father had not heard of the Indian scare, he and I passed over the strip of country over which the Indians were supposed to come through. We were driving a yoke of cows to a lumber wagon…, never dreaming of any danger, but when we struck the Beaver Valley about half way between Wilsonville and Hendley, just one man had stayed with his home. Several Indian scouts came in during the evening. Later it turned out that the Indians had passed over into Kansas and had tortured and killed everyone in the strip of country they passed through, those people had not received word that the Indians were coming, so were

---

3 Hotze.

taken unawares… My mother was at home with four of her little children with no near neighbors at that time.[4]

The news that the danger was past was greeted with a sigh of relief up and down the valley; however, not all were spared. Estimates of the number of settlers who fell to the Cheyenne vary with some saying that seventy-five to one hundred were killed in Kansas. A headstone in the Indianola Catholic Cemetery bears the inscription, *Antoine Stenner, killed by Indians, October 1, 1878, Luedell, Kansas.* (Luedell was on the Beaver Creek. Mr. Stenner's daughter was captured but later released.)

Both William H. Allen and his son E. E. Allen related the stories of Indian incidents their family experienced. There is some inconsistency in dates, and in all likelihood several events have, with the passage of time, lost distinction and merged into one story. It appears there were "Indian scares" in both 1876 and 1878. Because of the activity along the Beaver as the Cheyenne made this last attempt to return to their native lands in 1878, it is likely that Thomas Lynch's Indian encounter occurred at this time. Thomas Lynch and a young boy, who lived southeast of Stockville in Frontier County, were driving through with a herd of cattle when they stopped for their noon meal on the Beaver. As told by E. E. Allen:

> Hearing considerable shooting down the creek, he climbed a knoll and was in time to see the Indians kill a man and his boy and outrage the two daughters, the older one afterward being the mother of a papoose. Lynch and the boy hurried into a nearby dugout, which was occupied by a woman and two children – the husband absent – and while the woman molded bullets, Lynch loaded shells and shortly afterward the Indians appeared, and in trying to ascertain if the dugout was occupied, one exposed himself and Lynch got him. But one of them on top of the dugout roped the dead one and dragged him away and a young buck, thinking himself out of range, danced around with

---

4 Wilmeth.

one of the girl's aprons on, but Lynch bored him through the apron.[5]

The Indians weren't anxious to absorb any more gunfire, so they quickly cleared out, taking one of Lynch's best horses. Lynch was reported to be the only Frontier County man to run into these Indians. Less is known about the reactions of the settlers farther up the Medicine. Paddy Miles wrote of taking shelter in a cave, but the facts in his account have to be sifted out from the fiction. As Paddy told the story:

> In 1978 the Sioux Indians ran away from the Reservation in the Indian Territory and started back to northern Nebraska, their former hunting grounds. They whipped the soldiers, then killed and pillaged everything in their path. The commanding officers at Fort McPherson sent me notice by a soldier for everyone to run for their lives, as the soldiers could not protect the settlers.

> The settlers generally went to Cambridge in Furnas County and built a fort. I did not like to leave our little home and lose all we had so I went over and saw D. C. Ballantine and we decided to go in a cave on my ranch. This cave is ten by fifteen feet, under a bluff fifty feet high. The Medicine Creek runs within a few feet of the mouth. This we fortified and took in camp outfit and provisions for a siege. Dave Ballantine took in his wife and child. Miss Mamie Timmons and I assisted my mother and all went in the cave, from which we stood the bloodthirsty savages off, and they failed to get us out of the cave.[6]

It seems likely that the Miles and Ballantines did, indeed, seek shelter in a cave for a cluster of facts fit together – and there would have been no reason for Paddy to cite these details otherwise. However, it would have been 1876 instead of 1878. Fact: Paddy's sister, Ena, gave birth to Coulter Ballantine Jr. in August of 1876. Fact: Ena's cousin Mamie Timmons came from the south to spend some time with her after Coulter's birth. (This was the only trip Mamie

---

5 E. E. Allen, "Early Days in Frontier County," *Stockville Faber*, Aug. 10 – Sept. 28, 1916.
6 Miles and Bratt, p. 33.

Timmons made to Nebraska.) Fact: Paddy Miles' mother, Anne Palmer, died in April of 1877. And while the family likely did prepare for a standoff with the Indians, it is doubtful they actually had to fight off any "blood-thirsty" savages. There are no reports of actual Indian attacks in the area in 1876, and Ena made no mention of it in her journal. It is also a fact that Paddy Miles sometimes embellished his stories.

John L. Sanders, who settled on the Medicine near Stockville in 1874, recounted an Indian scare though he, too, may have been unclear on the date for he gave the year as being 1879 while it was probably 1876. At any rate, when they received news of an Indian uprising, Sanders sent his wife and children to the safety of Fort McPherson. The aspect to this story that Elizabeth Sanders surely never forgot was the delivery of a baby a few hours after returning home from McPherson. As Sanders told the story, "They got back about six o'clock in the evening. Before eleven o'clock there was another child born to us, and no doctor nearer than North Platte..." A wagon ride of more than forty miles over rough roads was no doubt a deciding factor in the birth of baby Georgia Sanders on October 11, 1876.[7] Andrew Webb and his family lived north of the Medicine several miles east of where Curtis is now located. When they received the news of hostile Indians on the move (again, the year is uncertain), Mrs. Webb and the children also sought protection at Fort McPherson. Andrew Webb, however, did not want to leave his herd of sheep. With guns close at hand, Andrew Webb and another fellow planned to take shelter in a natural cave located in the rocky cliffs on the south side of the Medicine should they get into a standoff with the Indians.[8]

Returning to the events of 1878: With horseflesh being valued as it was in those days, a bunch of cowboys in the vicinity of Stinking Water Creek in what is now Hayes County came out to the better as the Cheyenne passed through. The cowboys observed the Indi-

7 John L. Sanders as compiled by Ruth (Woodring) Young, "A Memoir," *Nebraska History Magazine*, Vol. VXIII, No. 3 (1932), p. 202. The Sanders also had a baby born in the fall of 1877, but circumstances suggest this Indian scare happened in 1876.
8 "Wm. Webb Here 63 Years, Lives in Part of Log House," *Curtis Enterprise*, July 30, 1936.

ans crossing the divide from the Republican River to the Stinking Water. They gave the Indians time to get to the Stinking Water and set up camp before picking up their trail. The Stinking Water Creek feeds into Frenchman Creek, and from a high hill on the Frenchman they could see the Indian camp. The Indians saw the cowboys and thinking they were soldiers broke camp in a hurry. Taking the Ogallala Trail, they traveled as fast as they could, leaving behind about a hundred head of horses. The cowboys quickly gathered up the horses. "Some of them were branded and evidently had been stolen from neighboring ranches. Those that were branded they turned loose, and the others they brought down the valley and sold for $5 to $15 each. A good many of them were sorrel stallions."[9]

Those in the Cambridge vicinity set out to improve their defensive position should the threat of Indian attack occur again. Some of the men in that area took spades and shovels and went to the mouth of the Medicine Creek where it empties into the Republican River. Leaving a triangular area of several acres with the creek on one side and the river on the other, they dug a trench to form the third side of their fort and used the dirt that they threw out of the trench for breastworks. Determined to "die in the last ditch," they girded the creek and river banks with rifle pits.

The settlers were still edgy when a few weeks later mounted men sped up and down the Medicine Creek with reports that once again the Northern Cheyenne were on the move. This time 2,000 Indians were said to be less than five miles from Wilsonville in Furnas County. The news of the previous attacks the Cheyenne had made on the settlers continued to filter into the countryside, and the earlier scoffers were now ready to bear arms. Andreas' *History of the State of Nebraska* describes the panic:

> This time the fright was a general one, and many who had been so brave when the first alarm began to subside, were now the first to flee. The settlers west of Beaver City almost in a body came tearing down the valley, stopping for nothing but to load in their families. Many of them

---

9 Dunning.

did not stop until they got out of the county and far down the Republican Valley.[10]

William H. Allen told the story of flight of those on the lower Medicine, saying that most of the settlers above him had vacated before he finally got scared. The prediction that this large group of Indians was expected to cross the Republican near Cambridge and raid the settlements along Medicine Creek had incited considerable fear. Having loaned his gun to a neighbor, who lived two and a half miles away, Allen rode horseback and got it back, along with three cartridges. While he retrieved the gun, the children were sent to notify the Wright B. Hammond family to the north and the John S. Tucker family to the south. Allen got word to Mrs. Light and children and Mike Yocum on Lime Creek. Both Wright Hammond and John Tucker were away, so it was their wives who had to decide whether they would seek safety with the Allen family or nervously await the return of their husbands. Although the other families left later, only the Hammond family went with the Allens. As told by William Allen:

> Hammond's and mine loaded up in wagons and on horseback making rather an imposing show. Started southeast [and] as we were raising the divide in that direction, we discovered some heads a bobbing ahead of us. Supposing them Indians, I made preparation with my gun, three cartridges and a ton of palpitating heart for battle. On raising the ridge, we found William Black and wife in a wagon going to Pat McKillip's, Black being in a state of defense, did not know the state of his heart. I know mine quieted several degrees. William said he took us for Indians trying to head him off. I said ditto.[11]

The little band of settlers under the care of William Allen drove to Mike Morrisey's, which is where the town of Holbrook is now lo-

---

10 A. T. Andreas, (Compiler), *History of the State of Nebraska*, 1882, <http://www.kancoll.org.>
11 William H. Allen, "Personal Recollections of Early Settlers on the Medicine in Frontier County, Nebraska," 1897, publication information unknown.

cated. The women and children all stayed in the house, which would have been a small log cabin at best. Mr. Allen camped under the wagon but did not sleep – keeping in mind his military training, "that a good picket did not sleep on guard." He emphasized that it was the aforementioned military training, <u>not</u> fear, that kept him awake. It was about midnight when William Allen heard a horse galloping up from the Republican River. Allen halted the rider, who turned out to be J. M. Gammill. Having been about fifty miles away when he heard of the Indian raid, Gammill had pushed his horse hard. Finding neither his brother Samuel nor the Allens home, Jim Gammill had gone on to the Medicine Creek Post Office, and finding neither there had followed the trail on down the river. His horse worn-out, Jim Gammill spent the rest of the night under the wagon with Allen, who was glad to have the company.

The next morning the two men went on horseback to Arapahoe where they found Sam Gammill. William Allen laid in one hundred rounds of needle gun ammunition only to learn that he wouldn't be needing it. The big band of Indians that had been seen south of the Beaver had passed through Arapahoe; however, they were Texas Longhorns on their way to the Platte. When the news came earlier that the Cheyenne were moving north along the Texas Trail, the cowboys chose a route much farther to the east. It was Captain George Culver of the Cambridge commanding forces who mistook the herd of Texas cattle for the Indians, a fact that was to cause him much chagrin in following years. Colonel J. W. Pickle commanded the forces at Medicine Creek Post Office, which, in Allen's words, "were in the main composed of crying babies and screaming women." Once the panic was over and the leaders swallowed crow, it was easy to look back and chuckle over the whole affair. The fact is, had the drove of Texas Longhorns been 2,000 hostile Indians, the settlers were woefully unprepared.

Following these Indian scares, the citizens made an appeal to Washington for help in protecting themselves and were issued army rifles with one hundred rounds of ammunition each. Charley Hotze posted the necessary bond and obtained one of the .52 caliber rifles, which was equipped with a bayonet. While the Cheyenne, in their desperate attempt to return to their homeland, were to leave an indelible chapter in Native American history, life for the settlers in southwest Nebraska returned to the ordinary events of daily living. Young William Hotze recalled that they felt a little safer with the government-issue rifle hanging over the door. It kicked like a mule, however, and tore game all to pieces, so his father used it mostly to kill skunks that prowled around the chicken coop.

14

John "Storm" King

The Indians that came through southwest Nebraska following the Cheyenne outbreak in 1878 were the cause of the last general "Indian Scare" in the region. And while nearly all the settlers on the Republican banded together and circled their wagons into hastily improvised fortresses, John "Storm" King decided to stick it out on his own. The Hotze family lived just to the south of King, so when he didn't show up at the enclosure by sundown, Charley Hotze went to investigate. He found the eccentric old hunter sitting on his door step; his dog lying by his side; his supper cooking on the stove and his Sharps rifle leaning against the wall. Charley Hotze made one last appeal, to which John King's reply was, "Na, Charley. I'll hide the ponies down under the creek bank. Bruno will watch, and I'll turn in after dark with plenty of shells handy. If I'm not around in the morning, you'll find some 'red devils' scattered about too."[1]

John King had been in his own share of scrapes with the Indians. On one occasion in the early 1870s, King and another buffalo hunter lost two ponies from their camp on the Red Willow. They followed the tracks and found two young Sioux in possession of the ponies. When the Indians refused to give up the horses, King and his companion shot and killed them. They marked the dead Sioux in such a way as to make it appear the deed had been committed by Pawnee. The white men had retrieved their ponies and saved their

1 Hotze.

own skins, but they did not anticipate the extent of the Sioux retribution. As told by William Hotze:

> In revenge for this, a hot headed band of Sioux broke from their reservation north of the Platte and, one thousand strong, descended upon the small Pawnee camp in [the] charge of Agent Williamson. Had they known the facts, they would have slain the white settlers instead. It is said that King's companion later confessed the deed when in a jovial mood at Fort Riley...[2]

Another story puts John King hunting alone near Courthouse Rock at the mouth of Pumpkin Creek in northwest Nebraska when he was attacked by Sioux. Though he had no shelter but a buffalo wallow and took several shots to his leg, he managed to stand them off. The Indians got away with his horses, which left King in a serious predicament; he was miles from anywhere with a wounded leg and no horse. When his leg healed, John King traveled by foot the one-hundred miles or so across the open plains to the Red Cloud Agency and demanded his horses from Chief Red Cloud, who had them returned to him.[3]

John S. King was the first real settler in what is now Red Willow County. He built a small log cabin near where Indianola is now located and sustained himself by hunting and trapping. Though it is thought he was from Pennsylvania, nothing else is known about his early life. The initial "S" may have represented a given name, but on the frontier it stood for "Storm." John King became known for showing up on the doorstep of the pioneers' homes in the midst of a storm. According to Paddy Miles, King was also sometimes known as "Crazy King." Paddy recalled that King would take his team and head out alone for a hundred miles, "building bridges over the streams, pulling through deep snows and fetching up at our camp every big snowstorm."[4]

The few white men on the Medicine in the newly organized Frontier County established a friendship with John King. It was

---

2 Ibid.
3 E. E. Allen.
4 Miles and Bratt, p. 21.

a wolf, which had broken the chain and drug one of John King's traps for miles before it succumbed, that inspired the naming of Wolf's Rest. Paddy Miles mentioned John King in his journal on March 18, 1872, saying he had traded him two cows for a mule. On the nineteenth Miles was on the Republican where he and King plowed the first furrow in that "splendid valley." Later in the month of March 1872, Paddy Miles' parents and newly widowed sister, Ena Raymonde, arrived in Nebraska. News of Ena's arrival spread like wildfire to the neighboring settlements. Not only was she a young and beautiful single woman, Ena's reputation as a crack shot had preceded her. Over on the Republican, John King got word of the newcomers on the Medicine.

> King mounted his best horse, gun in hand, hied [*sic*] away across the valley, the high lands and the canyons, forded the Medicine and called at Mrs. Raymonde's tent. After introducing himself, he invited Mrs. Raymonde out to shoot at a mark.
>
> "Certainly," replied Mrs. Raymonde. With gun in hand the new settler stepped out. "How far do you wish to shoot Mr. King?"
>
> "Say it yourself," replied the old soldier. Now the firing commenced a half a quarter toward the highland. "The sight of my gun has certainly got jarred out of place," said Mr. King.
>
> "Let me see your gun," rejoined Mrs. Raymonde, "that is a good looking gun. Let me have a cartridge," Mrs. Raymonde said. "And another one, Mr. King, and a third one, please." And all were placed precisely in the center of the bull's eye. "The fault is not your gun," said Mrs. Raymonde, "your nerve is not steady."
>
> King returned to his home in the valley but said very little about his visit to Raymonde Bend.[5]

---

5 John F. Black, "Pioneer Days in Red Willow County," circa 1918, quoted by Riley, Ballantine MSS. Ena Raymonde's surname was spelled "Ramon" in the article.

John "Storm" King may have said little of this first meeting with Ena Raymonde, but he did not forget the visit or the attractive woman who had outshot him. It was not unusual for John King to show up at Wolf's Rest on the Medicine. On April 10, 1873, Ena noted in her journal that Mr. King had spent the previous Sunday with them, "and he was charmed (so he said) with my 'den.' Says it is the most romantic and picturesque place he ever had the pleasure of seeing, etc." Small though it was, Ena's room in the cabin at Wolf's Rest was in stark contrast to John King's simply furnished cabin. Ena had brought her books, pictures, and other homey appointments from her old home in the South. And surely the very essence of Ena Raymonde's femininity was intoxicating to the old bachelor from the Republican Valley.

John King may have cleaned up a little before he journeyed over to "Raymonde Bend" on the Medicine; he may have attempted to refine his crude frontiersman's manner. But, alas, John "Storm" King was never elevated to a man of importance in Ena's life. On Sunday, June 9, 1872, Ena wrote in her journal, "Nothing of <u>him-portance</u> today!" She noted that two very good friends, Mr. Lewis and Mr. Dillard, had been there and then mentioned King almost as an afterthought: "Ah! I must not forget: 'Storm' King paid his respects also, and seemed less of a storm than usual..." Nearly a year later, in May of 1873, Ena wrote that Mr. King had come on a Tuesday...

> And not strange to say a storm [came of] snow, rain, sleet, and O! Such beating... blinding wind, which [bore] down upon us until Thursday night. Indeed! That made my den something of a bog-hole... [Leaks in the] roof dripped all over my romantic carpet and furs, and we dodged first a little [dab] of mud – or now a ball of damp clay. [We] dodged and talked; while I made ghastly attempts at a sort of desperate cheerfulness... But the storm passed, as all things early must. Mr. K. left us on Friday morning...

As the Republican Valley continued to be settled, John King's forays to "Raymonde Bend" most likely became less frequent. If he was captivated with "Little Curly Hair of the Medicine," he was one of a bevy of others to whom she was gracious and friendly but nothing more. The *History of the State of Nebraska*, published in 1882, counted John King as one of the leading men of Red Willow County and said that he was at one time a county commissioner. "Early in the year 1880, however, he became insane, and, in April of that year, he was taken to the Insane Asylum at Lincoln, where he died in a short time, and was lamented by all the old settlers of the county."[6] He was considered to be an old-timer – and so he was. The frontier had a way of grinding down a man, however, for John "Storm" or "Crazy" King was no more than forty years old at the time of his death.

---

6 Andreas.

15

Cowboy Shootout

The story is essentially a simple one: two cowboys had a shootout, and one ended up dead and was buried on the prairie. A few well-worn versions of the story provide an account of what happened on that fateful spring day in 1879. The winter of 1878 and 1879 was abnormally hard with relentless storms and blizzards battering the area. The rangeland was covered by deep snow during much of the winter, resulting in heavy stock losses. Similar conditions prevailed in the western part of Nebraska and on into Colorado and the Wyoming Territory, causing cattle to drift in a southerly and easterly direction. Large herds of cattle from the big ranches on the Platte wound up on the range in Frontier County. As the weather opened up in the spring, a hundred or so cowmen organized a big roundup with the intention of each outfit sorting off its own livestock.

Of necessity, each man was looking after his own interests; however, sometimes a man was looking after the interests of someone else. Such was the case of James M. Gammill who was charged with watching out for the concerns of a widow on the Platte Valley. The details have not been recorded, but Gammill's son J. N. Gammill summed it up in a few words: "And through recommendations of J. H. Morgan and Burke Brothers, (then on the Platte), my father took the job; and with success, by his fist under the chin of a big two-gun bully and telling him some things."[1]

On one leg of the drive, James Gammill was riding along beside a cowboy from the Ogallala area by the name of Isaac "Ike" Lowe. A young and inexperienced cowboy, Lowe had just bought a Colt six-shooter in North Platte and commented to Gammill, "That damn thing will probably get me in trouble." Lowe had reason to feel apprehensive, as he had been subjected to a considerable amount of harassment from Charles Ansley, an older, trail-wizened, and sometimes ill-tempered cowhand, who was a foreman for the big Bay State Company.

Riding hard and short on sleep, the cowboys were tired and irritable. It is no wonder that tempers flared with so many over-wrought men, and the winter-weary cattle not used to being herded. On the day before the fatal shoot-out occurred, Charles Ansley and Ike Lowe had quarreled long before the roundup reached the crossing at Mitchell Creek on the McPherson Trail where they made night camp. That night some of the horses were put in William Black's pasture, which extended across the Medicine. After breakfast the next morning, Ike Lowe set off to retrieve the horses. Ansley's horse had wandered across the Medicine and was with some of Bill Black's horses, so Lowe let it go and brought the rest of the herd to the campsite. Whether Lowe intentionally left Ansley's horse behind is unclear, but either way, he made a fatal mistake. Ansley was hot under the collar when he saw that Lowe had not brought his horse in with the others. The two men got into a bitter argument, and they finally agreed that the only way to resolve the matter was to shoot it out.

They rode into a side pocket upstream from Black's house. While Charles Ansley could draw a gun easily enough, Ike Lowe was not used to carrying firearms, much less pulling a gun on a man. When the signal was given, both men went for their guns. Lowe's six-shooter caught in the scabbard while Ansley got off two shots in rapid succession. The first shot hit Ike Lowe near the heart. As

---

1 Gammill.

he slumped backward, he pulled hard on the reins, which caused his horse to rear and take Ansley's second shot to the head. The only shot Lowe got off went wild and did no damage. Lowe was taken to Frank Griffith's place where Frank did all he could for the mortally wounded man. Lowe did not harbor hard feelings toward Ansley, conceding that if either he or Ansley had had the courage to back down no shots would have been fired. When Isaac Lowe died a few days later, Frank Griffith and a few of his neighbors made a rough box for a coffin and buried him high on a hill. Meanwhile, the roundup went on as though nothing had happened.

The duel had taken place in full view of witnesses, so there was no question as to who had fired the shot that took Lowe's life. In spite of the fact that both men had apparently agreed to the shootout, Ansley was justifiably concerned that killing Lowe might be considered murder. According to W. H. "Paddy" Miles, Ansley stood the witnesses off at gunpoint and then skipped out. Robert McKnight, who was sheriff at the time, deputized Miles and W. L. McClary to apprehend Ansley. Paddy Miles, however, took sole credit for the capture of Ansley in his version of the incident: "I was deputized by Sheriff McKnight to capture Ansley and after several days of hard riding up on the Platte River, I captured and brought him back for trial.

E. T. Jay, one of the first attorneys to settle in the area, was employed to defend Ansley. They went before a justice of the peace at the county seat of Stockville on a charge of murder. Miles recalled that when the justice of the peace asked Ansley if he was guilty or not guilty of the charge brought against him, Ansley answered that he was guilty. At this, Mr. Jay took the prisoner out behind the little log courthouse and explained one of the complexities of the legal system, "You don't understand the reading of the warrant. You must not say 'guilty'; you must say 'not guilty.' If you don't, you will be bound over."

Ansley replied, "I don't like to lie, but if I must, I will." Then he went before the court, and the question of guilty or not guilty was asked again. "Not guilty Your Honor," was the response. The judge acquitted and discharged the prisoner; Miles gave him back his pistol, and Ansley took off for Sidney, minus his horse, saddle, and the ten bucks he had to fork out to pay his attorney. All parties seemed satisfied with the decision to set Ansley free, given that no one could be found to testify against him. Miles justified the judge's handling of the case: "The prisoner could prove by half a hundred witnesses that he shot in self defense, there not being an instant of time between the report of the guns, while it saved a big expense to the county."[2]

Shootings at roundups in those early days were not unusual – some might say they were to be expected. Nevertheless, Ansley was destined to carry forever the heavy burden of having killed a man unnecessarily – a guilt that preyed on his mind, it is said, until he eventually became insane.

---

2   Miles and Bratt, pp 17-18. Other sources for this chapter are E. E. Allen and Mae (Griffith) Wilmeth.

16

The Hanging Tree

*V*igilante justice as meted out by a group of private citizens often provided an expedient solution to the lawlessness of the Wild West. Even after the establishment of a system of law and order, the appeal of being swift and sure occasionally induced the early settlers to take the law into their own hands. Such was the case when Jonas Nelson was hung from the limb of a large cottonwood tree in 1884. An old Swedish bachelor, known to have a foul disposition and unusual strength, Jonas Nelson was given wide clearance by the settlers on the lower Medicine Creek. In a fit of temper, he could perform such super-human stunts as picking up a piece of machinery and putting it in a wagon. Likewise, his rage was often directed at his neighbors or others who he perceived to be out to get him.

Jonas Nelson settled on Sand Creek in Lower Medicine Precinct (now Orafino Precinct) about eight miles southeast of Stockville around 1880. His homestead bordered that of Amanda Sherwood, a Civil War widow, and her son Eugene, and it was about a mile and a half from that of James M. Gammill. It seems there were several points of conflict between the Sherwoods and Nelson. The newspapers of the era reported that the trouble originated over the boundary line that separated the homesteads. Both claims were on good bottomland with nice stands of timber. This was advantageous to the landowners along the creeks and streams, as they could earn much needed income by cutting and selling the wood. Eugene Sherwood suspected his neighbor was working against the wrong property line to cut timber, and when a survey proved him correct, Nelson was furious and made repeated threats against Sherwood. Another survey made at a later date confirmed the first; Sherwood's timber was being harvested by Jonas Nelson.

Others say the trouble was over the clear, fresh water that bubbled from a spring near the headwaters of Sand Creek that ran through the Sherwood property. At the time he homesteaded, Jonas Nelson had paid a professional land locator a hefty fee to find him a desirable piece of land. Unfortunately, the locator (who soon made himself scarce) had lied to Nelson and told him that a large spring was on his land. In fact, the spring was on the Sherwood property. Nelson had made numerous threats to kill his neighbor and would have done so with a shovel early on, had someone not stopped him. As he sulked about and became increasingly paranoid, the homesteaders noticed Nelson carrying a couple of revolvers and sometimes a double-barreled shotgun. Realizing the problem was becoming bigger than he was prepared to handle, Sherwood entered a complaint before the county judge, William H. Allen, who placed Nelson under bond to keep the peace. Unfortunately, such a legal action held little weight with the ill-tempered Swede.

Whether it was over water or timber or both, the simmering issue of the boundary dispute finally reached the boiling point. Between nine and ten o'clock on the morning of Tuesday, December 16, 1884, young Eugene Sherwood was shot in the head and left to bleed to death where he fell. A short while later Jonas Nelson showed up at James Gammill's place where Gammill and his neighbor Elwood Clark were loading hay near the house of Orville Work. Nelson showed Gammill a bloody, wounded hand and pitched a story about having to shoot Sherwood in self-defense. Gammill, who was not afraid of Nelson and did not believe his tale, looked him straight in the eye and said, "You son-of-a-bitch, you have probably killed Sherwood."[1] Jim Gammill instructed Clark and Work to keep Nelson under guard with a shotgun, while he ran down to Sherwood's

---

1 Herbert C. Allen, publication information unknown.

timber to see if his suspicions were confirmed. The December 20, 1884 *Cambridge (Nebr.) Monitor* reported on what Gammill found:

> He came upon some woodchoppers, who had just discovered the dead body of Sherwood lying across his gun, which was a rifle of very large bore. He presented a horrible sight as he lay there with the top of his head blown off and blood and brains bespattered on the snow. They made a minute survey of the surroundings and followed Nelson's tracks in the snow up the path to his house, and when within ten or twelve feet of the house, discovered a pool of blood and drops of blood along on the snow up to the door, when they entered the house and found his shot gun on the bed with one barrel discharged, and after scrutinizing things pretty closely for some time also found one of his revolvers under the bed, covered with blood and one chamber empty.

William H. "Paddy" Miles was the county sheriff at the time, and because there was no county coroner, he impaneled a coroner's jury to investigate the apparent homicide. An inquest was held over Sherwood's body, and the jurors, "in consideration of the evidence" before them, found that Eugene W. Sherwood "came to his death by a shot fired from a double barreled breech loading shotgun loaded with leaden shot, fired by one Jonas Nelson with premeditated malice and forethought with intent to kill, and there and then, did kill the said Eugene W. Sherwood."[2]

Judge William H. Allen issued a warrant for the arrest of Jonas Nelson the following day. Because the log court house had burned, the preliminary hearing was held in Judge Allen's cabin on the eighteenth of December. When Dr. Seip soaked the bandage off Nelson's wound, powder burns were found – indicating a shot at close range. An old army surgeon, Dr. Seip testified as to the caliber of the ball and the distance the powder had penetrated, etc. From this evidence the *Cambridge Monitor* concluded "as Sherwood's gun was found to be loaded, it was clearly demonstrated that the old devil [Nelson] had shot himself."

---

2 Frontier County, Nebraska, Coroner's Report. Minor punctuation changes for clarity.

Prior to the hearing, Dr. Seip along with the state's attorney, E. W. Lewis, did some investigating. They found a couple of empty water buckets in front of Nelson's dugout with tracks going to them and leading away, indicating that Nelson had started after water when he caught sight of Sherwood going through the timber. The theory they presented at the hearing was that Nelson set down the buckets, went into his house and got his shotgun, and keeping out of Sherwood's sight, followed him into the timber. All indications were that Nelson then fired the fatal shot at the unsuspecting Sherwood from behind a large cottonwood tree. Twenty-two-year-old Gene Sherwood had on heavy mittens and had never cocked his gun. His grief-stricken mother said Gene had taken his gun with him when he went after some straying cows in hopes of getting a shot at a deer.

Herbert and Eugene Allen, the teen-age sons of Judge Allen, were naturally caught up in the feverish excitement. There was a large crowd present with a lot of talking and agitating outside the small log cabin that sufficed for a courtroom. Someone related that the previous year Nelson had difficulty with a neighbor living on the old E. G. Nesbitt place and shortly afterwards was seen one night fleeing from some burning haystacks on the neighbor's place. With the exception of one man who believed that he would come clear, the cantankerous Nelson was judged a guilty man. Even before Judge Allen issued his finding that, "There is a probable cause to believe that Jonas Nelson committed the offense charged," the conduct of the crowd was calling for a hanging. Eugene Allen recalled that, "One man from an adjoining county suggested that if the men hadn't enough nerve to hang Nelson that the women had. He was assured that the women would not be called out."[3]

For his part, Jonas Nelson stuck with the self-defense story and showed no remorse. He claimed that if the case went to trial, he would see to it that he got a jury of Swedes who would eventually clear him. In another haystack burning incident a year or so earlier – this one on the Platte River – he had been set free by a "Swede jury."

3 E. E. Allen.

Furthermore, he threatened to come back and do a general cleanup of all those who had anything to do with the trial.

Law and order were working as intended. The coroner's inquest had been conducted accordingly, and Judge Allen was judicious in conducting the preliminary hearing and ordering Nelson held for a trial in district court. If the citizens were impatient in wanting immediate justice, the newspapers were no less eager. The *Frontier County Faber* indicted Nelson in no uncertain terms: "He secreted himself behind a tree and waited until Sherwood was only a few steps from him before he discharged the fatal shot." The *Faber* further played to public sentiment in its December 19 issue by writing: "The sympathies of the public are with the murdered man, who was living with and providing for his mother." The *Cambridge Monitor* that rolled off the press on December 20, 1884, was even more inflammatory with their prediction: "We are not in favor of mob law, but we have good reason to believe that ere this has reached the eyes of many of our readers, Jonas Nelson will have passed into the great beyond, at the hands of excited and justly indignant neighbors."

On the other hand, the newspapers can hardly be blamed for the final outcome. Three days following the death of Eugene Sherwood and before either the Cambridge or Stockville newspaper had gone to press, Jonas Nelson's body was found. The *Monitor* added this late news flash: "Just as we are going to press, word is brought to town that Nelson was found, yesterday about noon by the sheriff, dangling at the end of a rope from a limb of the identical tree that he was standing under when he committed the murder." Jonas Nelson's guilt was, in the minds of the public, a foregone conclusion by the time Sheriff Miles headed for North Platte to secure him in the Lincoln County jail. As Miles told the story:

> I started to take him to jail in North Platte, as we had so little use for a jail in this county we have not as yet built one. It was very cold and the snow deep; we did not get along fast. When night came on, we stopped at a cattle ranch. There being no one at the ranch, we went in and

made ourselves at home, got supper. Dave Love was with me to help guard the prisoner.

At about ten o'clock there was a rush on us of masked men who took Nelson out in the night, back through the drifting snow. As we could do nothing, we waited until morning, then followed their trail to the woods and there, from a limb of the tree from which Sherwood was killed, hung Nelson.[4]

Once again there was an investigation and a coroner's inquest. When Sheriff Miles mounted his horse and made the rounds of the neighborhood to find out where everyone was on the night of the hanging, the answers he got were vague and conflicting. Mike Mousel and C. H. Siebecker were two of those said to have made the claim that they went to Cambridge to get a rough box in which to bury Sherwood. As Sherwood's body was to be shipped back East for burial beside that of his father, it was undoubtedly already gone or in Cambridge. Nevertheless, the sheriff was easily satisfied with the answers he received. Perhaps it would have been a farce for the sheriff to have conducted more than a rudimentary investigation, for it is commonly believed that he was sympathetic with, and quite likely a member himself of the hanging party. The report of the coroner's inquest filed by Sheriff W. H. Miles, acting as the county coroner:

Be it remembered that on the 19th day of December 1884 reliable information was given to undersigned Coroner of said County that the dead body of Jonas Nelson had been found in Lower Medicine Precinct in said County and the said Jonas Nelson was supposed to have come to his death by unlawful means. Therefore I summoned three lawful men of said County to appear before me at Lower Medicine Precinct forthwith, there and thence to hold an inquest upon the dead body of said Jonas Nelson there hanging and by what means he died. There upon at the time and place mentioned said jury to-wit, David Love, Orville Work, Joseph Barnhart, appeared and hereby duly impaneled and sworn, proceeded to make inquiry as to the

---

4 Miles and Bratt, p. 34.

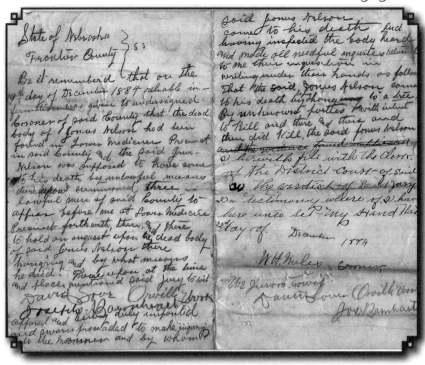

Sheriff W. H. "Paddy" Miles filed this report as the acting coroner following an inquest over the body of suspected murderer Jonas Nelson, who was found hanging from a cottonwood tree. The coroner's jury found that, "the said Jonas Nelson came to his death by being hung to a tree..."

manner and by whom said Jonas Nelson came to his death and having inspected the body heard and made all needful inquiries returned to me their inquisition in writing under their hands as follows:

That the said Jonas Nelson came to his death by hanging to a tree by unknown parties with intent to kill and there and thus and then did kill the said Jonas Nelson.

I herewith file with the Clerk of the District Court of said County the verdict of said jury in testimony whereof I have here unto set my hand this 22nd day of December 1884.

If some citizens felt a twinge of concern at the blatant display of vigilante justice, none doubted the guilt of the man who was buried beneath the hanging tree. E. E. Allen, who was only thirteen at the time, recalled other criminal cases that came before his father, the judge, when he hid behind haystacks or the stable and overheard prospective witnesses "arranging their testimony." In the case of Jonas Nelson, however, he said there was no "putting together of heads among those interested. It was simply murder in cold blood without the slightest provocation."[5]

The time that elapsed between the discovery of the murder of Eugene Sherwood and the hanging of Jonas Nelson was three days – swift and certain. Amanda Sherwood, the widowed mother of the slain man, was inconsolable as Christmas day came and went – she had lost her only child. The December 26, 1884 issue of the *Faber* reflected the prevailing mood of the community:

> The *Faber* is no apologist for "Judge Lynch," but when the circumstances are all well known, no reasonable man will blame the citizens for the lynching of Nelson. There is a sense of relief and security prevailing throughout the community since that hanging that tells its own story of approval of the entire community of this act of the Medicine Creek folk.

The Old West style of justice was not only swift but economical. Although there were other minor costs involved, the expense warrant filed by Sheriff Miles illustrates the point. W. H. Miles made a claim for $8.25, which included three days of custody and/or guarding the prisoner, three meals, serving of arrest warrant, and return of warrant.

Over the years, those involved in one way or another with Jonas Nelson related their stories. Mike Mousel may not have had a convincing cover story on the night of the hanging. Then again, he did clearly remember sitting with an ax on his lap the night the sheriff stopped at his place in route to North Platte with Nelson at the time of the haystack burning incident on the Platte. Herb Allen pulled the boots off the prisoner the night he was held under guard before the preliminary hearing. A small and peculiar incident perhaps, but

5 E. E. Allen.

it was a singular experience that involved the fifteen-year-old boy in an event that gripped the consciousness of the community for years thereafter.

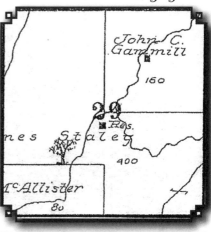

For the most part, the community was close-mouthed about which of their members were actually present at the old cottonwood tree on the pitch black night that Jonas Nelson was hanged. It is said, however, that when there was hesitation about who would put the rope around Nelson's neck, Paddy Peterson, a neighbor to the south, finally stepped forward and the deed was done. Elwood Clark lived about a mile to the west of

A tree-shaped emblem marks the location of Sherwood's murder and the hanging of Nelson in the SW¼ of Sec. 29, Twp. 6, Range 26 in Lower Medicine (now Orafino) Precinct in the 1905 *Standard Atlas of Frontier County, Nebraska.*

Nelson and Sherwood, and when he died in the 1930s, Herbert L. Allen's son Herbert C. Allen recollected, "When we heard of his passing, my father…told me he guessed it wouldn't hurt to tell me that Clark was the last of the men to help hang Nelson. Clark furnished the rope."[6]

---

6 Herbert C. Allen.

DRAWN BY *Rudolph Wendelin*

STOCKVILLE, Frontier County, Nebraska (CIRCA 1900)

Stockville, Nebraska, as it looked around 1900. The Bald Eage Hotel is the large two-story building left of center to the back of the drawing. See description on opposite page. Drawn by Rudolph Wendelin circa 1980. *Courtesy Robert Van Pelt Estate*

Rudolph Wendelin's Drawing of Stockville, Nebraska - Circa 1900

Following is identifying information for some of the buildings pictured in the drawing (opposite page) of Stockville. View is towards the northwest. Frontier County Courthouse is lower right-hand. Town windmill is at northwest corner of courthouse square.

Bearing east (right) from windmill, buildings facing courthouse are: Two-story building built by Miles Galland for boarding house (Citizen's Bank in 1898); Bradbury & Ward Hardware (Cash building in 1898); J. M. Parrott, dentist; J. A. Williams, attorney; *Republican-Faber* newspaper office & print shop.

Bearing south (left) from windmill, buildings facing courthouse are: Enterprise (Regulator) General Merchandise; Two-story Beggs' Building; two buildings used variously as grocery stores & other; Logan's Phoenix Drug Store; confectionary, served ice cream & malt hops; lodge hall & opera house (replaced with new building after 1913 fire); bank building (this building and four buildings north of it burned in 1913) There was a livery stable (not pictured) south across intersection.

Bearing west cattycorner across intersection from windmill: Two-story bank & other offices; Van Pelt Café, Dr. Case's office; Weikert Store; two buildings used as butcher & meat markets; Bald Eagle Hotel (big two-story building).

Across the street in the next block to the west are several residences and the Congregational Church, which was built in 1904 (the steeple was struck by lightning and burned. It was replaced by a steeple of a different style). Livery stable and blacksmith shop are across the street south of the Bald Eagle.

At left, center of picture, is the Methodist Episcopal Church, later used as a high school. To the right of the church is a lumber yard.

North at the edge of town (far right edge of drawing): Grade School (flag in front); between school and business district is Coun-

ty Fair Building; on hill beyond school is the Hopton family residence.

Dwelling in center at far left edge of drawing was occupied by
Ambrose Shelley from 1899 to 1905.

(This information is primarily from Robert Van Pelt's description that accompanied the drawing as it appeared in the *Nebraska
History* magazine, Fall 1984. Also information from George Shelley
as printed in *Stockville: Then and Now*, p. 30.)

17

The Death of Annie E. McClary

*I*f W. L. McClary let out a war-whoop and threw the reins over the back of his horses, whipping them into a run that caused the wagon accident, which killed his wife and unborn child, it appears he set in motion a series of events that resulted in years of feuding on the Medicine Creek. At first glance, it does seem the trouble started with the death of thirty-five-year-old Anne Eliza "Ena" Palmer Raymonde Ballantine McClary on July 13, 1884.[1] As it turns out, fissures in the complex relationship of the Palmer/Miles/Ballantine family had already appeared.

Nine years earlier, on October 5, 1875, Ena was married to David Coulter Ballantine Sr. As the new Mr. and Mrs. Ballantine faced together the struggles of wresting a living from the virgin land, it is perhaps natural that there was a weakening in the once strong connection between Ena and her brother. It has already been demonstrated that Wm. H. "Paddy" Miles could be unpredictable in his dealings with people. The draft of a letter (quoted in part in an earlier chapter) from Ena to her brother implies disputes over money had been the source of previous problems between the two:

> I write to you, because I pledged my word at our last
> settlement that I would never talk over [money] matters

---

1 Georgia census records in the Ballantine MSS show Ena as being two years old in 1850 and twelve years old in 1860 – making her birth year 1848, however, an entry in the Ballantine family Bible in Ena's handwriting gives her date of birth as being Sept. 28, 1851.

Ena Raymonde's marriage to David Coulter Ballantine Sr. was cut short when he was killed while trying to board a moving train. A successful cattleman and a senator in the Nebraska State Legislature at the time of his death, he left Ena with two small children. He is buried in the Ballantine family plot at Wyuka Cemetary in Lincoln, Nebraska. *Top photo courtesy Nebraska State Historical Society. Photo of gravestone by the author.*

again, and my experience here of late has only strength-
ened my resolution. And as to Mr. B. [Ballantine], he gave
me his word of honor to have nothing to do with the business between you and I, and I want you to understand that
it is solely between you and I, lawfully and individually...

Now what I propose is each one (you and I) write down
his own account and see how the two balance. None of us
look at the same thing alike, but we have a business basis
to go on. I am taking this stand because Mr. B. came to me
the afternoon you left and told me that you were coming
to him, not me, about money matters, and that if it was
my business, to say so. I want the understanding speedily
settled. I want you to know if I owe you anything – and if
so – I want all the time allowed me that anyone can hon-
orably have, to pay a debt of the kind because we have no
money to settle an unexpected debt...

I will not enter into any recrimination with you, Herbert. Poor Ma's last request to me was to have no money
matters with Willie. I have been warned of this, but what
is the use to talk to you. Do not think I am angry, or want
to make you so, but you must certainly know that I know,
you can talk one way today and another way tomorrow;
you contradicted your own word without any compunc-
tion a thousand times over – so knowing you as you are
– your good traits and your bad, I am not angry – only ask
you to let us get through this business...[2]

This letter was composed sometime following the death of Anne
Palmer and presumably before the 1880 death of Dempsey B. Palmer, as Ena made reference to the fact that she'd "had no peace all the
winter from Pa." Even though the bond between father and son does
not seem to have been particularly strong, Mr. Palmer did depart
"this life at the residence of W. H. Miles in said County on or about
the 25th day of February A. D. 1880..."[3] This is where we find another fly in the ointment. Mr. Palmer was the father of Paddy Miles

---

2 All letters to/from Annie Ena Palmer Raymonde Ballantine McClary, or to/from her
children, Coulter and Anna Ena (Ballantine) Adams, are from the Ballantine MSS.
3 All references to court proceedings in this chapter are from land abstracts in possession
of the author.

Annie Eliza "Ena" (Palmer) Raymonde Ballantine McClary had been married to W. L. McClary less than a year at the time of her death on July 13, 1884. She is buried beside her parents at Sunset Point Cemetary on the Medicine Creek. This photo was taken about 1874 in Freeport, Illinois. *Top photo courtesy of Nebraska State Historical Society. Photo of gravestone by Gail Geis.*

in fact, but not in name. Whether or not William Herbert Palmer assumed the surname of Miles because he committed murder in his home state of Georgia has never been established with certainty. What is known is that the young man on the run who hit the plains of Nebraska in 1869 was known as Paddy Miles.

Consequently, Judge S. P. Baker entered into the probate record of their father's estate the following: "On June 22, 1880, it is therefore declared by me that the said Annie E. Ballantine is the only lawful and legal heir to all the estate of the said Dempsey B. Palmer late of Frontier County, State of Nebraska, deceased." W. L. McClary, a trusted friend of D. C. and Ena Ballantine, was named administrator of the Palmer Estate. In spite of the fact that W. H. Miles filed suit against W. L. McClary as said administrator, agreeable terms were reached the following spring with an "amicable settlement of the suits and difficulties…" Miles filed a quitclaim deed to a quarter section of land, and the estate relinquished to Miles all interest in the cattle brands. It is not known what other concessions were made in order to settle the difficulties or whether they were mutually satisfactory to both parties.

On October 3, 1882, Ena Ballantine experienced the tragedy that would cut to the very depths of her soul. A local newspaper gave the details:

> D. C. Ballantine, who lived near Stockville in Frontier County, and who is the Senator from this District to the State Legislature, slipped while he was attempting to board a train at Benkelman on his way to McCook and was horribly mangled. He was brought to McCook, where he died three hours later.[4]

The young widow was left with two small children, two ranches, $5000 life insurance, and a broken heart. Less than a year later she married W. L. McClary and then, in July of 1884, Ena met her own tragic death. Several contenders jumped feet-first into the fracas over Ena's estate. Her brother William H. Miles acting in his capac-

---

4 Unidentified newspaper dated Oct. 5, 1882. Transcription in papers of H. P. Waite, High Plains Museum, McCook, Nebr.

ity as Frontier County Sheriff served notice to W. L. McClary that George W. Ballantine, brother-in-law of the deceased, had made application on August 6, 1884, to serve as administrator of the estate. This no doubt caught McClary by surprise as he was the widower of the deceased, and it was he who had served as the administrator of the estate of Dempsey Palmer. Then there was the sheriff, brother to the deceased, who perhaps viewed himself as a potential administrator

The turn of events caused by Ena's death merely complicated old grievances. McClary had been a presence in Ena's life from the time of her arrival on the Medicine in 1872. His name appears in her journals as early as December of 1872 and throughout 1873 – but just as a friend – never with a hint of romantic interest. After she was married to D. C. Ballantine, McClary obviously remained a confidant and demonstrated trustworthiness prior to his appointment as administrator of the Palmer estate. The gold Elgin watch still in the possession of McClary's descendents engraved, "*1879. To W. L. McClary from Mr. & Mrs. Ballantine,*" bears testimony to a solid friendship. McClary had apparently been the Ballantines' ranch manager and continued in that position following the sudden death of D. C. Ballantine in 1882. Regardless of the path he took to get there, Washington L. McClary became a fixture in the life of Ena Ballantine.

The circumstances of McClary's marriage to Ena add another dimension. As it has always been told (the McClary family genealogy has a similar version), the newlyweds were on their way home to Stockville from their honeymoon in Lincoln, Nebraska, "When… McClary threw the reins up over the horses' backs and whipped them into a run, a practice that he was known for. The wagon over turned and killed Annie Ena Palmer Raymond Ballantine McClarey [*sic*] at the age of 35 years."[5] This scenario presents problems in explaining the baby that Ena aborted as a result of the accident, as an out-of-wedlock pregnancy was uncommon in the 1880s. In fact, closer examination of the evidence shows it didn't happen this way.

---

5 *Curtis, Nebraska: The…*, p. 260.

Marriage records from Polk County, Iowa, show that the marriage between W. L. McClary and A. E. Ballantine took place on September 12, 1883, which allows plenty of time for a legitimate pregnancy. Nevertheless, Ena remained desperately unhappy, as she expressed in a letter to her cousin Mamie Timmons dated October 31, 1883, and finished the middle of November:

> My life is poor in purpose – broken and crowded with uncertainties. I, who used to be so sure of myself, never feel sure of anything now. I am glad to know that you are busy, "working" all the day and every day! May your strength to do it continue – it is the only thing that makes <u>life</u> possible. I am not as busy as I have been, and it is all the worse for me. I did not know what to do this winter. Our house is small, and I have to have just so many men. No room for a "hired girl," and Nora [a relative sent west by unknown kin in the south] and I could not do the work, so I decided at last to give up the ranche to the men (Mr. McClary has the business in charge) and three days ago moved down here to live.

She continued, "Am living in Mr. McClary's house – Coulter, Nora, baby and I. It is awfully lonely…" Then after several more paragraphs, she wrote, "What do you dream now? To dream is the horror of my nights now. I used to try so hard to dream of Mr. Ballantine but I have given that up. I rode up in sight of the ranche today but got homesick and turned back." In a November 15, 1883 letter to her friend, Mrs. Doane of Nebraska City, Ena again despaired that her life was "so hampered in a thousand ways – ways that Mr. Ballantine made smoother for me without my knowing it." Mr. McClary was not making life any smoother for Ena – at least not in the way Mr. Ballantine would have. Furthermore, this letter – two months after her marriage to McClary – and another in December are signed ~ A. E. B. (Annie E. Ballantine).

In the December 16, 1883 letter addressed to "My Dear Friend," Ena wrote: "Your kind letter was very welcome to me, yet I had no idea when reading your invitation that it would be scarcely possible to accept... I shall in all probability get Mrs. Garnisby to keep Nora

and come to you sometime shortly – this week or the first of next."
The next paragraph begins, "I am weary, almost into the weariness
of death of all the change and care and uncertainties that surround
me!" After several more sentences concerning the turmoil in her life,
the conclusion, "But my dear – what am I writing – pray excuse me
and only remember that we will see each other shortly, when we can
talk of all our hopes in the Ranche business, etc.," with the signature
~ A. E. B. Once again – where did "Mr. McClary" fit in? In the last
of Ena's letters known to exist, dated May 23, 1884, and again to
Mrs. Doane:

> How have you been all this long time and when are you
> coming out? We have things in a little better shape for liv-
> ing than when Mr. Doane was out; but really comfortable
> is a thing still <u>hoped for</u>! I have been miserably sick for a
> long time – am some better now but not at all strong yet.
>
> Have been busy with our garden. Raised a nice hotbed
> and have a fair promise of lots of nice vegetables this sum-
> mer. You can hardly realize the change that is going on
> around us.
>
> The whole country is alive with teams. The people have
> come en-mass and say they are going to settle the country
> solid…

Written in a day-to-day manner, this letter indicates that perhaps Ena was working through her sorrow and settling into her new
life as Mrs. McClary. It does seem, however, that the union between
Ena Ballantine and W. L. McClary was a marriage of convenience.
Ena's grief over the death of Mr. Ballantine was a constant if intan-
gible presence, and McClary's drinking didn't help matters. If the
McClarys' marriage failed to be fulfilling, it was soon of little consequence. Annie E. McClary died on July 13, 1884, from injuries
sustained in a runaway buggy or wagon accident. The date of the
accident is not known, but bills presented to the estate by Dr. J. A.
Gunn of Arapahoe, Nebraska, for visits he made on July 7, 10 and
12 indicate that Ena lived for at least a week. It is believed the baby
was buried in the same casket with its mother.

In his term as county judge, Wm. H. Allen established a reputation for being fair and thoughtful. In spite of the objections put forth by W. H. Miles and W. L. McClary, on August 29, 1884, the court recorded:

> NOW comes the above entitled matter to be heard on the objections of W. H. Miles and W. L. McClary to the appointment of George W. Ballantine as Special Administrator of said estate, and after hearing the proofs and arguments of counsel, said objections are over-ruled, and said George W. Ballantine is hereby appointed Special Administrator of the said estate of Annie E. McClary, deceased, and his bond as such Special Administrator is fixed at $10,000 – which bond as such administrator is filed by the said George W. Ballantine and approved by me, and I therefore issued to the said George W. Ballantine Letters of Administration of the estate of Annie E. McClary, deceased, this 29th day of August, 1884…

Judge Allen also appointed George W. Ballantine, the brother of David Coulter Ballantine Sr., as guardian of the children – Coulter Ballantine, age seven, and Anna Ballantine, age three.[6] Paddy Miles' objection to the appointment of George Ballantine must not have been particularly vehement, for Judge Allen appointed Miles along with County Treasurer John L. Sanders to appraise the real and personal estate. There were some small loans, store bills, and miscellaneous claims against the estate of Annie E. McClary; however, the bulk of the claims came from W. L. McClary, who was represented by his attorney, W. H. Latham. On February 26, 1885, Judge Allen ruled on a series of claims that had been made by McClary and which are summarized as follows:

• W. L. McClary filed a claim against the estate, "to work and superintend her ranch…" at $75 a month for 18 months for a total of $1350.

• W. L. McClary sold eleven head of horses on Sept. 8, 1883, to M. H. Clifford for $550 and sold another horse on Sept. 28 for

6 Although the daughter, Anna Ena Ballantine, was variously called Anna, Anne or Ena, the author has usually used "Anna" to avoid confusion with her mother.

$95 for a total of $645, which money was then used for the care and protection of the property now in the estate.

• W. L. McClary sold Annie E. McClary (then Ballantine) sixty-two head of cattle on May 6, 1883, for which she still owed him $450, sold her the rest of his cattle of that brand (twelve head) for $350 on Sept. 1, 1883, and sold her one mare for $60 to pay for hired labor, which left a total owed McClary of $860.

• Note for $1600 signed by McClary on July 30, 1884, (two weeks following the death of Annie E. McClary), which note he contended, "was actually made, executed and delivered by said McClary as Agent of the said Ann E. McClary in her life time and for her sole use, behalf and benefit." Total due McClary with interest $1639.84

Judge Allen took these claims under advisement and delivered the following terse ruling: "The whole of the above said claims are disallowed – excepting, $37.50 for labor dun [*sic*] after death of Annie E. McClary." McClary filed an application, "for an appeal from the decision entered against him…" On November 6, 1885, McClary's claim was again disallowed, however, with the following from the court:

> The Settlement this day made by the Administrator of said Estate in the case and claims of Washington L. McClary VS George W. Ballantine, Administrator of said estate, which claims amounted to about $4544.34 or thereabouts, by which settlement said administrator released and turned over to said Washington McClary certain property of said estate, now and for a long time in his possession *viz.* – a horse erroneously mentioned to administrator, one bed, bedding, bedstead – lounge and bureau…

Judge Allen had earlier disallowed the claim filed by Dr. J.A. Gunn for the three visits he made to Annie E. McClary before her death on the basis that "the services rendered were rendered to the deceased as the wife of W. L. McClary." Dr. Gunn also filed an appeal, which indicates McClary didn't readily come forth with the payment "as the husband of the deceased." Judge Allen was cautious

in allowing payment of claims against the estate of Annie E. Mc-
Clary. His concern was obviously that an adequate estate be left to
provide for the care of the minor children. George Ballantine was
authorized to spend "such sum of money as may be necessary for the
maintenance and education of said minor heirs, not to exceed $300
per annum for Coulter Ballantine and $200 per annum for [Anna]
Ballantine..." Only three years old at the time of her mother's death,
little Anna was taken into the home of Ballantine relatives. It is
generally believed that seven-year-old Coulter was passed back and
forth between McClary and Ballantine relatives.

Little more than a year following Ena's death – on October
28, 1885 – Washington L. McClary was married to Lillian Mae
Rummell at Indianola, Nebraska. Ten years following Ena's death,
eighteen-year-old Coulter Ballantine Jr. wrote to his mother's cousin
Mamie Timmons with queries of his own. Mamie responded in a
letter dated May 30, 1894:

> I am more than surprised at what you write me of Mr.
> McClary. I had no idea that he was that kind of man. I
> have a large package of his letters – wish that you could
> see them – he shows himself in different colors altogether
> – so good! – so noble! etc. I knew a little of him when I
> was West, but not much, and I was very much surprised to
> hear that your mother had married him. I didn't have time
> to realize that she was married before Herbert [Miles]
> wrote me that she was dead. Mr. McC. wrote me that she
> was paralyzed. I have never heard anything else, until now,
> from what you write.

> I do not wonder at anything that I hear of Herbert. I
> believe that he would be guilty of most anything – he is
> certainly a most wretched being!

Two years later, on June 22, 1896, Mamie responded to a letter
from Anna Ballantine, who was by then fifteen years old:

> Now, what is it that you want to know – what your
> mother's name was? Her name was Annie Palmer – spell
> it backwards and it is Einna Remlap – we commenced it
> in jest, at first, calling her Einna – after awhile we spelt it

Ena, and the name Annie was dropped forever. I always called her "Minna" – why, I do not know…

She was married to a Mr. Raymonde – I witnessed the marriage myself – after his death she moved to Nebraska with her mother and father. When your father met her, she was Ena Raymonde. It is so much the <u>best</u>, not to worry over what we do not know – your mother's troubles are over with now – let them rest!

The greatest sorrow that she ever had was your father's death – she was never the same after his death. I think that if I could of gone to her then, I could have prevented much after-trouble. I do not think that she would have married again. One thing you can be sure of; she loved you and Coulter, and she loved your father… Dear child, you are too young to think so much of these things, and I am wrong to be writing them to you. Think of the future and your dear brother…

Orphaned as young children, Coulter and Anna Ballantine had questions about their mother's death that apparently had never been answered to their satisfaction. In addition, there was the possibility that their mother may still have land holdings in Georgia. In her 1894 letter to Coulter, Mamie had asked if there were any homestead papers among his mother's papers. Writing that Ena did have land homesteaded in Georgia, Mamie added: "Herbert was anxious to find out something about it, and wrote me that if I had anything of the kind – deeds, etc., to send them to him – as they would be 'quite a curiosity.'" Two years later, on June 22, 1896 – the same day she wrote to his sister – Mamie wrote another letter to Coulter:

What is it that you wish me to tell you? You know I couldn't tell you anything but the truth, and I would hate to have to <u>refuse</u> to tell you anything. Don't you think that you would be happier to let everything rest as it is and not try to find out anything else? It is always best <u>not</u> to "stir a thing up"; it always makes it worse…

I asked a lawyer about this homestead affair. He says that homesteads are only given to the heads of a family –

if the husband or wife has it, it is good as long as they live, or to minor children if they die. It is out as soon as the children attain their majority, or 21 years, as it is made to protect the wife and minor children – that the papers, if found, would be of no value...

Everything connected with the land is so badly "mixed up," that it would be difficult to straighten. Your grandfather drank very hard – that is the secret of all the trouble... The cattle that they left with my father, they bargained away to J. W. Wallace as soon as they got to Brunswick...

Well, as I say, it does no good to stir these old things up – and it makes me sick to think of them. My dear child! I would let McClary alone and have nothing to do with him. I never heard anything at all about your mother's death – only what he wrote me that she seemed to be paralyzed.

McClary, though undoubtedly disgruntled with the estate settlement and bearing the reputation of being a scalawag, eventually stepped out of the arena of the Miles and Ballantine concerns. Young Anna Ballantine, by all accounts, grew to be a lovely young woman – well educated and a talented musician she, too, went her own direction. As he became an adult – and a complex one at that – it seems Coulter Ballantine Jr. was always spoiling for a fight with his uncle Wm. Herbert "Paddy" Miles. And what of Annie E. Mc-Clary's brother Paddy Miles? While surely not as "wretched" as Mamie Timmons portrayed him, Paddy could always manage to swing an old grudge around his head like a dead cat.

18

The Redemption of McClary

*T*he March 26, 1896 *Stockville (Nebr.) Faber* told the story in a nutshell: "W. L. McClary and Ira Shinley inverted a load of hay Saturday and 'Mac' crawled out with a damaged leg." So went the story of "Mac" McClary's life. McClary seldom crawled out of predicaments unscathed, but it seems he was able to shake off the dirt and get back in the saddle. An early arrival on the frontier, with a penchant for brandy, gambling, and women, McClary was a difficult fellow to peg. One old-timer declared that he "did not know what class to put him *IN*," but that "most everyone liked him with all his sins."[1]

Washington Lafayette McClary, the youngest of eight children, was born in Monroe County, Ohio. His date of birth is not entirely clear, with genealogical records giving the year as being 1851 while McClary himself made a note in his journal on Easter Sunday, April 18, 1897, declaring: "Forty-four years [ago] today I first saw the light of day…," which makes 1853 his birth year. Even if McClary hit the bottle a little heavy the night before, he surely knew his own birth date – but then again, maybe not.

Orphaned as a child, McClary was in the charge of his older sister Lydia for a few years, but after a quarrel with his teacher, he took off and headed west at the age of thirteen or so. The McClary family legend has him finding his way into an Indian tribe where he

1 William Shelley to Paul D. Riley, April 25, 1969, Shelley MSS.

was adopted as a tribal member. He spoke the Lakota or Sioux language fluently, and to the end of his life held a high regard and deep respect for the Indians. McClary's son Norman wrote that one of his father's treasured possessions was a hardcover "edition of the Holy Bible written throughout in the Sioux language."[2]McClary was involved in the usual activities of the frontier experience – principally as a buffalo hunter, trapper, and guide, and it was as such that he found his way to southwest Nebraska in the early 1870s. He filed a claim and with its proximity to the McPherson Trail, McClary's ranch became known as a place where news or information could be left or exchanged by those passing through the area. McClary platted the town of Stockville on his land using a lariat as his measuring tape. He seemingly moved about the country a lot in his early years on the frontier, and in one capacity or another he ranged throughout the territory that is now Kansas, Colorado, Wyoming, and South Dakota as well as western Nebraska. Again from his son:

> He was also a close associate of Wild Bill Hickok, well-known law-enforcer of that time. On the instigation of Wild Bill, he was in Deadwood, South Dakota, and but a block away when Bill was shot by Jack McCall [on August 2, 1876]. He was well acquainted with many of the people and incidents of that time. Many he held in high esteem, such as "Bat" Masterson, Doc Carver, etc., and many others (Buffalo Bill, General Custer, etc.) [he thought were] undeserving of the records credited to them.

Judging from McClary's reticence in later years to divulge information about his past, his claim to a connection with Hickok seems legitimate. He seemingly was not one to embellish his frontier credentials. It is also said he took part in the cleanup and burial after Custer's Last Stand near the Little Bighorn River in eastern Montana Territory in 1876. McClary's respect for Carver is notable given that he was also in the area and a contender for Ena Raymonde's attention during Carver's time on the Medicine. Given his proclivity

---

2 W. L. McClary's journals, genealogical & biographical information and personal observations of McClary's son Norman McClary are from the McClary Collection, NSHS (hereafter cited as McClary MSS).

It has been said that W. L. "Mac" McClary used a lariat as a tape measure when he platted the town of Stockville, Nebraska. He was the third and last husband of Annie "Ena" (Palmer) Raymonde Ballantine McClary. Photo taken circa 1895. *Courtesy Frontier County Historical Society.*

W. L McClary had a monument erected in Arbor Cemetary near Stockville, Nebraska, but was buried in Canada. The smaller headstone to the left marks the grave of McClary's brother-in-law William Hopton. *Photo by the author.*

for heavy drinking, gambling, and bedding women, McClary was in the same league as many of the legendary frontiersmen.

In addition to taking a turn as sheriff and county clerk, McClary was involved in a number of business ventures in Stockville over the years of his residence there. The McClary family history indicates he once acted as a purchasing agent for a Chicago packing plant, buying and shipping cattle to market. He was an ice dealer and kept at least one storefront on Main Street, but his most notable enterprise was as owner and proprietor of the Bald Eagle Hotel in the late 1800s. McClary's sister Lydia and her husband, Wm. "Bill" Hopton, moved from Ohio to Stockville, and Hopton was in on the ownership and management of the Bald Eagle Hotel. This establishment, the pride of Stockville, advertised itself as the headquarters for farmers and the traveling public. The Bald Eagle or "Baldy" and the attempts to sell it along with the headaches of maintaining it crop up in the journals McClary kept in the 1890s.[3]

McClary's life was often in juxtaposition with Ena Palmer Raymonde Ballantine's from the time he arrived in Frontier County until their marriage and her subsequent death in 1884. Yet there is stark contrast between the thoughtfulness of the young admirer as recorded in Ena's journals and McClary's apparent indifference to her death in the July 13, 1884 runaway accident. Bill Shelley's observation was that, "It did not seem to worry him to kill Ena in the runaway and abortion..." What appeared to be a callous disregard was more than likely McClary's predilection to let the bottle handle his troubles. There were too many years of shared experience between McClary and Ena for it to have been otherwise.

On October 28, 1885 – fifteen months following the death of Ena – McClary was married to Lillian Mae Rummell at Indianola. They were divorced seven years later at Broken Bow, Nebraska. The names of two women were reportedly branded with the "A" for adulteress in the petition for divorce. "Mac" McClary suffered intensely and paid dearly for his sins. He started keeping a journal following

---

3 Eliza Lydia "Lide" McClary was born in Monroe County, Ohio, in 1841. She married William Hopton in September 1865 and died in Stockville, Frontier Co., Nebr., on April 2, 1898.

the divorce but then destroyed everything he had written up until the middle of August 1892. In addition to the day-to-day happenings, selected excerpts from McClary's journal offer a glimpse into the heart of a man who suffered deep anguish before finally finding life again worth living. In addition to drinking from the cup of self-pity, McClary was also experiencing an assortment of physical ailments (he used a secret code for the segments appearing in italics):

August 25, 1892 –

Did not sleep any until the bell rang this morning… Talked trade some for the hotel – think I can make a deal.

August 26, 1892 –

Have not been feeling good. Sun has been shining all day, but it does not seem to shine for me. I see it and it is free for all, yet I do not seem to feel it. All seems dark and dreary!!!

August 28, 1892 –

Neuralgia in left side of my face – horribly swollen and very painful, but I am alone with no one but myself. What a dreary outlook to spend the balance of my days alone and then die by myself, but such I deserve and without complaint.

August 31, 1892 –

Half past twelve I was awakened by some noise at stable – got up and found I had a sick horse. Now I have a dead one. $200 more gone, and my larger team broken up. Such is life…

September 16, 1892 –

Went to the reunion at Curtis Wednesday and returned tonight. Met lots of the boys that I used to know years ago. Some from the Platte, others from White River, while some from Powder and Yellowstone River. People seemed to enjoy themselves quite well, although it was quite tame in many respects. The Sham Battle was almost a failure I thought. [A corresponding news item from the September 23, 1892 *Frontier County Faber* reported among other things that the different gambling devices on the ground attracted more attention than the campfire, a saloon was in full blast during the reunion, and "the woman who walked off the bank into the Medicine in the darkness was more scared than hurt."]

September 18, 1892 –

I feel that I am truly growing old as I had a tooth pulled last evening, and when we begin to leave pieces of ourselves along the road, we are preparing ourselves for the grave. I thought I would [let go of] them all together, but fate decreed it otherwise, but no matter – I brought no teeth into the world so if I lose them all will be in as good shape as I came in.

September 23, 1892 –

Found the people on the hill had left there yesterday, so I went over this morning – found chickens lying dead everywhere I looked – carried off all that was dead then looked all around for the cause of the wholesale slaughter. Finally Dawson came along. We cut one of them open and found nothing but corn in the craw – corn that had been cut off the cob. On examination it proved to be pickled corn. 'Twas the salt that killed them…

October. 7, 1892 –

Went to the place on the hill [where McClary and Lillian had lived]. Took all the papers out of the secretary. Made a thorough overhauling for a paper that I wished to find – had looked for it several times before – and found it. *It was a piece of poetry written by my baby Lill – I think, judging by a scrap of prose I find with it – last new years. It is this:*

> *"I have loved thee in life.*
> *I will love thee in death.*
> *I will love thee as long as*
> *God lendeth me breath*
> *And e'en when the death dew*

Is cold on my brow.
I'll love thee the same
As I'm loving thee now."

None can know the pangs of deep regret those lines sent tearing through my heart — nothing would quiet me until I took a good long cry.

Mrs. Shinley has returned. Says Charley is on the road and will be here in about four weeks. She wanted to live in the sod house until her husband [gets] in. I said yes. *Surely no one could suspicion her. I will risk it at any rate.*

October 8, 1892 –

Bought a pair of shoes today – price $5 – Almost the first thing I have bought all summer. Got one #9 and one a #8. They fit better that way.

No one can tell how much better I feel since I quit drinking...

Think my hotel deal has fallen through. Hear no more of it...

October 9, 1892 –

Every place I go, and every day I live makes me feel more blue. I never realized what it was to feel blue before... Could I but call back again our few short months, with the experience I have – how much different I could make my life.

October 16, 1892 –

Am going to bed as I did not have any sleep last night – was up all night *playing cards or poker. Am ashamed of it, nevertheless, it is a fact...*

October 17, 1892 –

Yesterday was windy and last night the wind was almost a hurricane. I went to bed but got so nervous and restless – had to get up – Walked about seven miles in the horrible wind...then I lay me down by the hay stack on Spring Creek *and prayed and cried until I fell asleep... Willingly would I give my life could I but repair the wrongs I have done thee my child* [Lillian]. *I long for thee, to be with you – but not in a selfish way that you might expect...*

October 18, 1892 –

Paid my real estate taxes – $94.06 – 'twas quite a surprise to me, as there was more taxes with less to be taxed, than last year. Think of it – paying more than $100 taxes and not money enough to buy a decent suit of clothes. Taxes growing heavier year-by-year, and the wherewithal to liquidate them growing smaller.

October 24, 1892 –

Mrs. Hopton and Annie are doing the work [at the Bald Eagle] now. Hop and Eva had a row Saturday...

October 25, 1892 –

Very pleasant and warm until late this evening – then it blew up from the North – cloudy and cold. Rained a few drops, but felt like snow... Hop has no girl yet, and Annie went home this morning but returned for supper... I helped make the mince meat for pies tonight...

Have been feeling strangely all day as though some change was going to take place. I wonder what it will be – whether for the better or worse. We cannot tell until those things come. Then we scarcely recognize the good from the evil – often taking the bitter for the sweet, for 'tis often that we cannot taste until we have chosen, and I am most always mistaken...

October 26, 1892 –

I ordered a monument today for my lot in the cemetery – but do not think I will ever be placed there. Do not know what to do *in regard to my first wife and our child that is buried up by Moorefield.* Want to get everything of that kind fixed up this fall, for I may never see the place again. I must do something for my Father and Mother's graves. As I remember them in my boyhood – they had nothing to mark them. I doubt if I could find them now though

The Enterprise General Merchandise store was owned by W. L. McClary at one time. Under a succession of owners and bearing many different names, the building was a landmark in Stockville, Nebraska, for many years. This photo may date to the early 1880s as there is not yet a building to the immediate south (left). *Courtesy Robert Van Pelt Estate.*

there are a few [people] left there yet who would probably know. I think that is all I care ever to see my old boyhood country for. Twenty-five years is a long time and many changes take place in that length of time.

Ah Time – Thou art the leveler of all things. Through thee, when thou art known by the Name of Death, we all meet on an even basis. 'Tis then we get our "chips" cashed in on an even basis. The game is at an end…

McClary's statement in regard to the grave of his first wife and child was his only reference to Ena's death. The next few entries, addressed to Lillian, are particularly poignant given that October 28, 1892, would have been their seventh wedding anniversary. McClary let down his guard in these lines and spilled out the anguish he would usually have concealed in code. Though he earlier claimed to have quit drinking, he apparently fell off the wagon for his handwriting became increasingly loose and fluid as the night passed into the wee hours of morning.

October 27, 1892 –

Tomorrow is a day I almost dread to see. How I will put in the day I do not know…You may have gone through what I am experiencing now, but I pray you may never have to do it again. With the setting of tomorrow's sun dies my last hope of you… I almost pray that I may not live to see the setting of tomorrow's sun – *Am I going crazy? I almost believe it – six months since you left…*

I am bankrupt and do not know that I can get "credit" to continue the business, yet this I can and will do. I will continue right along until "foreclosure" is commenced – will pay cash for what I do get, and as my main creditor would not get ten cents on the dollar (and the others nothing), they may give me a chance to get even…

October 28, 1892 (after 2:00 A.M.) –

Memories crowd upon my weary brain – or into my miserable head – so fast and furious that I do not know scarcely who I am… Oh! Vain regrets if you must come, why not come in time to save? I have been saved from a drunkard's grave but at what a sacrifice – how and for what…? Yet, I thank God, as well as thee, my child, that I have been brought to a realization of what I have done, of the confidence I have destroyed. I can look back now to many sleepless nights – nights of agony and suspense caused you…

I have wished to see you and do – 'tis the greatest wish of my life. But I do not wish to see you to annoy you or to try in any way to influence you from anything you think you want. I know you have a revengeful disposition – take your fill – gloat over it – get others to help you even though they are a thorn in your side forever after – anything to revenge yourself on me. *O, My God! What have we come to…?* It is now five o'clock [A.M.] of the 28th – the seventh anniversary of our [wedding day]. With today I shall close the book…

October 31, 1892 – And last day of the month.

My child, my sweetheart, my Baby Wife – must I bid you farewell forever? I miss you; I love you even yet… O' what a dreary waste my life is… Heaven forgive me – you will not…

On the first of November, the Rummells came for Lillian's piano. It seems her parents lived in Moorefield at the time, for McClary made several references to Moorefield in connection with the Rummells. Lillian had taken her personal items and with the moving of the piano, "almost the last trace" of her left the house.

November 14, 1892 –

Night before last I dreamed we were *again together and quarreled the first thing*…

Have bought no winter under clothing – don't think I will as I have only worn these three winters and [I will] try and make them do me for the fourth. Would be willing to *beg my clothes if I only had my debts paid*…

Sunday, November 27, 1892 –

Did not get up until 12:00 today. Then after dinner walked down to the Medicine Creek, then out south almost to the Cedar and all over the farm on the hill. I see the boys have been stealing my chickens quite extensively. They have been roasting them down on Spring Creek, so I am not [only] out the chickens but the wood they used to cook them with…

McClary's journal entry for November 28, 1892, inferred Lillian had taken up with another man and that she was being unduly criticized: "But if those with whom you have connected your life should abuse the trust and make your life worse than it has been heretofore, then Sweetheart, this vow that I register now 'to avenge you' will be strictly kept. I do not blame you – do not imply the same cause for your actions that others do, because I know you better…" He then questions his own strength: "I know that if I can keep my mind from the thought of revenge on those that have helped my downfall, I can in a few years do more than in a lifetime of experience of uncertainties…"

The last month of 1892 found the Bald Eagle still on McClary's list of problems. On December 12 he noted that Hopton had secured another woman to work at the hotel: "She has a small child with her. Do not think her help will pay for the annoyance of the child…" Then another dose of regret over the course his life had taken: "Memory – today drags me back over the past… There was so little in my childhood good to remember, and the rest of my life has been one long mistake…" He topped off the month with another runaway accident, which left him in even more misery:

> December 15 & 16, 1892 –
>
> I went to Indianola and McCook. Bought a few Xmas presents and started home from Indianola [at] 3:00 P.M., when going down to the Dry Creek, the team got the start of me and finally turned the buggy over. Since that time I have remembered little except the mutilated head and twisted neck. Frank Mc[Clung] was with me – he escaped with a skinned nose and general shakening up. He got me up to Whitneys' and he went to Stockville and sent Dr. LaRue over. Dr. pronounced no bones broken.
>
> December 28, 1892 –
>
> Don't know that I mentioned it, but Shinley and Jack Lynch are building quite an extensive livery barn here. They have it almost completed.
>
> December 31, 1892 – and last day of the year –
>
> I seem to improve so slowly. At this rate I will not be able to be out before spring. My face is almost healed up, but my neck and head still continue about the same – sometimes better and then worse. I got two presents [for] Xmas… Wonder if my life will pass out as quietly and peaceful as the old year?

At the age of thirty-nine, Washington L. "Mac" McClary was no longer the hot-blooded young carouser of a few short years ago. On New Year's Eve 1892, he was a man broken by love gone awry, nearly bankrupt, and still suffering the effects of the runaway accident. His sister Lydia as well as an unidentified friend had thoughtfully remembered him at Christmas. McClary jotted a few lines in his diary in January and February 1893 and then declared he must get away from Stockville:

> January 17, 1893 –
>
> Sold the place on the hill yesterday ($2550). It was with many a pang of regret that I let it go, but I felt as though I had to sell something or else let the Sheriff do it for me. <u>So she is gone</u>. Am getting better fast now – think I will go down to Jim Gammill's this P.M. Received letter from Broken Bow last night – *the divorce was granted the 21ˢᵗ day of June.*
>
> February 10, 1893 –
>
> I have indeed sold my place. I am now without home or friends. Think I will leave here by Monday, but do not know how long I will be gone or how far I will go…, but I must get away from here. Tomorrow night I will stand square with the world. No – but almost…
>
> February 19, 1893 –
>
> My diary, this will be about, if not the last, I will see of you for some time to come…Today I visited most all of the places having pleasant histories – was at the gulch, the park and have been walking all day…

McClary then left for a trip East to the land of his birth. He started a new journal and on March 21, 1893, wrote from a boarding house in Hunter, Ohio: "I find the landlord's mother is dead in the house, but there is no other [place] to go so will have to remain." A week later he had traveled across the state to Woodsfield in Monroe County. He did not like the country – specifically the muddy roads: "I want to leave here just as soon as possible. Have a mind to take my Father and Mother's remains up and move them west where they should have taken me before I was born, then I would never have known there was a country such as this." From Woodsfield, McClary hired a livery rig to take him as far as the old grist mills on Sunfish Creek. He then struck out on foot to visit the cemetery and to see what remained of the McClary home place:

> Am almost in sight of the Old Place – the place that gave me birth. Yet I have a mind to go back to the Station without going there. No one knows of me being here and I almost dislike to meet them. All that I cared for are either dead or else have left here…

> I am sitting on the steps where for the first time I asked a girl for the honor of her company home. I remember well the queer feeling I had at that moment – yet strange as it may seem, I do not remember the girl's name.

> Twenty-five years ago I was running around here looking like all boys of fourteen or fifteen – as though they knew everything worth knowing – and was only awaiting a chance to put their knowledge to usefulness for the benefit of mankind…

Less than a month later, McClary was back in Nebraska. While he hadn't cared for the mud in the East, the prolonged drought that held the Midwest in its grip was quite another matter. On the twenty-third of April McClary noted that he'd "had very little use for my rubber boots since I came to Nebraska…" Toward the end of May he queried, "I wonder if God could make a man out of this dust?" It wasn't until the end of May that the country received a good rain. McClary had bet another fellow that they would have a good rain before June 10, and on May 30, 1893, he collected: "Have my bet already as we have had a good rain and 'tis still raining. Everybody seems happy. Water is running down the street for the first time since last September." The widespread drought along with other factors had plunged the nation into a severe economic downturn, and on September 2, 1893, McClary reflected: "One would scarcely believe times are so dull and money so scarce as it is. I am wondering if we know how close times are in other places. And we have not seen the extent of them here. This winter is what is going to count…"

Apparently the excursion to the East did snap Mac McClary out of the doldrums, and with the advent of spring, he threw himself into gardening and planted 3000 hills of cabbage. McClary also stepped back into the mainstream of life and began keeping company with the ladies – several of them. Miss Whitaker and Miss Black, both young school teachers, took the risk of setting tongues to wagging when they associated with the twice-married man with an assortment of bad habits. But then, it was no secret that McClary had the ability to attract women:

May 12, 1893 –

Yesterday I went up into Lincoln County – visited Miss Whitaker's school or visited her. We drove down where her sister is boarding. Had quite a pleasant visit though I fear she will get a scolding when she gets home. How foolish and perverse people are. They are always contrary. 'Tis no wonder so many are driven from home.

May 14, 1893 –

Letter from Maywood – *Will have to go up there Thursday* – I am wondering what the people will say *about Miss Black going out riding with me – Enough though I suppose.*

May 26, 1893 –

Started to write letter to Maywood. Don't know that I will ever finish it or not, but presume I will whether I send it or not…

June 1, 1893 –

I am wondering again. Wondering what will be the result of my visit up the country yesterday. *There was no decision or conclusion arrived at yesterday… I bought a book – Campbell's poems – and took up for her.* Oh, what a wonder…

June 3, 1893 –

Miss Black did not get back tonight. I miss her more than I thought… Suppose she was detained on account of the rain.

June 5, 1893 –

Got letter from *Jennie B*. Had quite a shower of rain about half past four.

June 6, 1893 –

Got a letter from Maywood. Will have to go up there tomorrow.

The letter from Jennie B[annerman] on the fifth of June signaled a turning point. The correspondence with other women continued, but gradually they were winnowed out. Miss Whitaker seems to have fallen by the wayside by July, while Miss Black – McClary sometimes referred to her as M. E. B. – stayed in the running through August.[4] There were also sporadic letters to several other young ladies, and for a while indecision seemed to haunt McClary as he lamented, "*O, when will we be able to know ourselves!*" In due course, McClary knew. For reasons that weren't explained, Jennie Bannerman spent part of the summer in Greeley, Colorado. In early autumn McClary traveled to Colorado, though it isn't clear whether or not he got any farther than Holyoke:

July 3, 1893 –

Had a splendid visit while at Gothenburg and one that I shall never forget. Jennie crossed the Platte with me and I went part way up the river with her. Wonder what will be the outcome of this visit. I feel satisfied twill not end… but may end with an exclamation point!!! Time will tell, as it does all else.

August 28, 1893:

The mail has just came in and brought me two letters from Jennie – and in them – not a scolding, but some-thing – a lecture which I richly deserved for the letters I had written her. But …*she knows I did not mean* what I had written. Must write her tonight…

---

4 Mary E. Black died two years later at the age of twenty-four and is buried close to the McClary monument.

The storefronts on the west side of Stockville Main Street across from the courthouse. This photograph was taken sometime after 1904 as the belfry spire of the Congregational Church (built in 1904) is visible in the background. Under new ownership, the name of The Enterprise store has been changed to The Regulator. It is said that Paddy Miles once shot up the Phoenix Drugstore. *Courtesy Robert Van Pelt Estate.*

Oct. 1, 1893:

> Holyoke – This is Sunday in a strange town. 'Tis cold
> and windy. I will write a few lines to Jennie, can do no bet-
> ter than pass the day with her even though we are miles
> apart. I know she will be writing to or thinking of me –
> and I <u>think</u> she will be doing both...

On July 26 McClary had noted, "Coulter Ballantine came in
tonight. What a surprise it was to [see him]." Two days later Ballantine rode up to Curtis with McClary to see a baseball game between
Stockville and Curtis. Coulter Ballantine, McClary's stepson, was by
now almost seventeen years old, and although McClary's references
do not indicate friction between the two, there may have been a
lot left unsaid. Replies Coulter received in 1894 and 1896 from his
mother's cousin in response to his letters to her reflect a rocky relationship between Coulter and his stepfather. Needless to say, given
what would prove to be Coulter's skewed approach to life, the circumstances of his mother's death, and the resulting fight over the
estate, difficulties between the two were probably inevitable.

Reflecting on his trip East, McClary made the last entry in another journal:

Oct. 20, 1893 –

> This is the last record in this book. I commenced it the
> first day of March 1893 when I left Stockville for the
> East. I sometimes wish I had never gone; and still I do not
> know but what it done me good in more ways than one.
> Still there will always be something clinging to me from
> that trip. It is like giving children a glimpse of something
> unobtainable – creating an appetite for something they
> cannot have, then leaving them struggling in the surf...

W. L. McClary was married to Janet "Jennie" Bannerman on
February 6, 1894. About twenty-one years of age, Jennie Bannerman
was born in Walkerton, Ontario, Canada. Her original surname was
McPhail, but following the death of her mother, she was raised by
her mother's parents. It is presumed they met while McClary was in
the East. Jennie Bannerman married a man who had been broken

by his own recklessness. McClary didn't shed all his bad habits immediately, but having sown his wild oats, he now shouldered the responsibilities of a family man. In December of 1896 – nearly three years later – McClary took up pen and ink:

> December 1, 1896 –
>
> Almost if not quite two years have passed since I made any attempt to put down or keep track of passing events. Yes, it must be almost three years, for since that time I have married and can count two children – a girl and boy. We were married February 6, 1894, at Colorado Springs, Colorado.
>
> Our little girl, Irica…, was born April 26, 1895. I had been down in Indian Territory all winter. Arrived home the morning of the 26th. Had traveled for two nights – was feeling tired and sleepy. Went to bed and awoke only a few hours before our daughter arrived. She is now hanging on the side of the table trying to help me write…
>
> I used to tell the story of eating mush and milk out of an old yellow bowl together with a yellow pup. But Irica eats three times a day out of the same dish with her dog. He is a little black fellow named Boss.
>
> December 10, 1896 –
>
> [Our son] was born on the 21st day of August 1896 and named Bryan before he was ten seconds old… Ivor Bryan McClary. Now my dear boy, I want to say right here that your birth came very near making me a widower… We had a hard time for six weeks trying to pull her [Jennie] through, which we did at last. You did not seem to take much interest in the struggle, but seemed to be well pleased if you could only get enough to eat…
>
> Now my boy, when you grow up you must try in every way in your power to make up to your Mama for what she has gone through for you. Never forget that your mother is the best and truest friend you have upon earth – or that

you will ever have. Never fear to confide your troubles in her, and also to make hers as few and as light as possible.

January 25, 1897 –

Sister, I am wondering if you will remember the punishment I gave you tonight when you grow up. I do not see how we are going to manage to live with you unless we can induce you to change some of your habits. You are the most mischievous, contrary child I ever saw. You want in every drawer and box around the house. In fact, you <u>want</u> everything that you should <u>not</u> have and care nothing for those you could have… So far your Bro. Bryan has shown a very quiet, happy disposition, but I expect him yet to show his Canadian blood.

February 7, 1897 –

Mama seems sad and downhearted for some cause or other. Sister, I wish you were big enough to help and cheer your mother instead of being a continual source of worry and trouble. You will never know how much trouble you have been unless you have children of your own. You will then find that they are not <u>dolls</u> that you can throw away or pick up at <u>will</u> – but something that demands your attention no difference what else has to wait.

Writing to his children, McClary revealed himself as a dedicated husband and loving father. Another span of time and with his family on an extended trip – probably to Jennie's family home in Canada – McClary took solace in his journal. It appears he was residing at the Bald Eagle:

November 12, 1898 –

Will [Hopton] and I have concluded to keep the [Bald Eagle] hotel open until after court – unless I sell it.

November 18, 1898 –

Mama, I do hope [to] be able to get this place off my hands at once. If I fail at this attempt, I will close it at once… Mama, Mama! How I wish you was with me tonight. And the babies – I miss them, oh, so much.

December 11, 1898 –

Yesterday I went out into the country twenty miles to arrest one Patrick Kelley for trespass… [Sheriff] Bradbury was sick and did not feel like making the trip, and I know that I should not have gone. Got up out of bed tonight for the first [time] since I returned.

December 13, 1898, 6:00 P.M. –

Came in tonight and found the chamber work still undone. Washbasins and slop bowl both full and the lamps unfilled. If the present [managers] think I am going to do the chamber work for their guests, they will find themselves mistaken…

December 16, 1898, Friday night – About 2:00 the 17th A.M. –

The day past for winter has been beautiful, clear, calm and quite warm. During the early morning the smoke would rise straight up for distance of 100 feet, then lazily spread out until it formed clouds, which would evaporate and disappear.

December 18, 1898 –

Do not know what to think about putting up ice, as I am going to have my hands full next week. Hay to haul, corn to draw, and I expect…Shinley will want me to help haul away his wheat about next week. And besides it is almost impossible to do anything while court is going on…

December 25, 1898 –

Xmas and all alone… It has been a beautiful day – clear, calm, and very pleasant for this time of year… The last of the Old Year. How I wish we could have been together today – or tonight [to] commence the New Year together…

January 7, 1899 –

Well, Mama, we are moved… Hopton and Annie helped us, and I want to say right here that if you do not help to move the next time we will be apt to stay here the balance of our lives. We are in here but have not room to turn around and still have not all the things that we should have. But I intend to wait until you come home and see if you can find any place to put them. I do wish you was here tonight to spend with [us] the first night out of the hotel. We will continue to board [take meals] there until you return, except my midnight meal.

January 9, 1899 –

I made another trade with [R. D.] Logan. Traded him three lots for a colt and the use of his barn until the 1st of March next. Tried to make a deal with Biggs, but he is entirely off. I intend to try Frank Florom tomorrow, as I must have a wagon and cannot pay the cash for it.

Another year passed and once more Mrs. McClary and the children were away over the holiday season – something that McClary had hoped would not happen again. A brief note indicates they came home on January 20, 1900, which worked out to the better for McClary:

Thursday, December 12, 1899 –

I am sorry to say it but went up town and got a black eye – one that I fear I will carry when Mama comes home. I am sorry for it all Mama, but it is now too late to prevent it. It may prove a good thing yet – who can tell. I will keep it [ ] up in beefsteak tonight and try to draw some of the color out of it all I can. Can you, will you forgive me, Mama? I did hope you would be home tomorrow, but now I hope you will delay your coming for a few days.

A third child, Norman, was born in Stockville on March 25, 1904. The May 31, 1906 *Republican Faber* reported that McClary had built for himself a first class water-works system – with a 300 barrel capacity cistern on the hill west of town from which he could pipe water to his residence. By 1909, however, the McClarys had moved to Lewellen, Nebraska. It is there the twins, Wayne and Dorothy, were born on April 16, 1909. McClary farmed and ranched at

Lewellen for a few years, and in 1914 the family migrated to Canada, Jennie McClary's homeland, where he "ranched in the Caribou…"

The reflections of Washington L. McClary's son Norman portray a man who, matched with the right woman, learned from his mistakes. At about the time the family moved from Frontier County, McClary also quit drinking. Norman McClary gathered that in the later stages his father "would consume the greater part of a bottle of brandy before breakfast, and follow with many others through the day." When McClary quit drinking, he quit cold. His own reason was, "If I cannot control it, I neither need nor want it."

Largely self-educated himself, McClary accumulated a vast library of scholarly works over his lifetime, and it was from this collection that the McClary children received the bulk of their education after they moved to the remote back country of Canada. The children obtained only limited knowledge of their father's early years as it was against the decorum of the era to ask one's parents about such things. In describing the discreet questioning of their father, Norman McClary recalled that his father was "in no way given to voluntary recall and elaborate disclosure of past experiences or history." The older children, however, became "adept in ways of getting him started, such as starting an argument over some interesting incident or place, and then appealing to him for clarification." With astute and careful questions, the children "could sometimes keep him going for quite a time and [get] a lot of information."

Another observation by his son testifies to the fact that McClary did grow in character from having once been to the depths of despair himself: "He was deep natured and somewhat reserved with an understanding and quiet compassion for the weakness and frailties of mankind, and with rigid and unyielding personal codes, ethics and principles." McClary's daughter, Iraca – who her father had once declared would never know how much trouble she had been until she had children of her own – died in childbirth on November 3, 1920. Mac and Jennie McClary raised Iraca's baby daughter.

Washington L. McClary departed this life in Canada on April 6, 1938.[5] Jennie McClary, who was about twenty years younger than her husband, died in 1946. Norman McClary put forth one more query in the examination of the multi-faceted "Mac" McClary – once known as the rapscallion of Stockville. Considering that Jennie (Bannerman) McClary was a member of the proud, conservative Bannerman family rooted in the elite area of Bruce County, Ontario, Canada – "Question: How in heck did a sheltered virgin maiden come into emotional contact with a 'lone wolf' representative of the Wild West, whose home range was nearly two thousand miles away???"

---

5 Although he had a monument bearing the name McClary erected in Arbor Cemetery near Stockville, Nebraska, W. L. McClary was buried in Canada.

19

The Body in the Well

Thomas Jensen's remains might still be at the bottom of an abandoned well in southern Frontier County – his fate sealed forever by rotting layers of straw, manure, and other rubbish – had it not been for the suspicions and timely observations of several area residents. It was Tuesday, August 9, 1898, when a party from Stockville followed up on their hunches and journeyed seven or eight miles south to Knowles Precinct. As reported by the August 11, 1898 *Stockville (Nebr.) Faber*:

> J. W. Melvin, of this town, heard of Andrew Hawkins' hauling a load of manure two miles, from his place to the old A. Y. Lincoln place, and throwing it into an old well, and decided that it would be a good scheme to investigate. On Tuesday a party from here, accompanied by the county attorney, coroner, sheriff and *Faber* man, went to the well, which is located on the west half of the west half of section 12, township 5, range 27, on the east side of Knowles precinct, and young Frank Green went down.

> Four ten-gallon kegs full of dirt were taken out, then twenty-five kegs of manure, then four kegs of hay and the bare feet and trousered legs of a human body were disclosed. It was getting night and nothing else was done until the next day (Wednesday), when about 1 o'clock p.m. the body was raised to the surface. The corpse was fully dressed, having on also an overcoat, except that the feet

were bare, and the hat was missing. The shoes, however, were found in the well and were covered with rubbers. No hat was found, neither was the leather grip with which he was last seen. A notebook was found in one of his pockets, which contained a certificate of deposit on a Kansas bank for $2500 and a check on a Topeka bank for a large amount. The body was so badly decomposed that it was impossible to readily identify the remains, but probably the coroner's jury will endeavor to do this.

Frank Green, the son of the pharmacist at Logan's Phoenix Drugstore in Stockville, was the young fellow who accepted the offer of twenty-five dollars to dig through the putrid mess in the well on that hot August day in 1898. Spurred on by curiosity and the bravado of youth, Green no doubt took on the endeavor with enthusiasm. At one point though, as Green complained about the stench, Bob Richey and Dr. Parrott, the dentist, began giving him whiskey to induce him to keep digging. Green was more than ready to conclude his part in the mission when they finally pulled him out of the well, retching and vomiting all over the pasture.[1]

A widower in his seventies, Thomas Jensen was originally from the state of New York, but at the time of his disappearance he was headquartered in Beatrice, Nebraska. A dealer in real estate, he had become quite wealthy by buying up mortgages and making loans to the farmers. At various times throughout the year, Jensen would be in the Red Willow and southern Frontier County area for several months, traveling from farm to farm to collect debts. He was too frugal to hire a livery rig, so he walked from place to place unless someone gave him a lift. It was also reported – and this became an important aspect of the case – that he carried a black bag, which was thought to contain a substantial amount of money.

It was back in the spring when Jensen's son L. H. Jensen, who lived in Tacoma, Washington, became concerned after not having heard from his father in the customary length of time. Failing to come up with any clues to his father's disappearance from his own

---

1 Samuel Van Pelt with Introduction by James W. Hewitt, "All's Well That Ends Well: The Murder Trial of Andrew Hawkins," *The Nebraska Lawyer*, October 1998, pp. 16-18. Also William Shelley to unidentified recipient, Oct. 27, 1964, Shelley MSS.

The body of Thomas Jensen, a landowner and money lender, was found at the bottom of a well in Knowles Precinct in southern Frontier County, Nebraska, in August of 1898. *Courtesy Robert Van Pelt Estate.*

inquiries, the younger Jensen hired Beatrice attorney A. H. Kidd to conduct an investigation. Attorney Kidd came to Indianola about the first of June 1898, but after several weeks of diligent effort, he had accomplished little more than to narrow down the last sighting of Mr. Jensen, which seemed to be December 13, 1897. At that point, Kidd recruited the help of Frontier County Sheriff Bradbury, who suggested offering a reward for information, on the theory that rewards have a way of "loosening tongues." When word got around that a reward of $500 was being offered, anyone who had been associated with the missing man fell under an implied cloud of suspicion.

Over the next few weeks the combined efforts of the attorney and the sheriff put the focus of the investigation on one Andrew Hawkins, a farmer in his mid-fifties, known to be in debt to Jensen. Although he was married, his wife, Elizabeth Hawkins, also had a farm several miles away where she lived much of the time. Andrew Hawkins farmed both of the farms and lived back and forth between the two places. They had a fifteen-year-old son, Bert, and Elizabeth Hawkins had a daughter from a previous marriage. This daughter lived in southern Lincoln County and was married to William Conklin – one of the Conklin brothers who would figure into the case as it unfolded. Andrew Hawkins was illiterate, but he was shrewd and got by about as well as the general run of farmers. And while he was in the words of Sheriff Bradbury, "a mite scaly," the February 6, 1896 issue of the *Faber* reported that Andrew Hawkins and his wife had united with a neighborhood church following a series of revival meetings.

When questioned, Andrew Hawkins was tight-lipped, but he was fully aware that his interrogators knew he had been with Jensen on December 13. Hawkins acknowledged that Jensen had bummed a ride with him early in December but insisted he had let the old man off sometime in the late afternoon. The investigators did manage to get the names of Jesse Carroll and Emory Conklin as being the other two fellows who had been seen with Hawkins and Jensen. It took no stretch of the imagination to picture Carroll and Conklin involved in some scheme with Hawkins, as the opinion locally was

A typical sod house, this was the home of Andrew Hawkins, the man accused of murdering Thomas Jensen. *Courtesy Robert Van Pelt Estate.*

that they were cut from the same bolt of cloth. Emory Conklin, the brother of William Conklin, was an illiterate farmer living east of Stockville, while Jesse Carroll had lived with Hawkins for a short time before purchasing the A. Y. Lincoln land adjoining Hawkins' farm.

The investigators then looked into the financial transactions Hawkins and his cohorts had made since mid-December. It was found that Jesse Carroll's initial payment of $100 on the A. Y. Lincoln property had been made by Hawkins, with Carroll being expected to work for Hawkins to pay off the debt. Hawkins had also made a significant number of purchases in addition to paying off an old note in Bartley and a longstanding doctor bill in Cambridge. The Hawkins' buying activity at the small general store at Freedom had previously been small purchases made on credit, however, Frank Vernam, the proprietor, had noticed a shift to larger purchases made in cash since January. The farm economy in the Midwest in the late 1890s was tight, and the less prosperous farmers were generally mortgaged to the hilt, which cast suspicion on these sudden cash transactions. Several people had observed that Hawkins carried a large amount of cash with him. This apparent sudden affluence was suspicious but inconclusive, and Hawkins maintained the money was from the sale of his 1897 crop. Neither Emory Conklin nor Jesse Carroll, who had made the December 13 wagon trip with Hawkins and Jensen, had made any noticeable change in their spending habits.

In the meantime another event occurred that added a new twist to the investigation. Sheriff Bradbury received word that Hawkins, along with Emory Conklin and his brother Reuben, had made a trip to North Platte for no apparent reason. The three Conklin brothers, including Hawkins' step-son-in-law who lived about eighteen miles south of North Platte, were questioned individually regarding this trip. It took a certain amount of pressure, but in the end the brothers told essentially the same story. Hawkins had come up with a scheme to go to North Platte, a division point for the Union Pacific Rail Road and stopping off place for a large number of the hobos who commonly rode the rails in those days. They would locate an unidentifiable tramp, kill him, and bring him back to Frontier County where they would pass him off as the confessed murderer and collect the reward money.

Reuben Conklin was interrogated first and insisted that other than overhearing the proposal at Mrs. Hawkins' place, he had no further involvement in the plan. Emory Conklin admitted he went along on the trip to North Platte but only to try to keep Hawkins out of trouble. William Conklin, the last of the brothers to be questioned, added some almost unbelievable detail, saying that Hawkins "even had it figured he'd prop the stiff up in the wagon seat, stick a pipe in his mouth, pull a hat down over his eyes, and haul him home in plain sight." Conklin continued, "I was plumb scared he was loco enough to do it; maybe even kill one of us. That's why we all went along 'till we talked him out of it."[2] For whatever reason, the plan to kill a hobo was not carried out. After dropping William Conklin off at his farm south of North Platte, Andrew Hawkins and Emory and

---

2 "Wagon Ride to Death," reprinted in *McCook Daily Gazette*, July 16, 1965.

County officers as named below in front of Frontier County Courthouse at the time of the August 1898 coroner's inquisition and preliminary examination of Andrew Hawkins, the accused murderer of Thomas Jensen. *Courtesy Robert Van Pelt Estate.*

Left to right: Clerk of District Court Reed, Judge E. W. Pyle, R. D. Logan, Sheriff E. L. Bradbury, and County Clerk W. H. Wilson. *Courtesy Robert Van Pelt Estate.*

Rueben Conklin returned home. Though Hawkins did not know it yet, his would-be partners-in-crime were not sharp enough to keep even a crime never committed from working against him.

Another interesting bit of information had been brought to Sheriff Bradbury's attention. Mrs. Weikert, who, with her husband, ran a small general store in Stockville, hurried into Bradbury's office in Stockville one morning and informed him that Mrs. Hawkins had purchased some merchandise in the Weikerts' store the previous evening. Mrs. Weikert was having difficulty figuring the bill because she couldn't find her eyeglasses. She finally asked to use Mrs. Hawkins' glasses. Mrs. Hawkins handed over the pair of glasses, and Mrs. Weikert put them on and added up the bill. Mrs. Weikert had known Thomas Jensen very well, for he would often forgo the expense of a restaurant meal, instead purchasing cheese and crackers in the Weikerts' store. While Mr. Jensen was visiting and eating his cheese and crackers, Mrs. Weikert would sometimes use his eyeglasses. She told Sheriff Bradbury the eyeglasses Mrs. Hawkins was using in the store the night before were Mr. Jensen's.[3]

The clues, though each of them small in and of themselves, continued to accumulate and to point towards Hawkins. An undercover man operating under the guise of a drifting farm hand recommended the investigation of an old well in the canyon north of Hawkins' place. Other parties had also mentioned the peculiar straw and manure, rather than more substantial well-settled dirt, being used to fill the abandoned well. Jesse Carroll, who had purchased the land on which the well was located, was among those questioned about the unusual activity around the well. Though defensive, given the nature of the questioning, he did admit Hawkins discussing the issue with him, and insisting he was going to fill the well. Hawkins had also encouraged Carroll to fence the canyon road and post no-trespassing signs in order to keep out undesirable neighbors.

Though still not certain they were on solid footing, the party that went out to inspect the abandoned well on August 9, 1898, was fully prepared for the grisly discovery they found. Once the well

---

3 Van Pelt.

The unpleasant task of examining the remains of Thomas Jensen fell to County Coroner Dr. E. S. Case (left). Pictured in front of the courthouse with Dr. Case is R. D. Logan, proprietor of the Phoenix Drug Store. *Courtesy Robert Van Pelt Estate.*

was cleared of the fill material that had been dumped into it, the next problem was to raise the body without any further damage. Frank Green, who had already taken on the brunt of the dirty work, descended into the well again and decapitated the body with a corn knife. The head was then secured in a half-bushel basket padded with gunnysacks and raised to the surface. The rest of the body was brought out of the well in a makeshift sling.

While Andrew Hawkins, his wife and son, Jesse Carroll, and Emory Conklin were held as witnesses, Coroner Case immediately summoned six citizens to act as the coroner's jury. The body of the deceased man and the witnesses were brought into Stockville where the coroner's jury continued its work. Meanwhile, additional witnesses were called including A. Y. Lincoln, who lived in Iowa, but who had owned the farm where the body was found at the time it was supposed the murder occurred. Other than the land-sale transaction he had made with Hawkins, A. Y. Lincoln had little to offer as material evidence. He was no doubt greatly relieved when the attorneys for the prosecution requested the Faber print a public exoneration of any charges, as they were convinced Mr. Lincoln had no connection with the case. A rumor that had circulated to the effect that Hawkins had traded him Thomas Jensen's black bag and silver watch was found to be just that – a rumor.

The Conklin boys told the "killing the tramp" story; although, it took being recalled to the stand after Reuben had told the story before Emory coughed up the details of the proposed plot. They believed at the time that the reward was $6,000. According to the report in the August 25, 1898 issue of the *Faber*, when County Attorney J. H. Lincoln asked Emory who was to kill the tramp, he said, "Hawkins, I suppose." When asked how the killing of the tramp was to secure the reward unless Jensen's body was found, he said, "I asked Hawkins about that and he said, 'O, I'll fix that.'"

For his part, Hawkins claimed he only filled the well as a safety measure; he was unaware there was anything at the bottom. He passed the whole tramp-killing thing off as merely a joke that was immediately forgotten. On the evening of August 18, the coroner's jury returned its verdict, which *The Faber* – over the jury's objec-

Interested spectators converged in Stockville during the preliminary hearing of murder suspect Andrew Hawkins in August 1898. The view is looking north up Main Street. The windmill was located in the northwest corner of the courthouse square. The Citizens Bank and Cash Store are visible across the street to the north in the top picture. Note the open windows in the courthouse in the lower picture. *Courtesy Robert Van Pelt Estate.*

tions – published in full, explaining that it felt a full and truthful report would accomplish much good in counteracting the influence of false rumors. In a special dispatch to the *Omaha World-Herald* and reprinted in the August 26, 1898 *Curtis (Nebr.) Enterprise*, the content of the coroner's report was concisely worded: "The jury found in substance after a thorough investigation that Thomas Jensen came to his death on or about December 13, 1897, by blows upon the head, struck by Andrew Hawkins and other parties unknown." Indicating that a bitter legal fight was expected, the *World-Herald* also listed the legal counsel for both sides. W. S. Morlan and C. E. Eldred of Mc-Cook would assist County Attorney J. H. Lincoln in the prosecution, while J. L. White of Curtis and W. R. Starr of Indianola were retained for the defense.

A warrant charging Andrew Hawkins with the murder of Thomas Jensen was immediately sworn out, and he was brought before Frontier County Judge E. W. Pyle the following day. He pled "Not guilty," and the preliminary examination was set for the following week. Hawkins was remanded to the sheriff's custody, and a cognizance bond of $500 each to appear at the preliminary hearing was set for A. Y. Lincoln, Jesse Carroll, and the three Conklin brothers. The preliminary examination, held on August 26, 1898, in the Frontier County Courthouse in Stockville, did not reveal any new evidence of significance, but it was of immense interest to the crowd in the courtroom, many who had not previously heard any of the facts in the case. There was a large crowd in the morning, but an even greater crowd was present in the afternoon. The August heat was nearly unbearable, as described by the weekly edition of the *Faber* that hit the newsstands on September 1, 1898: "It was a hot day and the crowd surged forward, anxious to hear every word of the witnesses, unmindful of the efforts of the sheriff to secure working space for the attorneys, witnesses and reporters, until it seemed almost too suffocating to breathe." Unable to endure the heat, many of the spectators left the courthouse "to form groups on the streets engaged in animated and excited discussions of the evidence presented and of vague and, in most cases, groundless rumors with which the community is flooded."

Coroner Case described the position of the body in the well and the severity of the wounds – triangular and jagged with the bones mashed in and imbedded in the brain. He further confirmed the situation of the wounds would indicate falling in the well did not cause them. Dr. J. M. Parrott identified the false teeth taken from the body as being those of Mr. Jensen. The man who had sold Jensen his rubber over-shoes in December testified they could not have had more than fifteen miles wear on them, as the ink stamp was still visible. Robert Richey testified to meeting Hawkins last winter with a load of manure with which Hawkins said he was going to fill up an old well.

B. F. Sibbitt testified Jensen had told him on a previous occasion that he (Jensen) was afraid to go to Hawkins' place because Hawkins had threatened to "stomp" him if he came on his (Hawkins') farm again. This testimony was stricken from the record on grounds that Jensen's statements were not made in anticipation of death. Irvin Frizzell testified to being at Hawkins' place when Mr. Jensen called to collect interest, and that Hawkins refused and abused the old man and called him names. At the conclusion of the testimony, Judge Pyle decided the evidence was sufficient to warrant the holding of the prisoner to the next term of the district court for trial and remanded him to the charge of the sheriff until that time. In addition the *Faber* reported: "The recognizance of William, Emory and Reuben Conklin as witnesses was set at $800 each and that of A. Y. Lincoln, N. Portz, Chris McKinney and Irvin Frizzell was fixed at $200 each and all gave the required recognizance except Emory and Reuben Conklin, who were locked up in the town 'cooler.'" Following the hearing Hawkins was taken to the jail in Indianola, Nebraska, for safe-keeping, Frontier County having only a "cooler." If Hawkins was not appreciative of this accommodation, he should have been – as pointed out by the *Faber*:

> That the dastardly murder of Thomas Jansen [*sic*] has awakened public interest and aroused public indignation was fully attested by the immense crowd in attendance at the opening of the preliminary examination of Andrew Hawkins before Judge Pyle on Friday afternoon, and many quietly expressed but stern threats were heard as to what should and what would be done with the cold-blooded murderer should his identity be clearly established, and it is not improbable that short work would have been made of the guilty party had the evidence clearly shown whom he was.
>
> This is the second murder known to have been committed in this county, that of Eugene Sherwood, who was shot by Jonas Nelson nearly fourteen years ago, being the first, and Jonas Nelson's lifeless body was left hanging to

the limb of a tree on his claim in Lower Medicine precinct, at the scene of the crime by a mob.

The Conklin brothers, unable to come with the $800 bond and confined to the cooler, were in a more precarious position. The news item that appeared in the September 1, 1898 *Faber* may have been a cover-up for the attempted lynching of the Conklin brothers:

> Reuben and Emory Conklin, who were confined to the cooler until they could secure bonds for their appearance at the November term of district court as witnesses in the Jansen [*sic*] murder case, gave leg bail Sunday night. They effected their release by removing some of the bars from the window with the aid of a cross bar, which they twisted off from an inside door. Sheriff Bradbury recaptured them next day. They will be taken to the Indianola jail for safe-keeping.

In later years it was told that a so-called vigilante committee from Stockville took two brothers from the jail down to a little creek to scare them into a confession by hanging-by-degrees. The story is that the brothers were big and tough, and when one got his hands loose and cut the other loose, the committee scattered fast.[4] Apparently the fleeing lynching "committee" was a little slow on the take-off and ended up on the receiving end of the injuries. As the story is told:

> It was Mrs. Van Pelt who took kettles of boiling water to Logan's drug store when Logan and Dr. Case washed and sewed up the wounds of leading citizens of Stockville who took part in the attempted lynching of the Conklins prior to the Hawkins' trial. Like Logan and Dr. Case, she would never disclose the names of the Stockville citizens who carried scars to their graves as a result of this attempt to take the law into their own hands.[5]

---

4 Shelley, Oct. 27, 1964.
5 From biography of Sarah Van Pelt, believed to be authored by her son Robert Van Pelt. Date and publication information unknown. Robert Van Pelt Estate.

In the late 1890s Frontier County relied on a "cooler" (built of 2x4s stacked one on top of the other) or sent their prisoners to other counties. This photo, taken in 1986, shows the bars, which came across from both sides to secure the door. Two witnesses in the Jensen murder case escaped in 1898 by removing the bars from one of the windows. *Courtesy Frontier County Historical Society.*

(Note: Though it is not clear how he became involved, McClary's journal entries confirm that there was an attempt to lynch the Conklin brothers. On December 14, 1898, McClary noted: "Had quite a long talk with Mose Conklin. He says he will surely prosecute the mob provided they do not come to his terms. But it seems to me that he is bluffing." On December 27, after the trial was over, McClary wrote: "The Conklins are in town trying to compromise with the parties in the mob matter." The following day: "Mr. Conklin asked me to help him in settling up the matter…" On December 30: "Have been fooling all day with *Mose Conklin* trying to settle up that *mob deal.* Think that is all okay now or will be after tomorrow…" The next day, writing in code, McClary indicated he would have to go to McCook, Nebraska, "*to meet Mose Conklin and finish the terms agreed upon and see that he fulfills his part.*" Finally, writing from Room 9 of the Commercial Hotel in McCook on January 1, 1899: "*I came to watch old Mose Conklin out of town. And the state – with promises that he would not return – or allow his boys to do so. They are gone – leaving nothing but their promises behind.*")

Washington L. McClary and his brother-in-law William Hopton were the proprietors of the Bald Eagle Hotel in Stockville at the time, and McClary noted in his journal on November 12, 1898: "Will and I have concluded to keep the hotel open until after court – unless I sell it." Two days later McClary wrote: "District Court convened today. Hawkins and witnesses are here – it is not yet decided whether the case will be decided this term of court or next." On November 17, 1898, McClary wrote that court had adjourned until the thirteenth of December, when it was expected the Jensen-Hawkins murder trial would come up. McClary did not mention the trial again until December 11, 1898: "Morlan and Jensen was over yesterday – went down and looked the country over so as to be familiar with the surroundings when it comes to examining the witnesses."

District Court reconvened on Tuesday, December 13, 1898, with Judge George W. Norris at the bench. It was a year to the day from the presumed date of Thomas Jensen's death. The outcome of the trial was not a foregone conclusion as the evidence, though convincing, was wholly circumstantial. Andrew Hawkins maintained his innocence throughout the trial, though he offered no alibi or other theories to account for the evidence. The black bag in which the deceased man carried his money was never found. The only reported piece of material evidence that a murder might have occurred at the Hawkins' place had also disappeared. Jesse Carroll's wife revealed that while she and her husband were staying at Hawkins' place the previous January, Hawkins had asked her to wash a bloodstained comforter. The weather was bad, which would have prevented her from hanging the comforter outside to dry, so she had not taken on the task. That was the last the comforter was seen.

W. R. Starr, one of the attorneys for the defense, was rooming with W. L. McClary at the Bald Eagle. Starr was not the most reputable attorney in the area, but he was considered to be a very capable criminal lawyer. A heavy drinker, he was in good company with McClary, whose reputation for tipping the bottle was well known. McClary's position on the case was no doubt influenced by his close proximity to Starr. McClary's journal entries reflect the tension in the courtroom:

> December 15, 1898 –
>
> Starr and White are working a strong effort for Hawkins, but I think part of their testimony is slipping away from them, little by little. The other side has been doing more than people gave them credit for, too. It now appears as though they have had a "spatter" after every witness that testified, before the coroner's jury and at the preliminary examination. Some of others they have frightened until they are ready to almost swear Hawkins did the deed. So it is in order to save themselves from prosecution as they are made to believe.
>
> It is an old saying "There is honor among thieves." And there may be at times – at times, but not always – about as long as it will shield themselves. If one wishes to keep clear of suspicion, 'tis best to keep clear of bad company.

About 2:00 A.M. the 17th –

Starr just now woke up, and I asked him what kind of a case the State has made. He said, "I do not believe they would convict if we put in no testimony at all." (I should have mentioned that the State has rested their case.) I promised him I would go over and watch the jury awhile tomorrow and give him my opinion of them [the jurors] individually.

(Later the same day): Somehow, I do not like to see Hawkins convicted. While I think he knows and probably committed the deed, I do <u>not</u> think he was the instigator of it. There is someone else into it as deep, or even deeper, than he.

While Starr was overly confident, McClary echoed – to some extent – the sentiment of others in the community. Hawkins was not of exemplary character, but many were reluctant to believe he would commit murder, and it was generally believed that Mrs. Hawkins had done the planning. And while he continued to insist he had not committed the deed, Hawkins did not implicate his wife or anyone else; no one else was ever indicted in connection with the crime.

It was after midnight – the very early morning – of December 20, 1898, and the occupants of McClary's room in the Bald Eagle had not yet retired as McClary noted: "Starr and I have been sitting here talking for a long time, and Starr had just gone to bed when Bradbury came in for him to go over – said the jury has come in with verdict. They have all gone over. Poor fellow – I know it is guilty." The jury of twelve citizens of the community did, indeed, find Andrew Hawkins guilty of murder in the first degree. Court was adjourned until eleven o'clock the next day in order to give the defense attorneys time to prepare a motion for a new trial. As had been the case throughout the trial, the courtroom was crowded by the appointed time. District Court Judge George W. Norris had his own distinct memory of the occassion:

Just as the attorneys for the defense finished their motion, the sheriff came into the room, took the defendant by the arm, and led him into the clerk's office without

The courtroom (top) in the Frontier County Courthouse has changed little in 120 years. District Court Judge George W. Norris was at the bench when he narrowly missed taking a bullet from the accused in the 1898 murder trial of Andrew Hawkins. Countless hands have gripped the banister (right) of the stairs leading to the courtroom on the second floor of the historic courthouse. *Photos by Gail Geis.*

saying anything to me. Shortly after, he brought him back. I overruled the motion for a new trial and sentenced Hawkins to the penitentiary for life.

Later, I asked the sheriff why he had taken the man [Hawkins] out of the courtroom without asking permission. He reached into his pocket and pulled out a .38-caliber revolver with just two loads in it.

"That is why I took him out," he said.

Apparently someone had given Hawkins the gun… He sat not more than six feet from the elevated bench. He knew that if he killed me, he would be mobbed, and he had a second load in the gun for himself.[6]

Andrew Hawkins was sentenced to life imprisonment at the Nebraska State Penitentiary where he became prisoner number 3385.[7] The fate of one man has an effect on his fellow man, whether it is in a negative or positive manner. Still, once that effect has been acknowledged, each man must then get on with his own life. Washington L. McClary was affected by the trial of Andrew Hawkins, but he had his own concerns. McClary made his final comment on the trial from his room at the Bald Eagle Hotel on December 21, 1898:

A stealth-like stillness roams over the house tonight. Court is over and everyone has gone home.

Hawkins was sentenced to the pen for his natural life and has been taken to Indianola until next Saturday when they expect to take him to Lincoln.

When I got up this morning, I found it raining. The rain soon turned to snow, but broke by noon and tonight the stars are shining bright as ever.

---

6 George W. Norris, *Fighting Liberal*, (New York: The Macmillan Company, 1945), pp 75-76.

7 Affidavit of Andrew Hawkins, Feb. 10, 1912. In this affidavit, Hawkins implicated several other people, including Jesse Carroll and two of the Conklins. He portrayed himself as a bystander who knew full-well that murder had been committed, but who had taken no active part. The records of the Nebraska Department of Corrections as quoted by Jason Strong in "A Mysterious Murder in Frontier County: The Andrew Hawkins Murder Case," show that on Nov. 23, 1913, Andrew Hawkins was placed on parole.

20

Coulter Ballantine Jr.

ituated at the very tip of a gently sloping divide, Sunset Point Cemetery overlooks the Medicine Creek Valley in southwest Nebraska. It was here, on a cold December day in 1959, that Coulter Ballantine Jr. was buried. He had departed this life the day before Christmas at the age of eighty-three. Almost immediately, Coulter Ballantine became a part of the folklore of the Medicine Creek Valley as had his mother, Ena Palmer Raymonde Ballantine McClary, and his Uncle Wm. H "Paddy" Miles of Wolf's Rest. If the spirit of Coulter Ballantine haunts the Medicine Creek Valley today, is it the bronzed young man with finely sculpted features wearing a fawn-colored felt hat and mounted on a spirited stallion? Or is it the cantankerous Coulter who put the spurs to his horse as he and Paddy Miles shot at each other up and down the creek? Perhaps it is the wild eyed, eccentric old man, driving a herd of unbroken horses down the road, frightening anyone he chanced to meet. When did the shroud of legend envelop the reality of the life of Coulter Ballantine Jr.?

David Coulter Ballantine Jr. was born in North Platte, Nebraska, where his mother spent the last few weeks of her "confinement." Ena Ballantine noted the event in her journal: "August, Monday night, 21st, 1876 – our baby was born. The papers spoke of him as a 'beautiful, ten pound boy.'" Though he eventually took his father's name – David Coulter or D. C. Ballantine – the family Bible gives his name as being Coulter Bertram Ballantine. Ena took time a year later to note her son's first birthday: "Our baby's birthday! One-year-old today! Our precious, beautiful boy! Our dearest measure on earth!" A few weeks earlier, baby Coulter had exhibited a developing affinity for horses. Ena recounted the incident in her journal: "Baby gave me a fearful fright today – got out of the house and was under my horse's feet, almost, when I found him."

By the time baby Anna Ballantine was born on February 24, 1881, her father had been elected as a senator to the Nebraska State Legislature and had moved his family to Lincoln. That same year, Ena Ballantine and her children escaped the Nebraska winter and visited her homeland in the Deep South. Years later, a relative wrote of this visit to the South. She recalled:

> Coulter was a fine, bright boy, and very large for his age. He had very large ideas also, and when playing built "railroads" around and among the orange trees, and planned largely for the future. He… proposed that I should <u>marry him</u>, and go West, where he said that he "would build railroads and cities and also plant orange groves there!" My mother often remarked that he did not think in small groves.[1]

Following their return in the spring of 1882, Ena and the children were again living on the ranch near Stockville. Mr. Ballantine attended to his duties as a state senator and also traveled back and forth between the ranch and Denver as a cattle buyer. It was on a cattle buying trip that the accident occurred that would forever change the lives of Ena Ballantine and her children. The *Indianola News* reported: "Senator David Ballantine, with headquarters on upper Medicine Lake Creek shipped cattle from Benkelman and in attempting to board the moving train, fell under the cars. The stock train was given special rights to McCook and made a non-stop run, but he died on arrival there."[2] David C. Ballantine Sr. left his widow with two small children. In the months that followed, Ena often mentioned the children in her letters. She described Coulter

1 Ola Mattlette to Anna Ballantine, April 21, 1912.
2 Sutton, p. 60.

David Coulter Ballantine Jr. as he looked at the time of his marriage in 1895. Photo was probably taken when he attended college in Boulder, Colorado. *Courtesy Nebraska State Historical Society.*

as being a "big, rough boy," and on another occasion she described the children's playing church: "Coulter is a great preacher – congregation consists of Nora [the hired girl], Austin (my house-keeper's little boy) and baby Ena…Coulter is very Orthodox – if you are good you go to Heaven, if bad, to Hell."[3]

The grieving young mother was united in marriage to W. L. McClary in September of 1883. Ten months later she met an untimely death as the result of a horse and buggy accident. The death of Annie Ena McClary on July 13, 1884, left the Ballantine children orphans. George W. Ballantine, the children's uncle, was appointed administrator of Annie E. McClary's estate as well as guardian to the children. By all indications, he was a responsible and diligent guardian, who held the children's inheritance together while assuring there was provision for their education and other needs.

Three-year-old Anna was raised by Ballantine relatives, but it is believed that Coulter was passed back and forth between the Ballantines and his step-father, W. L. McClary. Little more is known about the childhood of Coulter Ballantine Jr., but the scenario can be imagined. McClary remarried shortly after the death of the children's mother, and that marriage was fraught with difficulty. If McClary was drinking and carousing, it is doubtful he was particularly attuned to the needs of a young boy who had just lost both his parents. The growing boy may have been little more than cheap labor to McClary. And while the Ballantine relatives no doubt doted on the cute little Anna, they may have been at a loss when it came to raising Coulter Jr. While the children weren't parceled out like so many heads of cabbage, Coulter may never have felt as though he belonged anywhere. It is known that as an adolescent he attended the Davenport Academy, a military preparatory school in Davenport, Iowa.

As a young man, Coulter matriculated at the University of Colorado at Boulder where he took business courses. He met his future wife, Jemima "Mima" Leach, either at the university or while working for his Uncle George Ballantine, who was at that time affiliated with the Denver Union Stock Yards. Coulter Ballantine Jr. was not

---

3 Ena Ballantine to Mamie Timmons, May 22, 1883.

yet nineteen years old when he married the pretty twenty-one-year-old Mima Leach on June 2, 1895. Coulter's marrying at a young age suggests that his inheritance along with working for his uncle had given him a measure of financial stability. It can also be assumed that after years of being somewhat displaced, Coulter was anxious for the security of his own home – something and someone that belonged to him. Around 1900 Coulter and his wife moved into the sod house on the place his mother had referred to as the "Lower Ranche" on the Medicine Creek.

Legal wrangling started even before then. In April of 1899 Nellie Miles sued Coulter and his sister for $250 plus interest (Coulter eventually bought out his sister's share in the land). The Miles apparently attempted to seize a parcel of the Ballantine property to settle this debt, for the October 19, 1900 issue of the *Curtis Enterprise* reported the "Case of Miles vs. Ballantine, attachment proceedings, was dismissed after the jury was empanelled."

The tables were turned in another suit reported in the same issue of the *Enterprise*: "The case of Ballantine vs. Miles ejectment proceedings from real estate was tried before a jury and decided in favor of the plaintiff and damage in the sum of $85 was awarded plaintiff for damage for retention of the land." This decision was apparently appealed before the Nebraska Supreme Court. In the brief filed before that court W. S. Morlan, the attorney for Coulter Ballantine Jr. and his sister, noted the contradiction of Miles' testimony: "Reference is made…to the testimony of Mr. Miles that he paid the $50 to keep [Jacob] Walker [a tenant] away; that is he paid $50 to keep Walker off of property that year, when at the same time he swears that it was not worth more than $30 a year." This brief also noted the previous decision of the court: "William H. Miles was WRONGFULLY in possession of the property and that the defendants in said case should recover the same."[4]

It seems there was an on-going animosity between Paddy Miles and Coulter Ballantine, as the old-timers recalled them riding up and down the creek shooting at each other. These disputes continued

---

4 Supreme Court of the State of Nebraska, No. 12320, Error to District Court of Frontier County, Brief of Defendants in Error, Ballantine MSS.

even after Paddy Miles moved to California. The January 15, 1904 issue of a Curtis newspaper reported under County Court Affairs: "The preliminary hearing in the case of the State against Coulter Ballantine for destroying fence around a cemetery was held Tuesday. W. H. Miles is the complaining witness. The defendant was bound over to the District Court in the amount of $300." Sunset Point, the family cemetery, was surrounded by land owned by Coulter Ballantine, but there is no explanation as to why he destroyed the fence. Most likely he was trying to eke out a little more grazing for his cattle, but he may have been avenging some grudge against his uncle. Coulter was not as wild a canon as his Uncle Paddy Miles, but he was every bit as ornery.

Another legal issue that consumed a great deal of Coulter Ballantine's energy and contributed significantly to his eventual indebtedness was his battle against the straightening of Medicine Creek. Around 1910 there began to be talk of moving the channel of the Medicine Creek to eliminate some of the loops and bends. The railroad was anxious to reduce the number of trestles needed to cross the winding creek, but it was the landowner who stood to gain the most. Crop growers on the bottomland had the advantage of sub-irrigation, and straightening the creek would give them the opportunity to develop larger fields. Although the majority of landowners between Curtis and Cambridge were behind the proposed plan, Coulter Ballantine fought it tooth and nail. Recognizing the increased likelihood of flooding as well as a decrease in the sub-irrigation potential, he retained legal counsel and put together a comprehensive and forceful argument for an injunction against the implementation of the project. Coulter was unsuccessful in his fight, however, and the Medicine Creek was straightened in the early 1920s.[5]

Regardless of his legal difficulties, young Coulter envisioned himself following in the footsteps of the Ballantine men. His father had been a successful business and cattle man, and his uncle and mentor, George W. Ballantine, was president and general manager

---

5 Unknown entity to D. C. Ballantine dated Aug. 25, 1914.

Jemima "Mima" Leach as she appeared at the time of her June 2, 1895 marriage to Coulter Ballantine Jr. *Courtesy Nebraska State Historical Society.*

of the Denver Union Stock Yards.[6] The relative from the south, who years earlier declared that Coulter "did not think in small groves," predicted his ambitions accurately. Coulter Ballantine was intent on building a cattle empire come hell or high water – and in time both hell and high water did come. Coulter was single-minded in purpose, and all else was seemingly sacrificed as he expanded his herd. Pulling in the same harness, his wife, Mima, did her part. In addition to the usual housework and cooking, she set the hens and raised the baby chickens, fixed the fence, repaired the outbuildings, and cared for the baby calves as well as a myriad other tasks around the place. While the neighbors were building frame homes, the Ballantines lived in the sod house Coulter's parents had built years earlier. Eager to supplement the calves he raised, Coulter traded firewood for calves in the early years although this method did not always meet with the approval of all parties involved. Perhaps Ed Nelson had made a deal with Coulter Ballantine to trade a load of firewood for the calf – perhaps not. Whatever the case may be, the Nelson children had played with and grown quite fond of the calf in question. Ed Nelson was not at home when Mr. and Mrs. Ballantine drove up one day, dumped off a load of firewood and started to take the calf. At this, the children started to scream and yell, so Coulter got down on one knee and talked to them. He explained at length how much happier the calf would be if it were allowed to run free out in the pasture with other cattle. Once the children were quieted, Coulter made off with the calf. The children's mother, Garnette, later recalled that from that time on she knew who Coulter Ballantine was.[7]

The Ballantine cattle business – High Line Breeders – eventually achieved a degree of success though it never became an empire and

---

6 George A. Carlson, Governor of Colorado, was among those giving toasts at George W. Ballantine's retirement as president of the Denver Union Stock Yard Company on Jan. 30, 1915. George Ballantine's son, Norman S. Ballantine, a year younger than Coulter Ballantine Jr., was the founder of the Ballantine Land and Cattle Co., one of the largest stock-raising yards in the western United States. According to his obituary, Norman Ballantine also acquired and operated extensive mining properties in Colorado and located and patented a 12,000-acre tract of oil shale land in eastern Utah. He was president of the Mountain States Rubber Co., manufacturer and distributor of mechanical rubber goods which produced the first automobile tire.
7 Garnette Nelson.

Shortly after 1900, Coulter Ballantine Jr. (center) and his wife, Mima (wearing hat), returned to the sod house his parents had built on the "lower ranche" in the early 1880s. The identity of the other couple is uncertain, but it may be Paddy and Nellie Miles. *Courtesy Nebraska State Historical Society.*

may never have been on truly solid footing. Coulter's first registered cattle were shorthorns, but he later switched to registered Herefords. The business undoubtedly reached its peak during the 1920s when cattle prices were good and before the stock market crash of 1929 wrecked havoc on the nation's economy. By this time a number of the cattle on the Ballantine range were the progeny of Beau Mischief, the famous Hereford bull belonging to the Mousel brothers at Cambridge. It is said that at one time buyers from Chicago and Denver came to Coulter Ballantine's well-advertised sales.

In addition to the Great Depression that affected the entire nation, the 1930s also brought severe drought and the resulting Dust Bowl, which further depressed the economic stability of the Midwest farmer and ranchman. With the specter of debt already at his door, Coulter Ballantine's operation saw a consistent decline during those difficult years. His reason for having his wife declared insane and being named her guardian in 1932 was for the purpose of securing control of her interest in the land so he could sell off a quarter-section. The only D. C. Ballantine Hereford sale catalog known to exist is for the sale held on December 6, 1937. By this time the business had taken a number of hard hits, and Coulter had been forced to sell some of his herd to meet financial obligations. While the catalog was professionally produced, and most of the "9 Bulls" and "31 Females" described still carried the Beau Mischief bloodline, the breeding stock offered was marginal at best and would not have attracted buyers from a distance.

It was during this time period that Coulter Ballantine wrote lengthy letters seeking help from elected officials. He was still fighting the battle as he wrote to United States Senator George W. Norris on May 11, 1939:

> I am at this time taking the liberty of writing to you pertaining to my own case of trying to keep the Federal Land Bank of Omaha from entering a decree of foreclosure of mortgage on my land, livestock and machinery. I am hoping at least to save…my farm home or enough of it that I will not have to quit farming as you know farming and stock raising has been my life business continuously on this place for 38 years, and a fellow don't like to be driven from the home he has become attached to after these many years, neither can he stand to take the whip of threats of foreclosure that are handed to him apparently to make him dig, when it is impossible for him to do so and continue to operate.[8]

With a Federal Land Bank first mortgage on his land and a second mortgage on his livestock and machinery, he wrote: "A person cannot…butcher a hog without taking mortgage property." Less than a week later, on May 16, 1939, Senator Norris replied: "This is a matter entirely outside of my control… Nevertheless, I am taking this matter up with the proper officials in the Farm Credit Administration…" In June Senator Norris received a letter from an official with the Farm Credit Administration outlining their position:

> The land bank has carefully considered the information regarding the borrower's farming methods and the system of management employed, and it has reached the conclusion that further forbearance on its part would result only

8 All letters to or from Coulter Ballantine Jr. in this chapter are from the Ballantine MSS.

This undated photo titled "hunting camp" shows the Ballantines and friends in a light-hearted mood. Coulter is seated center holding gun, and Mima is to the far right. Others are unidentified. *Courtesy Nebraska State Historical Society.*

in further delinquencies. It is reported that the farm is not being operated at reasonable capacity, and with the handicap of a heavy outside indebtedness, the bank feels that the situation is now such that it should no longer delay the consideration of foreclosure. [9]

Still fighting to hold off foreclosure, Coulter Ballantine appealed to Carl T. Curtis, the United States Congressman from Nebraska in a September 22, 1940 letter:

320 acres of this farm were my parent's homesteads of 1871 and 1875... I live moderately...; farm with horses and do not owe any finance on car or machinery... On account of lower prices, floods, cyclone, grass hopper and drought conditions, about everything that could happen since 1929 – most of which you know about. Also two bank failures... Last November 20 I got a nine-months stay hoping to be able to reinstate myself. But this year with poor pasture...two floods and two hail storms left

9 H. A. Lake, Assistant Deputy Commissioner, Land Bank Division, Farm Credit Administration to George W. Norris, June 10, 1939, Ballantine MSS.

me without crops except what feed grew after the last hail storm… I wish for another year's stay here to save my home for my wife and self and without losing title to the land, as I have a deep pride in retaining my parents homestead, and if I can't save the 720, I would like to have a chance to save half of it… P.S. This land is advertised to be sold Oct. 7, 1940.

Congressman Curtis replied in a letter dated October 5, 1940: "The farmers of Nebraska can stand one or two years of crop failures, but when it persists for so many years, things happen entirely beyond their control… Unfortunately, I know of no possible government loan or other assistance that would…stop this foreclosure." Coulter Ballantine was able to save a portion of his land but lost the home site. He then relocated to a site on the north side of the Medicine, where he moved in a frame house and situated it on a cement foundation built into a bank with two walls exposed. The frame portion of the home, however, was never finished off, and it was not connected to the lower level with a stairway. While the upper level was used primarily for storage, Coulter and Mima lived in the lower level. Still with no electricity, they heated with wood and used a kerosene lamp for light. Their water came from a hand-pump just outside the kitchen door, and a privy stood out back. Though they never had a telephone, they did have one luxury – a Victor phonograph and a large number of records.

Mima Ballantine was showing signs of mental instability as early as 1905, and by the 1920s she slipped in and out of "spells" or episodes of losing touch with reality. For his part, Coulter continued the shooting up and down the creek. Sometimes he was expressing his aggravation with a neighbor; more often than not he was only shooting over the head of someone who was hunting on his property. With the undercurrent of suspicion that Mima was a little off, it is no wonder the Ballantines created a stir when they went into town in a horse-drawn cart. One fellow remembered that as a young boy growing up in Curtis in the 1920s, Coulter and his wife "scared the hell out of him and that all the kids would stay off the streets until the Ballentines left town."[10]

The neighbors thought it somewhat out of the ordinary when Coulter Ballantine took a baby calf in the house and tied it to the bedpost. But then it has also been said that he sometimes tied his wife to the bedpost. On July 18, 1932, the Commissioners of Insanity of Frontier County, Nebraska, adjudged Mima L. Ballantine to be insane and mentally incompetent. It was stated in Coulter's petition for guardianship that Mima had been insane "for more than three years last past" and was a patient at the Asylum for the Insane at Ingleside, Nebraska.[11] Although Mima was institutionalized more than once, these confinements were for fairly short periods of time. By the mid-1930s, Coulter no longer took Mima out in public. For the most part Coulter kept his wife at home, and no doubt he did eventually devise ways to restrain her. Though it is believed he usually locked her in the house, he may very well have tied Mima to the bedpost or a fence post at times. On occasion he had someone come in and stay with her when he had to leave the place for an extended length of time.

And Coulter did leave the place. Besides the essential trips to conduct business, Coulter nearly always went to the saloon or to a dance – or both – on Saturday nights as long as he was able. Remembered by anyone who ever met him, Coulter presented a strong visual impression and was generally described as being colorful. With his highly defined facial features and dark complexion, many incorrectly believed him to be of Native American descent. He wasn't tall in stature, but he was quick and wiry. He wore a broad-brimmed hat and always wore a kerchief at his neck – a colored one during the week and a white one on Saturday night. There are women alive yet today who remember dancing with Coulter Ballantine, and he was described as being "a magnificent dancer."

Subject to the influence of the bottle throughout his life, Coulter was no doubt "on the sauce" when the Saturday night trip into

---

10 Leonard Carlon, as quoted by Steve Herman in unpublished manuscript, circa 1973.
11 The petition for guardianship is an exhibit on file in a land abstract. The Ingleside Hospital for the Insane is now the Hastings Regional Center at Hastings, Nebraska.

town put his name in the November 20, 1903 *Curtis Courier*: "A little disturbance occurred Saturday between John Cunningham and Mr. Ballantine on the street. No serious injuries followed and peace again reigns." Coulter inadvertently taught one sharp-eyed young fellow the value of a bottle of bootleg booze during Prohibition some twenty years later. Kenneth Phillips, a freshman in high school, was sitting at the soda fountain counter in a Curtis drug store in the 1920s when Coulter and the druggist came out of the back room. Seeing that he was being observed by the young fellow at the counter, Coulter ordered something – a soft drink or malt – and handed the druggist a five-dollar bill. The druggist gave him a few cents change, and Coulter left with a bottle in his pocket. The price for the whisky was fairly steep considering a man could only make about two dollars a day shucking corn.[12]

Pauline Nutt remembered Coulter's Saturday night trips to town during the 1930s and early 1940s. Coulter would spend the evening drinking beer and eating peanuts, and by the end of the evening he was pretty well "tanked up." There were a couple of ninety degree corners between the Nutt's place and Coulter's, and Pauline said Coulter would invariably run his Model T off the road. Because he was the one to get the knock on the door when Coulter needed pulled out of the ditch, John Nutt would often comment on Saturday night that they most likely wouldn't get much sleep.[13]

After Coulter lost his home place and moved to the north side of the Medicine Creek, he often rode his horse across the creek on a Saturday night, tied the horse in John Nutt's barn, and went into town with the Nutt's. He would usually spend the night "sleeping it off" in town and catch a ride back to the Nutt's with one of his drinking cronies on Sunday morning. Feeling a little sorry for Coulter's horse (Coulter kept his horses "starved down" so the balance of power was in his favor), John Nutt got in the habit of giving the horse a scoop of grain when it was tied in his barn. After awhile

---

12 Kenneth Phillips, conversation with author, Cambridge, Nebr., Dec. 7, 2004.
13 Pauline Nutt, conversation with author, Curtis, Nebr., June 4, 2004.

Coulter told John that he would prefer John didn't grain the horse, as it was becoming a little too frisky.[14]

Being particularly fond of horses, Coulter always kept a number around, and he drove a horse-drawn rig long after the general population had automobiles. He also farmed with horse-drawn equipment throughout most of his active working life. In 1939 he still owned seventeen head of work horses. His horses were usu-

Coulter Ballantine Jr. in the one-horse cart he drove into town as late as the 1920s. *Courtesy Nebraska State Historical Society.*

ally only green broke – if that. Kenneth Phillips bought a couple of horses from Coulter when he started farming in the early 1930s. He paid sixty dollars apiece for them, but they turned out to be as wild as mustangs – not even halter-broke. (Kenny broke the horses and traded them for a '34 Model B John Deere tractor.) Some years later Harry Corlett, a dyed in the wool horseman from Maywood, Nebraska, tried to buy some horses from Coulter, but Coulter refused to sell. His logic may have been askew, but it was true to Coulter's line of reasoning. He told Harry, "You can't have a hoss ranch if you don't have any hosses."[15]

Coulter Ballantine left other impressions as well. Remembering his ability to manage animals, Garnette Nelson said his favorite stallion, Old Chief, would sometimes get "kind of violent," but he would quiet right down when he heard Coulter's voice. According to Garnette, "He had that quality that he could control animals with his voice." Garnette described Coulter as being a "Stallion Man"; he wouldn't ride anything but a stallion. She also recalled that though Coulter liked to have a lot of help around his place; he wanted to make sure he was getting his money's worth. He was always riding

14 William "Bill" Nutt, telephone conversation with author, August 11, 2009.
15 Blaine Farrar, conversation with author, Curtis, Nebr., Dec. 11, 2005.

around his place horseback and "made you think of one of those Southern overseers of the plantation."[16] Coulter kept meticulous time and payment records. He knew exactly how many bushels of corn a man shucked in a day. If he advanced a man forty-five cents for mittens, it was recorded; if he paid the fellow in tobacco, it was recorded.

As Coulter aged and his star continued to fall, his livestock suffered as surely as did his wife. While it was said that as a child, Coulter "planned largely for the future," it was John Nutt's observation that in the end he was short-sighted and failed to look ahead for what tomorrow would bring. Never prepared for a change in the weather, Coulter would wait until a snow storm settled in, and then he would ask his neighbors to help him bring in feed. In the later years he kept his cattle tied to fence posts. This proved to be disastrous during the 1947 flood, as Coulter lost a number of cattle that were tied in the barn or to fence posts and couldn't seek higher ground. It is said that Coulter and Mima took refuge from the raging flood water in the trees, but not until after Coulter tried to save his bridge across the Medicine Creek by roping it while horseback.

There remains the nagging question – what about Coulter's wife? Mima Ballantine's story will be told later; but the question has to surface now. Did Coulter push his wife over the edge into insanity, did Mima's insanity contribute to Coulter's eventual downfall, or did they pull each other into the quicksand of hopelessness? When Sheriff Swanson asked John Nutt to help him get Mima Ballantine out of a tree so he could take her to the asylum, John stated bluntly, "You're taking the wrong one." On the other hand, when Forest Whelan went to the door of the Ballantine home, and Mima doused him with kerosene it was clear in his mind that she was the crazy one. In a time when there was very little understanding of mental illness, how much could Coulter endure before he lost his grip? Some of the neighbors said Coulter beat his wife and most likely he did. Some men believed it was their right; others maintained it was their duty. No one knows what really happened behind the closed door of

16 Garnette Nelson.

the Ballantine home, but those who heard Mima Ballantine screaming as she ran through the hills, were left to wonder.

Coulter Ballantine developed a reputation for dealing with life
in contradictory ways. Though an unannounced visitor might stare
down the barrel of a shotgun, Coulter could as easily deal with matters in a diplomatic fashion. Bill Shelley recalled the finesse Coulter
could use with people if the occasion so warranted, "Coulter himself
could have got along nicely with the queen of England when he was
younger, but [he] would have had a better time with someone like
Winston Churchill."[17] In 1948 Coulter solicited the legal services of
Robert Van Pelt, a Stockville native who at that time was associated
with the law firm of Van Pelt, Marti & O'Gara in Lincoln, Nebraska. It seems that Coulter had gotten into a little difference over
some money matters with a fellow by the name of Levi Pedersen and
Levi's father, R. P. Pedersen, who was at the time acting as Frontier
County Deputy Sheriff. Although Van Pelt had urged him to settle
out of court, Coulter apparently believed a little pressure from an
attorney would help resolve the issue. In concluding a letter to Van
Pelt pleading his case, Coulter added a postscript: "I know Pedersen
will try to whittle, but do the best you can, Robert. I will split and
compromise, and I will be satisfied, and I know you will try but you
know and they know I am not going to get into much trouble over
it. And if you can hold them to what they say and set them on that
they will do OK. That's the main point."[18]

It was cold and the snow lay deep when Mima Ballantine died
in December of 1955, so Coulter wrapped her body in a blanket and
left it in an unheated room. Never one to want anyone knowing his
business, he planned to wait until the ground thawed enough to dig
a grave and bury her right there on the place. He was soon persuaded
that this wouldn't do; it wasn't even legal. Contrary though he was,
Coulter did not want to do anything that would incur government

17 William Shelley to Dan Danker, Sept. 27, 1962, Shelley MSS.
18 D. C. Ballantine to Van Pelt, Marti & O'Gara, Nov. 10, 1948.

interference, so Mima Ballantine was buried properly. It cost Coulter $495 for a casket.

If living with Mima was hell, living without her was lonely. Some say Coulter went downhill fast after his wife's death. He held a selling-out sale on October 29, 1956. There wasn't much to go on the auction block. In addition to the livestock – seven young bulls, twenty-two cows and heifers and seven calves – other items listed included a few tools, 12 gauge Winchester repeating shotgun, .22 caliber repeating rifle, hand corn sheller and grader, John Deere General Purpose tractor in running order, folding ironing board, "much old iron accumulated over 50 years," and "many other useful items." There were also five Belgian Red Carneau pigeons.

A draft of a letter that Coulter wrote to an unknown recipient reveals his resignation to the difficulties of old age:

> In reply to your suggestion that I seek another place to go or live at my age involves too many complications at this time. The [ ] familiar is ever present – we are here to-day and there tomorrow – a very slight matter may end us and all our hopes and our plans are naught. We are prone to plan for the better. I know of my parents' plans and hopes, and how plans can be ruined without a second's notice.
>
> I may be able to go to Old Mexico with my old rheumatic bones to spend the winter. I have thought of it a good many times when I see the wild geese and hear their honking…The thought comes – would it give me peace of mind? I have promised [my sister], when I wake in the morning, I get up as soon as I come to my senses and sometimes do not get anything done [ ] until noon. My renter came…this morning and brought the mail. His

little ones go to school in Curtis. There are no country schools here now.

> Complications are so many and so fixed, they set my old brain rattling a plenty, and before long I would be ready for the Six Gun route. Hope you understand me at this time, and that a change soon will be impossible.

In his last years, Coulter became a recluse. He lived as though he was destitute and no doubt would have done so regardless of his financial situation. While his Social Security checks lay on the table unopened, his sister Anna E. (Ballantine) Adams sent him money on a regular basis. (There was an unsubstantiated rumor that a bag of $10,000 in gold coin was found buried under his house after his death.) Mrs. Adams made regular trips from her home in Springfield, Missouri, to be with her brother in spite of the fact that he became increasingly ornery to her. The accommodations were, of course, no better than the way in which Coulter lived – with no electricity, telephone, or indoor plumbing. Coulter saw no necessity in having much of anything other than beer, crackers, and cheese in the house for provisions. Attention from his sister continued without fail during the last year of Coulter's life. She sent letters almost weekly, a beautiful Valentine's Day card in February and a box of "eatables" later in the year. In one letter she wrote her brother that she was glad he had his cats.

As the end of Coulter's life drew near, he was faced with some difficult decisions. Marion Johnson, Coulter's neighbor, went to the house one day and finding Coulter in bad shape, gave the ultimatum: "You're going to have to go to the hospital or lie in that bed and die." Coulter reluctantly permitted Marion to take him to the hospital in Gothenburg, Nebraska. As Marion was leaving the hospital, one of the nurses came running after him exclaiming, "Mr. Johnson, Mr. Ballantine won't let us take off his shirts." Marion had encountered the same resistance when he was getting Coulter ready to go to the hospital. He, too, could dig in his heels and realizing further diplomacy wasn't going to work, Marion Johnson went back into the hospital, pulled out his pocket knife and cut off Coulter Ballantine's shirts.

After a few days in the hospital, Coulter began to improve and naturally wanted to go home. The hospital, however, would not release him to return to his home unless he had someone to stay with him. It was Christmas Eve when Marion Johnson gently explained this to Coulter, telling him that the only way he could leave the hospital was to be admitted to a nursing home. In the end, Coulter Ballantine had it his way; he died that night.[19] A graveside service was held three days later. Once more a little group of mourners gathered at Sunset Point Cemetery. Among them was Merle Roach, who was Coulter's banker, a few neighbors, and Ed Vreeland, who ran the local pool hall. Coulter's sister was the only relative. George Wetzel and George Stewart from the mortuary along with John Nutt's son, Bill, and some of the other younger fellows were called upon to carry the casket up the steep hill. A couple of neighbors had taken on the job of hacking out the grave from the frozen ground. David Coulter Ballantine was buried beside his wife on December 27, 1959.

He died in the mid-twentieth century, but in many respects his spirit and soul remained in an earlier time. Rigid and unyielding, Coulter Ballantine hung on to vestiges of the old life to the end. Determined never to be without adequate firepower, he sent off for two boxes of hard-to-get .32 long rim cartridges not too long before his death. He still had six or seven horses though they were underfed and gaunt, and there wasn't one among them a man would want to ride. The old hat he'd worn for years had been stitched up time and again, and his saddle – held together with wire and straps – wasn't in much better shape. He had stacks of reading material, including the *Literary Digest*, but only a kerosene lamp by which to read. John Nutt went to see him a short time before he was taken to the hospital during his final illness. As John told it, Coulter was sitting with his feet on the open stove door and "a gun in every corner."

---

19 Marion Johnson, conversations with author, Curtis, Nebr., 2007/2008.

21

The Woman in the Tree

hen Sheriff Swanson came to the Ballantine farm to take Mima to the insane asylum, he found her in a tree. This was where she often took refuge when it felt as though caterpillars were weaving webs across her brain, and she could no longer discern between reality and her own tortured fantasies. What had transpired in the forty or so years since the pretty, fresh-faced young woman at the tender age of twenty-one married David Coulter Ballantine Jr.? How are the years reconciled between the young, cultured Mima and the crazed woman who ran screaming through the hills of the Medicine Creek Valley sixty years later? Did the experiences of living on the frontier grind down the idealism and hopefulness of youth? Perhaps the mindset of the man she married would have eroded the vitality and mental well-being of any woman.

Jemima Leach was born on the twenty-first of March 1874 and preferred to be called Mima because she disliked the name Jemima. Her family lived in Kansas, and though there may have been more siblings, it is known for certain she had two sisters, Ida and Alpha, and a brother Fred. Mima said she was a first cousin to Dwight W. Morrow, father of Anne Morrow, who became the wife of the world-famous aviator, Charles Lindbergh. The Lindberghs became household names after the kidnapping of their young son in 1932, but Dwight Morrow, an American diplomat, was well known in his own right. The family connection was through Mima's mother, who was an aunt to Dwight Morrow. The familiarity with which Mima referred to "Lindy and Anne" Lindbergh in her writing lends credence to her claim.

Although the only extensive examples of Mima's writing are from the period in her life when mental illness had wrecked its havoc they, nevertheless, reveal high intelligence. She had a command of the language along with the ability to articulate her thoughts, irrational though they might have been. Her family evidently prized education, and it is believed by some that she was an instructor at the University of Colorado at Boulder at the time Coulter met her. Others contend that Mima was a secretary at the Denver Union Stock Yard, and that Coulter became acquainted with her there while working for his uncle. Regardless, the girl from Kansas obtained an education and successfully made her way in the city. Mima acquired a stylish wardrobe and with her fashionably small waist and engaging smile, she struck a fetching pose. David Coulter Ballantine Jr. noticed. There was a courtship, and the young couple was married on June 2, 1895.

Though the extent of her dowry is unknown, Mima likely came into the marriage with little more than a trunk-full of nice things and perhaps a few pieces of furniture. Having had her own source of income for a period of time prior to the marriage, she was able to acquire some of the things young women of her time felt to be essential. With linen tablecloths and napkins, Mima Ballantine was able to set a nice table. As for her fine clothes – the satins, laces, fur trimmings and fancy hats – they were soon packed away and remained there until Mima's death. Likewise, Mima put away any personal hopes or dreams she may have had.

Presumably there were good times in the early years of the marriage. Several snapshots bear witness to light-heartedness and camaraderie with neighbors and friends. There weren't babies, however, and in those days babies were an almost inevitable result of marriage. Whether this was a point of contention or disappointment to either Coulter or Mima is, like much of their story, open to speculation. Freedom from the tether of motherhood may have given Mima a lesser sense of purpose in life. The paper trail is meager – some led-

The young Mima some sixty years before her death in 1955, her mind ravaged by mental illness. *Courtesy Nebraska State Historical Society.*

ger books, a few letters, and scraps of paper that were left to the ravages of weather, mice, and pack rats before they were collected and preserved. The first is a July 6, 1905 journal entry: "Temporary illness comes to almost everyone. Continued illness is an evidence of weakness of character, ignorance or vice…"[1] It can be inferred from this statement that Mima was intolerant of what she perceived to be character weakness. It is also an indication of storm clouds on the horizon. The next journal entries are from 1923 – nearly twenty years later:

June 1 – Coulter to Curtis – Eggs $1.53

June 2 – 122 chicks to date – Wedding Anniversary.

July 20 – Worked in house

July 23 – Washed

July 24 – Ironed

July 25 – Baked bread

July 26 – Went fishing in evening

July 27 – Cut weeds

July 28 (Saturday) – Cleaned house

July 31 – Hottest day of season – Coulter gone all day

August 21 – Went to pasture – Coulter's birthday

August 26 – Alone all day except for Spirit nuisance – "For in much wisdom is much grief and he that increases knowledge increases sorrow." ~ Ecclesiastics 1:18

August 28 – Puttered

August 30 – Coulter returned

September 10 – Eclipse – Gerald here

September 15 – Went to Owens to dance

---

1 Mima Ballantine, Ballantine MSS. All journal entries, letters, essays, etc. attributed to Mima Ballantine are from this source.

September 16 – Jess and Towne helped operate on [baby calf?]

September 23 – Ann and Jess here in evening. Townes in P.M.

October 2 – Churned

October 13 – First hard frost

October 20 – Coulter left for Syracuse

October 22 – Made cellar door – baby calf born

October 23 – Cow that lost calf up in Whipple cornstalks

October 25 – Coulter returned

November 8 – Ironed

November 9 – Fixed fence – fine weather

November 29 – Thanks day – very beautiful in atmosphere

Stark in their simplicity, these entries are noticeably lacking in emotion. The wedding anniversary is seemingly no more significant than baking bread. Mima noted an eclipse on September 10, and there was, in fact, a lunar eclipse on that date. The insertion of the verse from Ecclesiastics on August 26 is significant as is the reference to a "spirit nuisance," which indicates a psychic disturbance beyond Mima's control. Further evidence of this is found in the following piece written by Mima at about the same time:

Woman (Woo-man)

I am merely a procurator – "A female of the species." Sometimes God chooses his meanest instrument through which to display Himself. After a given period, I will be back in my allotted sphere, for I am intensely democratic and happily content to shine in reflected glory.

A female was never born with a bigger desire for finery [and] elegance than I possess. Fortunately, I have been deprived of the use of money and found more worthwhile remuneration by indulging my mind with the mysteries of the occult.

This bit of prose offers several insights into the unraveling of Mima Ballantine. Her admission to indulging her mind with the mysteries of the occult predicts the psychotic behavior to follow. Her relationship to man as a "female of the species" content to shine in reflected glory – indeed, to "woo man" – runs counter to a deeper, underlying current of discontent. And finally: "A female was never born with a bigger desire for finery [and] elegance than I possess. Fortunately, I have been deprived of the use of money..."The insinuation here is that Coulter did not allow his wife spending money. Mima *did* desire nice things but for all practical purposes, she was living in poverty. If Coulter held off the hard edge of life with the proverbial bottle, his wife escaped – willingly or not – to the darker recesses of her mind.

In the early years Mima knew when she was going to "have a spell." According to her neighbor Garnette Nelson, "She could tell when she was gonna have one. She said it was like a web goin' across her brain. Just like caterpillars weavin' a web across her brain." Garnette added, "When she was well you couldn't know a finer person."[2] A June 2, 1923 newspaper clipping of a poem by Henry Wadsworth Longfellow is pasted inside the cover of the ledger book in which Mima kept a few personal notations and her journal entries:

We Are Potters All
I took a piece of plastic clay
And idly fashioned it one day
And as my fingers pressed it still
It moved and yielded to my will.

2 Garnette Nelson.

Mima Ballantine and Nellie Miles are amused at being dressed in men's clothes while Coulter Ballantine Jr. (middle) wears a woman's dress. Photo circa 1909. *Courtesy Nebraska State Historic Society.*

I came again when days were past
The bit of clay was hard at last
The form I gave it still it bore
But I could change that form no more.
I took a piece of living clay
And gently formed it day by day
And molded with my power and art
A young child's soft and yielding heart.
I came again when years were gone
It was a man I looked upon
He still that early impress wore
And I could change him nevermore.

Jemima Leach married a man who had been orphaned a month before his eighth birthday. His father's death in 1882 changed young Coulter's life forever, but the death of his mother two years later affected him in subtle ways that were ultimately more destructive.

Mima Ballantine would pay dearly for the maternal love that was taken from her husband that July day in 1884. Coulter Ballantine Jr. no doubt shielded himself from the pain of further loss by erecting an emotional barrier that excluded even his own wife. The lines, "He still that early impress wore, / And I could change him nevermore," speak poignantly to the situation in which Mima Ballantine found herself.

What Mima perceived as inferior education in the public school system was addressed in a number of letters and essays. In a 1923 letter to the teacher of rural School District No. 99, Mima contends, "Frontier County has more or at least as many inefficient boys and girls as any other county in the U. S." In a letter to C. K. Morris, who was superintendent of Nebraska School of Agriculture in Curtis, Nebraska, from 1919 until 1933, Mima's disapproval is explicit: "Why in the name of all that is divine, do you tolerate a virtue destroying Jew in your faculty as instructor of mathematics? You know as well as I do that mathematics is the most potent branch of every training schedule. If an individual is a failure with dimension (knowledge is soul measuring), he or she is a misfit everywhere you place them." The most significant examples of Mima's writing come from the early 1930s. Her intolerance for what she perceived to be a host of human ills and sins, magnified by her own psychotic thinking, are apparent in several lengthy, rambling essays. Her penmanship was fluid – more so in some of the essays than in others – and she used the signature "Solitary." The female teacher was the specific target of Mima's caustic criticism:

> Sum up the ailments and casualties of the heathen footgear of the average teacher of today with her "spiked" heels. Each year it costs the taxpayers of our county thousands upon thousands of dollars, confiscated dole, to employ the "coveted maid servant" to demonstrate to our youth the sacred values of making the head save the heels…

> If the teachers of our county want to wriggle around on their bellies on our sidewalks or hop along on all fours, the place for this type of joke is in the zoo, not in the business world with men.

At the time of their deaths in the 1950s, the Ballantines lived in the lower level of this house overlooking the Medicine Creek Valley. They had no electricity or indoor plumbing. Water was supplied from a hand pump in front of the house. *Photo by Gail Geis.*

> Our state has a surplus of many thousands of she-teachers. But you cannot expect a philandering man to marry what the devil wouldn't have – a domineering old maid schoolteacher. Most men choose the companionship of the breadlines rather than having to dodge the broom-stick of the academic wife...

Mima Ballantine was deemed insane by the Commissioners of Insanity of Frontier County, Nebraska, on July 18, 1932. She was at the time a patient at the Asylum for the Insane at Ingleside, Nebraska. Furthermore, the guardianship petition filed by her husband indicated she had been insane for the past three years. Mima believed that the vitriol with which she attacked the public school system was the reason for her confinement at Ingleside. In an undated letter she wrote, "I landed here because of my attitude towards Our Public Educational System: The sole purpose of our Educational System, churches included, is to infallibly interpret The First Law – Self-preservation…" In a letter dated March 8, 1934, she wrote:

> I am only one in millions deprived of my sacred right, "to do what she chooses with her own." Forced to forsake my home and comply with a governmental regime is just another name for abject slavery. Forced labor is libel against the Monroe Doctrine…here the small business of the attendants is to insist that the goofies do the dirty, hard work.
>
> Over in the sewing room, a patient said, "Today is my birthday. I was brot [*sic*] here when I was [fifty] and for 25 years, excepting two weeks of sickness when I came, I've worked in this sewing room. I've made enough garments to carpet Nebraska many times and what have I to show for my labor? Not a thing! All I get is my eats, room and a few cheap clothes and dogged around from morning till night and then try to sleep on a ward with a lot of noisy people. My life is similar to putting snow into boiling water."
>
> I said, "Listen, little Mother – keep right on doing your level best, smile through your tears, and thank God Almighty you're not an educated slave driver; the lowest species of human in God's workshop…"

Here, again, Mima vilifies the school system. Another letter, dated March 25, 1934, and addressed to her husband begins with a softer tone. Mima had turned sixty years old four days earlier and mentioned that she had been "nicely remembered." She commented that Nellie Miles (who lived in California at that time) had said she could forward the letters she received from Mima on to Coulter as it would "make one letter day a double-doer." Writing of a recent blizzard, Mima said she "could not keep my mind from picturing the ranch hardships on such days." She then launched into a tirade against the government with references to her confinement and conversations with her doctors:

> But the way our present style of Government Service is gradually taking over the control of every industry, we

won't possess even a home; we will be taken into custody and assigned work without pay while the slave-drivers draw the salary and get cock-eyed and chesty like a pouter pigeon. I'm right in it now and know what I'm talking about. It doesn't make any difference that you are one of the biggest taxpayers in Frontier Co. and said county is expected to fork over some of that tax money for my care here. I am expected to get right into the collar here to help keep the patients and Service looking as if they had health and brains to rent or will and b'gooh [*sic*] they haven't either.

Prof. Flint, alias Doc Farrell, says, "As always, [you] hew right to the Truth, regardless of where the sparks hit and that's what makes a truthsayer indestructible and expedient." I have learned, since being parked here that the M. D. who advised you to so do and Dr. Farrell are inseparable pals. Farrell says, "There is great ability in knowing how to conceal your ability." But I'm telling you I cannot enthuse over the picture of being "a possible teacher emeritus of Ingleside." Yet it is hard to estimate the ability of a female of the soil just by feeling her pulse…

The remarks attributed to Dr. Farrell imply the doctor's recognition of Mima's intelligence and perhaps even validation of some of her views. It seems the doctor felt she could improve her situation in life by subduing the expression of her radical opinions. For Mima's part, she apparently believed she had been understood on an intellectual level. While most of her letters ended in incoherent rambling, Mima's summation that "it is hard to estimate the ability of a female of the soil just by feeling her pulse," is reasoned and perceptive, whether or not viewed in the context of her illness.

Institutional treatment at that time was little more than custodial, and although Mima was committed to Ingleside several times, it appears these stays were of a short duration. Though Coulter kept Mima at home most of the time, he was ill-equipped to know how to deal with his wife's mental derangement. John and Pauline Nutt were neighbors of the Ballantines from 1933 until 1949. Pauline recalled that Mima Ballantine had no social life during those years.

Jess and Annie Marsh, who had been neighbors for years, were the only people that Coulter let in the house. Pauline Nutt said that to her knowledge, the last time Coulter took Mima anywhere was to Curtis in the 1930s to see the newly paved streets. The Nutt's young son Lee would ride his pony over and spend an occasional afternoon with Mima Ballantine. Mima raised squabs (domestic pigeons), and Lee liked the pigeons. Pauline Nutt was a little afraid of Mrs. Ballantine, but when she expressed concern about Lee going to the Ballentine's, John would assure her that it was okay; he was glad his son could give Mrs. Ballantine some pleasure in life.[3]

Eventually both Coulter and Mima Ballantine suffered rope-burns from trying to hang onto the situation as it spiraled out of their control. In the later years of her life, it seems Mima was never released from the torture of her illness. People who came to the house to see Coulter were likely to get up to the door, only to have Mima come running around the corner, screaming at them. If she happened to have an old revolver in her hands, she was all the more terrifying. Other times the neighbors heard her wild screams as she ran over the hills and through the canyons. Perhaps the last person to bear the brunt of her rage was the doctor who gave her medical attention in the last days of her life. Mrs. Ballantine began to shriek and told Dr. Magill in no uncertain terms to get his cold hands off her.

Following Mima's death in December of 1955, her body laid wrapped in a blanket but otherwise unattended in a cold room for several days before Coulter was persuaded to follow the proper procedure for her burial. There was a heavy blanket of snow on the ground when the undertaker made the trip over the rough country road to the Ballantine home. When asked about a dress in which to bury his wife, Coulter indicated that her clothes were in the trunk. On opening the trunk, all that was found were the beautiful clothes that Mima had worn as a young woman some sixty years earlier. Freda Wetzel, the wife of the funeral director, bought a dress in which to lay Mima Ballantine to rest. She also cleaned and arranged

---

3 Pauline Nutt, conversation with author June 4, 2004.

the long gray hair of the deceased woman. There was no funeral, but a small group of neighbors gathered two days before Christmas for the burial. It could scarcely be called a graveside service, for although a minister was present, Coulter had requested no words of comfort be spoken. Several of the neighbors carried the casket up the steep hill to Sunset Point Cemetery. Perhaps needing to add some semblance of ceremony to the occasion, someone from the funeral home asked the small gathering if they would like to have the casket opened. There was an answer in the affirmative, and the casket was opened. This was the first and only time sixteen-year-old Opal Buker ever saw

Coulter Ballantine Jr. and his wife, Mima. This photo was probably taken in the mid to late 1920s. *Courtesy Nebraska State Historical Society.*

Mrs. Ballantine. It was the only time in many years that anyone had seen Mima Ballantine in a state of calm and repose.[4]

One photo of Coulter and Mima as a couple is known to exist. It is a snapshot of a smiling Mima with her hand firmly planted on Coulter's arm and Coulter – receptive to her touch – proud to be photographed with his attractive wife. Putting a date on this photo is difficult. Women's skirt-lengths didn't generally get to just below the knee until the mid-1920s when Mima would have been fifty years old. Likewise, her writings in 1923 reflect emotional flatness and at least some mental instability. In the photo, however, Mima

4 Opal (Buker) Crow, conversation with author, Oct. 22, 2008.

appears healthy and relaxed; her eyes and expression do not reveal the developing insanity. And finally, there is the issue of the dress – conservative by the standards of today – but seductive in rural Nebraska in the 1920s. A short, form-fitting satin dress does not seem to be the type of garment Mima Ballantine would have worn. Yet, construction details of the dress indicated Mima may have actually fashioned it herself from some of the dated clothes of her youth. The photo presents more questions and answers none. What the photo does do is give a lasting impression – one indelible image – of Coulter and Mima Ballantine as a happy couple.

Coulter Ballantine Jr. and his wife, Mima, are at rest in the Sunset Point Cemetery on the Medicine Creek in Frontier County, Nebraska. *Photo by Gail Geis.*

22

Of Men and Snake Skins

O ne of William McKnight's early boyhood memories was of Paddy Miles riding through the McKnight place after sleeping off a drinking binge in the town jail. As McKnight told the story: "Old Paddy would go up to Curtis on his spotted pony. He always carried two guns – one on each side. He'd go up there and get drunk. He'd shout – tobacco juice all over his face. You could hear him talk for miles. They'd throw him in jail and let him out in the morning, and he'd come down through our place. I'd see him, and I'd hit the house right now. Dad would stand out there, and they would talk and laugh, and I was afraid he'd shoot Dad."[1] Young Will McKnight was scared to death of Paddy Miles, but he needn't have worried about his father; Robert McKnight could hold his own.

Other than having been on the frontier for a number of years, McKnight and Miles did not have similar backgrounds, but it seems they both had fiery tempers and each served a term as sheriff in Frontier County. Born in Ireland in 1839, Robert A. McKnight immigrated to Canada as a young man and later drifted down into Wisconsin where his two brothers, John and William, and sister Sarah joined him. The four siblings eventually found their way to Nebraska where Robert McKnight went to work for John Bratt as an all-around cowhand and foreman of the barn at Bratt's Home

---

1 William S. McKnight, tape recorded interview by Reiney Martins circa 1980. All quotations attributed to William S. McKnight are from this source.

Ranch on the Platte River. From there McKnight eventually came on down to Bratt's Curtis Creek Ranch, which was located just at the point where Curtis Creek fed into the Medicine Creek. Bratt's cowboys had homesteaded the locations for some of the line camps along the waterways to assure access to water. Apparently the cowboy on the Curtis Creek Ranch wanted to leave, so he relinquished his homestead, and McKnight then filed on it and later built a little more onto the log house. This became the location of the Curtis Post Office after a postal district was established, and Robert McKnight was appointed the first Curtis Post Master.

Will McKnight told of yet another time as a youngster when he "took for the house." It was his recollection that this incident happened when his dad was sheriff, but Robert McKnight's term of sheriff was actually before Will was born in 1882. In any event, Will remembered that on occasion a remnant band of Indians would be in the area: "The house where we lived – the Indians came right through our yard. Dad would go out and talk to them. I stayed hid under the bed…" One time the Indians had stolen some horses, and "they come through there – wanted to sell Dad a horse. He went to the house and got his rifle. There were six or eight of them. He made them go down there south of Tyra Nelson's [who lived just to the east]. There was a high round-up corral – it was high and made of rails. Paddy Miles came along, and they took the horses away from the Indians. Then some of the old-timers rounded them [the Indians] up and put them on the railroad in a boxcar and sent them out of town."

Robert McKnight was almost forty-two years old when he married Mary E. (Gordon) Williams on June 20, 1881. The new Mrs. McKnight had been married once before and had a five-year-old daughter. In the next twelve years she gave birth to seven children and her youngest children, the twins, were not yet four years old when Mary E. McKnight died at age forty-seven in 1899. This Mary McKnight was, in fact, the second Mary McKnight, for Robert McKnight had also been married previously. McKnight family records show that he married a woman by the name of Mary Colston in Wisconsin on September 20, 1873. There was a son named

Robert A. McKnight settled on John Bratt's Curtis Creek Ranch and was the first postmaster of the Curtis postal district before the town was organized in 1886. *Courtesy Anna Marie Hansen Memorial Museum.*

George, but it is not known for certain whether Mary Colston came into the marriage with the son or whether he was a product of the marriage. It is also not known just when or how this first Mary McKnight died. Ena Raymonde, in a September 3, 1882 letter to her cousin, wrote: "Mrs. McKnight, Mary, that you knew, committed suicide in Cheyenne some seven months ago. You knew that McK. was married again? A nice looking woman. They have a baby." (William S. McKnight was born May 20, 1882.) The death of the first Mary McKnight most likely occurred earlier than the seven months ago of which Ena wrote. And though she may, indeed, have committed suicide, some have suggested that Robert McKnight's first wife died either directly or indirectly as the result of a fit of rage on her husband's part.

The McKnight's only daughter, Anna, became the victim of sorts – not to her father's Irish temper but to his inconsideration. Anna McKnight was sixteen years old and had only recently lost her mother when she was united in marriage to William H. "Bill" Seide in 1901. Born in 1876, Bill Seide spent half of his growing-up years in an orphanage in Brooklyn, New York, where his mother – unable to provide for him – had left him when he was eight or nine years old. While in his teens, he found his way west and came to the Curtis area as a well-digger in 1899. After four years and two sons, the union between Anna McKnight and Bill Seide ended in divorce. It seems Anna's wishes had never been considered in the first place, for she later referred to the marriage as the "R. A. McKnight and W. H. Seide Business Deal."[2] McKnight had moved to a location in Lincoln County northeast of Curtis by this time; perhaps Bill Seide dug a fine deep well – the equivalent of forty ponies – in exchange for the hand of Anna McKnight.

It was around the turn of the century – 1901 or so – when Will McKnight struck out looking for a job. As he told it:

> I'll tell you one thing I done. I'd never do it again, and I wouldn't advise anybody else to. I left home about the last of March on a three-year-old buckskin pony – hunting a

---

2 *Curtis, Nebraska: The...*, p. 305.

job. I…[went up] to North Platte and went up to some folks at Hershey. There was a fellow that was a school-teacher that had a store there. I went to school to him. I never found a job, and I started home and met some folks in a covered wagon by the name of Johnson. We got to talking, and they talked me into tying my pony on behind and going with them to Gering. I had an uncle up there who was a foreman on an irrigation ditch. We went up there, and I worked on the irrigation ditch. Drove a team with a slip for the foreman.

We finished that, and then they wanted me to go up to Mitchell almost to Cheyenne to work widening the rail-road track. You take a team and slip and go down and get dirt and bring it up and dump it to widen the fill on each side of the rail. We lived in tents and cooked in tents and that's all we knew was tents. Every week they'd bring the mail in there. I was about ten miles from Cheyenne, and I should have stayed, but I got homesick. It was hard work – ten hours a day. I got on my pony; the woman gave me a lunch and the young girl cried when I left…

I started out on that pony. I never walked him a mile; I never loped him. He just trotted – he trotted easy. I only had fifteen dollars – I'd sent the rest of my money home. I got a dollar and a quarter a day. Come night I pulled into a feller's place. Sure I could stay. Turn your horse loose in the pasture. I slept in his bed – got a pancake or two. I got my pony, and he charged me seventy-five cents. I knew my money would run out before I got home at that rate. I didn't have a rope to put on my pony – just the bridle and a saddle and an extra coat tied behind and a pair of shoes wrapped in my coat. That's all I had except the clothing I wore. I had a watch. I'd turn that pony loose – it was all prairie. You wouldn't see a house in a day's travel. I'd spread out the blanket and lay down with the saddle for a pillow – turn that pony loose and he'd fill up and then come and lay down within three foot of me. We'd rest for three hours, and then we would travel night and day – travel three hours and rest three hours. I ate cheese and ginger snaps and some bologna.

I'd come to a water tank and water the horse and drink
out of the horse tank myself if the windmill wasn't runnin'.
One night I was layin' there in the evening, and there was
a rattlesnake comin' with his head up lookin' at me. I got
up and took the bridle and killed him and skinned him. I
put the hide over the back of the saddle. I come to a store
– a post office. I went in and bought some cheese and ginger snaps and some bologna. I tied them in my coat. Two
fellers standing there and one said, "I wouldn't get in that
saddle with that damned hide on there for five dollars."
Just the other side of Big Springs – I had an uncle lived
there and stayed a day there and then rode on into Curtis.
I often thought – turning that pony loose – he could have
left me...

Will McKnight had a lot of grit. As for his father, Robert McKnight played an important part in the early development
of Frontier County – when it truly was the frontier. Located on a
branch of the old McPherson Trail, his log cabin was a stopping-off
place for travelers in addition to serving as the first Curtis Post Office. Besides stints as sheriff and post master, Robert McKnight also
acted as a land agent and helped locate settlers in the area. Without
a doubt Robert McKnight passed down a hard edge to his son.[3] On
the other hand, it took a lot of nerve and a thick skin to settle and
survive in a newly opened territory fresh on the heels of the Indians.
John Y. Nelson, Hank and Monte Clifford, Paddy Miles, Doc Carver, Mac McClary, Ambrose Shelley, Coulter Ballantine, and Robert
McKnight are just a few of the hardy breed of men who stand out
on the pages of the history of southwest Nebraska. Any one of them
– and a number of women as well – would have been comfortable
with the skin of a rattlesnake draped across the back of the saddle.

---

3 Robert McKnight was married a third time to Mrs. Margaret Bowen in 1904. He died on
August 17, 1922, and is buried in the Curtis Cemetery. Also: *Curtis, Nebraska: The...*, p. 261;
Curtis 75th Jubilee program; Email from Ruth (McKnight) Hughes, June 7, 2004.

Bibliography

Abbreviations

Ballantine MSS   Ballantine Collection MS1730, Nebraska State Historical Society

FCHS   Frontier County Historical Society

NSHS   Nebraska State Historical Society

Unknown   Publication information unknown

Articles & Books:

Allen, E. E. "A History of Frontier County." *Stockville (Nebr.) Faber*, Aug. 10 – Sept. 28, 1916, reprinted in *(Maywood, Nebr.) Eagle-Reporter*, Sept. 23 – Sept. 30, 1932.

Allen, Herbert C. "1884-1984." Circa 1984. Unknown.

Allen, Wm. H. "Personal Recollections of Early Settlers on the Medicine in Frontier County, Nebraska." 1897. Unknown.

Andreas, A. T. (Compiler) *History of the State of Nebraska.* 1882. <http://www.kancoll.org.>

Belden, George P. Ed. by General James S. Brisbin. *Belden, The White Chief: or Twelve Years among the Wild Indians of the Plains.* 1870. Digitized image, <http://moa.umdl.umich.edu.>

Black, John F. "Pioneer Days in Red Willow County." *Indianola Reporter*, June 27, 1918. Quote used by Riley in Ballantine MSS.

Bratt, John. *Trails of Yesterday.* 1921. Reprint, Chicago: University Publishing Company, 1980.

Bridger, Bobby. *Buffalo Bill and Sitting Bull: Inventing the Wild West.* Austin: University of Texas Press, 2002.

Carver, Wm. F. *Life of Dr. Wm. F. Carver of California: Champion Rifle Shot of the World.* 1878. Digitized image, <http://books.google.com.>

Cody, William Frederick. *The Life of Hon. William F. Cody.* 1879. Reprint, Lincoln, Nebr.: University of Nebraska Press, 1978.

Curtis, Nebraska: The First 100 Years. Dallas, Texas: Curtis Media Corporation, 1986.

Curtis 75th Jubilee program. *Curtis Enterprise*, 1961.

Dunning, John. "Why We Went West." Circa 1930. Unknown.

Gammill, J. N. "Jim Gammill Writes Interesting Early History of Frontier County." *Indianola Reporter*, August 7, 1941. <http://rootsweb.com.>

Gilman, Musetta. *Pump on the Prairie.* Detroit, Michigan: Harlo Press, 1981.

Harvey, Robert. "The Unwritten Story of the Establishment of the Second Standard Parallel." *Eustis News*, Eustis, Nebraska, January 20, 1911. Reprint, FCHS newsletter, Vol. 17, issues 1, 2 & 3 (2002).

Hayden, C. D. "Frontier County Trails." *The Curtis Enterprise*, July 30, 1936.

Holmes, Louis A. *Fort McPherson, Nebraska; Fort Cottonwood, N.T.* Lincoln, Nebraska: Johnsen Publishing Company, 1963.

Hotze, Wm. H. "Indian Scares and Massacres Marked Early Settlement in Red Willow County." *Nebraska State Journal* (*Lincoln Journal Star*), October 9, 1933.

Jacobs, Emma V. (Ruff). *Dimming Trails, Fading Memories.* Kyle, South Dakota: Little Wound Day School, 1983.

Johnson, Dean. "A Paddy Miles' 'Believe it or Not.'" *Curtis Enterprise*, date unknown.

Lewis, Emily H. "Shadows of the Brave." Circa 1962. Reprint, FCHS newsletter, Vol. 7, Issue 4 (1992).

McKee, Jim. "The Cow That Started a 40-year War." *Lincoln Journal Star*, date unknown.

McNeill, T. A. "The Last Indian Raid in Kansas." 1920. <www.rootsweb.com.>

Miles, W. H. and John Bratt. *Early History and Reminiscence of Frontier County, Nebraska.* Maywood, Nebraska: *The Eagle*, 1894.

Mousel, Charles. "The Murder of 1884 – Frontier County, Nebraska." Reprint, FCHS newsletter, Vol. 8, Issue 3 (1993).

Nordin, Charles R. "Dr. W. F. Carver," Jan. 10, 1928 address before the NSHS. *Nebraska History Magazine*, unidentified issue.

Norris, George W. *Fighting Liberal.* New York: The Macmillan Company, 1945. O'Reilly, Harrington. *Fifty Years on the Trail.* 1889. Reprint, Norman, Oklahoma: University of Oklahoma Press, 1963.

Paine, Bayard H. *Pioneers, Indians and Buffaloes.* Curtis, Nebraska: *The Curtis Enterprise*, 1935.

Price, Wayne. "The Mystery behind the Nelson Buck Massacre." *Rural Electric Nebraskan*, Vol. 60, No. 7, (July 2006).

Riley, Paul D. "Frontiersmen of Fort McPherson, 1870-1875, and the Writings of Ena Raymonde Ballantine." Circa 1970s. Unpublished, Ballantine MSS.

Rosa, Joseph G. *They Called Him Wild Bill.* Norman, Oklahoma: University of Oklahoma Press, 1964.

Russell, Don. *The Lives and Legends of Buffalo Bill.* Norman, Oklahoma: University of Oklahoma Press, 1960.

Russell, Don. *A History of the Wild West Shows.* Fort Worth: Anon Carter Museum of Western Art, 1970.

Sagala, Sandra K. "Buffalo Bill V. Doc Carver: The Battle over the Wild West." *Nebraska History*, Vol. 85, No. 1 (Spring 2004).

Sanders, John L. as compiled by Ruth (Woodring) Young, "A Memoir," *Nebraska History Magazine*, Vol. XIII, No. 3 (1932)

Shelley, Ambrose. "Early Frontier Days." (*Maywood, Nebr.) Eagle-*

Reporter, Sept. 15, 1928.

Shelley, Ambrose. "When I Slept Under a Dead Indian." 1928. Reprint, FCHS newsletter, Vol. 14, Issue 2 (1999).

Smith, Kristine H., Compiler. "Burt Grant Moulton and Ann Isabella Gammill Moulton." Circa 1960. Reprint, FCHS newsletter, Vol. 15, Issue 3 (2000).

Stockville, Then and Now. Stockville Women's Club, 2005.

Strong, Jason. "A Mysterious Murder in Frontier County: The Andrew Hawkins Murder Case." May 4, 2004. Reprint, *Hi-Line (Curtis, Nebr.) Enterprise*, July 28 – Sept. 8, 2005.

Sutton, E. S. *Sutton's Southwest Nebraska and Republican River Valley Tributaries.* Benkelman, Nebraska: E. S. Sutton, 1983.

Thorp, Raymond. *"Wild West" Doc Carver: Spirit Gun of the West.* London: W. Foulsham & Co. Ltd., 1957.

Van Pelt, Samuel with Introduction by James W. Hewitt. "All's Well That Ends Well: The Murder Trial of Andrew Hawkins." *The Nebraska Lawyer*, October 1998.

Westgate, Berl. Letter to *Curtis Enterprise*, 1932. Reprint, *Hi-Line Enterprise*, Jan. 1973.

Wilmeth, Mae (Griffith). "History of Orafino Post Office," 1936 Golden Anniversary Edition of the *Farnam Echo*. Reprint, FCHS newsletter, Vol. 10, Issue 2 (Spring 1995).

Yost, Nellie Snyder. *The Call of the Range.* Denver: Sage Books, 1966.

Yost, Nellie Snyder. *Buffalo Bill: His Family, Friends, Fame, Failures, and Fortunes.* Denver: Sage Books, 1979.

Private Papers:

Ballantine MSS, NSHS. Journals, letters to/from from Annie "Ena" (Palmer) Raymonde Ballantine McClary and to/from her children, Coulter and Anna Ena (Ballantine) Adams, and other misc. This collection also contains the journal entries, letters, essays, etc. attributed to Jemima "Mima" (Leach) Ballantine, wife of Coulter Ballantine Jr.

Carver Collection, MS3623, NSHS. This collection contains letters written by W. F "Doc" Carver as well as other items pertaining to Carver.

Herman, Steve. Unpublished manuscript about D. C. Ballantine Jr. with research notes, circa 1973.

Lofton, Neva. Unpublished manuscript, circa 1985.

McClary Collection MS3775, NSHS. Collection contains journals of W. L. McClary as well as subsequent letters relating to McClary papers.

Miles, Wm. H. "Paddy" Palmer. Journal, photocopy, FCHS.

Miles, Edward B. to Robert Van Pelt, Dec. 17, 1986. Robert Van Pelt Estate.

Raymonde, Annie E. "Frontier Life," unpublished manuscript, circa 1874,   Ballantine MSS.

Seymour, Richard. Journals written on odd pages of Ena Raymonde's journals. Ballantine MSS.

Shelley, Ambrose S. Letters in Ballantine and Shelley collections, NSHS.

Shelley, George to Robert Van Pelt, April 3, 1986. Robert Van Pelt Estate.

Shelley, William M. Letters in Ballantine, Carmody and Shelley collections, NSHS.

Van Pelt Estate. A collection of papers and photographs from the Robert Van Pelt Estate still held in the Van Pelt family.

Waite, H. P. Transcriptions of late 1800's news items and observations of Mr. Waite.

High Plains Museum, McCook, Nebraska.

Official Papers:

Affidavit of Andrew Hawkins, State of Nebraska, Lancaster County,

Wolf's Rest
Feb.10, 1912.

Court documents associated with Nelson/Sherwood murder case in possession of Henry Koch, McCook, Nebraska.

Court documents pertaining to Miles and Ballantine are exhibits associated with land abstracts in possession of author.

Marriage license for Antoine Barrett and Nancy Wheatley. Photocopy, Robert Van Pelt Estate.

Marriage certificate for Antoine Barrett and Nancy Wheatley. Photocopy, FCHS.

Supreme Court of the State of Nebraska, No. 12320, Error to District Court of Frontier County, Brief of Defendants in Error. Ballantine MSS.

Other Newspapers:

Cambridge (Nebr.) Monitor, Dec. 20 1884.

Curtis (Nebr.) Courier, Aug. 26, 1898; Nov. 20, 1903.

Curtis (Nebr.) or *Hi-Line Enterprise*, Oct. 19, 1900; Jan. 15, 1904; July 30, 1936, Jan. 1973.

Lincoln County (Nebr.) Advertiser, Sept. 4, 1872.

McCook (Nebr.) Daily Gazette, July 16, 1965. "Wagon Ride to Death," reprinted from *Frontier Times Magazine*.

New York Times, digitized images on Internet: July 6, 1878; July 16, 1885; July 30, 1891; Nov. 19, 1893.

Stockville (Nebr.) Faber, Dec. 19 – Dec. 26, 1884; Sept. 23, 1892; Feb. 6, Mar. 26, & June 11, 1896; Aug. 11 – Sept.1, 1898;

Other Sources:

"Cheyenne Outbreak," <www.nebraskahistory.org.>

McKnight, William S. Tape recorded interview by Reiney Martins circa 1980. Transcribed by Joan Wetzel, Curtis, Nebraska.

Author's Bio

The descendant of a pioneer farm family, D. Jean Smith lives in the home built by her great-grandparents overlooking the Medicine Creek Valley in southwest Nebraska.

After eight years of schooling in a country school, the author received her secondary education at the University Of Nebraska School Of Agriculture at Curtis, Nebraska, graduating in 1960. She graduated Kearney State College in 1980 as an English major with a Bachelor of Arts in Education.

A member of the Nebraska State Historical Society, her enthusiasm for writing, history and genealogy has been parlayed into her dedication to preserving the stories of the past.

jean@djeansmith.com
www.djeansmith.com